KU-116-635

WAYWARD DAUGHTER

An Official Biography of Eliza Carthy

By
Sophie Parkes

soundcheck books
the stories behind the sounds

First published in Great Britain in 2012 by
Soundcheck Books LLP
88 Northchurch Road,
London N1 3NY
www.soundcheckbooks.co.uk

Copyright © Sophie Parkes 2012

ISBN: 978-0-9566420-7-3

All rights reserved. No part of this book may be reproduced or transmitted
in any form or by any means, electronic or mechanical, including
photocopying, recording, or any information storage and retrieval system
without permission in writing from the publisher.

This book is sold subject to the condition that it shall not, by way of trade
or otherwise, be lent, resold, hired out or otherwise circulated without the
publisher's prior consent in any form of binding or cover other than that
in which it is published and without a similar condition being imposed on
the subsequent purchaser.

We've made every effort to fulfil requirements regarding the reproduction
of copyright material. The author and publishers will happily rectify any
omissions at the earliest opportunity.

Book design: Benn Linfield (www.bennlinfield.com)
Printed and bound by CPI., Croydon, CR0 4YY
www.soundcheckbooks.co.uk

WAYWARD DAUGHTER
An Official Biography of Eliza Carthy

C333101657

Contents

Acknowledgements viii

Foreword x

Family Tree xii

Prologue 1

1 Don't Put Your Daughter On The Stage, Mrs Waterson 4

2 Little Gypsy Girl 31

3 'The Future Of British Folk Music' 59

4 Where's My Fiddle? 68

5 This Fiddle Kills Fascists 105

6 What A Beau Your Granny Is 128

7 In London So Fair 150

8 Follow The Dollar 177

9 Stumbling On 192

Afterword From The Fans 213

Endnotes, Sources & Further Reading 241

Author Biography 249

For Dennis Crisp

Author's note

I met with Eliza Carthy several times throughout the course of 2011. Sometimes she answered my questions via text, email and telephone conversation, too. I also had the privilege of interviewing over thirty friends, family members, fans and industry peers. All interviews have been conducted by me, unless otherwise stated.

I have tried to ensure that the narrative is as chronologically clear as possible, but with many of Eliza's projects and ideas happening in tandem, the timeline often leaps forward before taking a step back, only to trip forward once again.

Sophie Parkes

Acknowledgements

Never meet your heroes, or so the saying goes.

Well, I've had the pleasure of meeting with mine many times over the past year or so and she has never been anything other than accommodating, enthusiastic, entertaining and helpful. She and her family have made me feel welcome in their home, at gigs, on the end of the phone and via email.

Enormous and heartfelt thanks to Eliza Carthy for making this project so enjoyable and fulfilling. I can only hope the final result goes some way to doing her justice.

There have also been overwhelming amounts of people who have given up their precious time to speak with me, sharing opinions and memories, as well as helping me source contact details, provide recordings and articles and set up interviews. They are:

Lucy Adams, Keith Ames, Ian Anderson, John Atkinson, Kit Bailey, Sophie Baker and all at *Mslexia*, Jen Blacker, Jon Boden (and a rather windy Jacob), Joe Boyd, Billy Bragg, Pauline and Dennis Butterfield at Mulgrave Cottage in Goathland (and their lovely son who drove us all the way to Malton station), Martin Carthy, Shirley Collins, Matt Wayland Copley, Ash Dosanjh, Michael Doward, Simon Emmerson, Tony Engle, Eleri Evans, Fyling Hall School, Matt Gannicliffe, Tristan Glover, Goathland Plough Stots, Claire Godden, Ash Green, Martin Green, Hannah Griffiths, Cathy Hornung, Emma-Victoria Houlton and Henrietta Rowlatt at Smooth Operations, Hannah James, Sophie Jones, Johnny Kalsi, Nancy Kerr and James Fagan, Oliver Knight, Stewart Lee and Sally Homer, Liz Lenten, Chris Long, Jenny McCormick, John McCusker, Heather Macleod, Cerys Matthews, Jo Mall, Jed Mugford, Peter Nash and Monty Funk Productions, Liz Newell, Van Dyke Parks (who believes I don't know how to spell my own surname!), Kevin Pepper and Debbie Metcalfe at the Streonshalh Guest House, Beth Porter, Tim Powell-Jones, Mark Radcliffe and Emily Rees Jones, Shelley Rainey, Peter Robinson, Saul Rose, Al Scott, Derek Schofield, John Spiers, Barnaby Stradling, David Suff, York Tillyer, Sam Thomas, Keith Thompson, Richard Thompson and his publicist Mick Houghton, Becky Travers, Jock Tyldesley, Lucy Ward, Marry Waterson, Norma Waterson, Andrew Wickham and Kate Fraser, and Kellie While and Lizzie Hoskin.

... and anyone else I have neglected to mention. Thank you.

Special thanks to the public transport networks of Britain and all those who work on it – I managed to reach all the strange places which tend to be inhabited and frequented by folk musicians without any mishaps (barring the Huddersfield to Leeds train on one occasion – see below).

Special gratitude to my family, particularly my mum and dad, Matt and Graham, and, of course, to Chris, for answering silly questions in the middle of the night, and for putting up with lonely weekends whilst I'm off gallivanting in Yorkshire. Thanks for not getting a weekend girlfriend, despite all the threats.

Thanks to my friends for their patience in politely asking 'how's it going?' and listening whilst I replied *at length*. You didn't try and wrestle the airtime back from me once and now I feel embarrassed.

Thanks, though. I'll shut up now.

And massive, deepest thanks to Phil and Sue Godsell at Soundcheck Books who have been nothing but extremely generous, patient, enthusiastic and kind from the very beginning.

In true Eliza Carthy style, no thanks to:

Dodgy phone signals and slow motion Skype, Facebook (AKA The Enchantress) and the Huddersfield to Leeds train which decided to break on a Saturday morning, meaning our journey from Manchester to North Yorkshire took a whole six hours.

Foreword

The family chronicles of the Waterson Carthy clan are stitched into the story of British folk, but even given her illustrious pedigree, Eliza is special.

For a whole new generation of roots music explorers, discovering the songs and tunes for the first time, she represents an organic link with what's gone before whilst simultaneously taking us somewhere new. She blazes the trail for young women to believe it's okay to enter this world of long observed traditions and yet dance in high heels and dye your hair pink.

She was nominated for the Mercury Music Prize, making her almost a pop star, which brought her to the attention of new fans who might never have investigated folk otherwise. She has assembled meticulously crafted and lovably eclectic albums which she effortlessly transfers to the stage, often sharing the spotlight with wonderfully talented young musicians she's picked up along the road. In every aspect of her musical life, she clearly respects all she's learned and absorbed, but makes it distinctively her own.

And she is never afraid to make it fun. She knows what matters about the music and when to take it seriously, but she also understands that when we go out of a night, sometimes we're in need of a party.

I like her enormously as a friend. We've presented the television coverage of the Cambridge Folk Festival and countless radio programmes together. I'm deeply ashamed to say that on one occasion I turned up on the train from that there London, where I'd been attending the *Q* magazine awards, heroically or perhaps horrendously drunk. It wasn't my fault really. The hosts had kindly, if unwisely, loaded the tables with not only free wine but complimentary spirits, too. Sitting between the charming but abstemious Jo Whiley and the raffish and newly sober Russell Brand, I thought it would look ungrateful to leave all the booze untouched and so, out of politeness, drank for all three of us. There are still a couple of hours I lost that day that can't be explained. Perhaps alien abduction played a part.

Anyway, as a result of *Q*'s cavalier approach to buckshee brandy, I turned up at Studio Five in Manchester minutes before air-time and listing heavily. This, for a show broadcast nationally on Radio 2. Eliza, who for once had arrived more or less on time, took stock of the situation and effortlessly guided me through the next two hours with a smile, a song and the odd touch on the tiller. I guess she was used to dealing with inebriated men many years her senior.

But that's Eliza. She has so much charm, ability and charisma that she can fill any situation, room or stage with genuine warmth. And she has the filthiest laugh you will ever hear.

Eliza is a genuine phenomenon, a bit of a one-off really, and no small part of why folk is such a vibrant and progressive force right now. Above all, she understands what is precious, and that makes her precious, too.

Mark Radcliffe
On the banks of the ship canal. 13.01.12

Family Tree

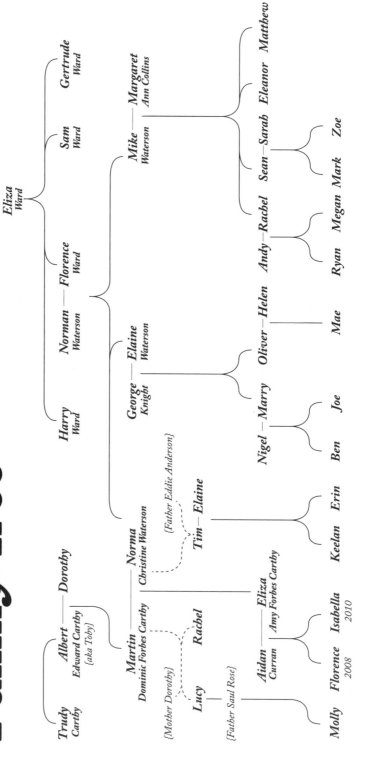

The Return Of The Wayward Daughter

*It's funny that you should be doing this at this point in my life
because potentially this is very much a year zero for me,
a re-evaluation … I really hope this is the beginning of, if you like,
the rest of my life. I'm close to actually being settled.*

Eliza in conversation with Sophie

It is the weekend before Easter 2011 and the Waterson Carthy household is bustling, busy with children, happenings, things.

Conversations are repeatedly punctuated by the charming Florence, Eliza's two-year-old, who runs in, usually with a gift for mum – a flower, a pancake, a Cadbury's Roses chocolate – and runs out again. Megan and Molly, Eliza's nieces, keep their auntie updated with Florence's activities, whether it's trying a pancake for the first time or asking to play dress up, whilst baby Izzy, at this point only four months old, is gazing peacefully up at a window, decorated in bright patterns by another young family member.

Eliza's mother, Norma Waterson, is in nearby Whitby hospital where she has been recuperating from a life-threatening illness for the past five months; though, fingers crossed, she is due for a visit home during the week. It will be the first time she has been there in six months, and will be visiting only briefly, an occupational therapist in tow. The latter will assess that the house passes the health and safety audit, is free from potential hazards and suitable for a convalescing folk singer who has only recently begun to walk again.

Eliza's dad, Martin Carthy, is due to visit Norma. He is going to the renowned Botham's of Whitby for bread on his return trip from the hospital, though he worries that there won't be any left by the time he gets there late on a Saturday afternoon. The door closes, he is gone, and Eliza will join him soon at her mother's bedside.

Eliza, meanwhile, asks me to help her carry some luggage from the boot of her car into her parents' home. There are some bin liners filled with clothes, a framed picture or two, something that must be a magazine rack. She tells me it's good to have her clothes back, that it's been too long without them. Inside, the bags and boxes are left in the doorway of the front room, a room which already hosts other similar-sized packages containing, it can be assumed, more of the same. A baby grand piano sparkles invitingly from the corner of the room.

What is bothering Eliza is not the amount of stuff that she needs to find a home for, in a house that already seems full to bursting, judging by the vast quantity of children's toys underfoot and the books, framed photographs and DVDs that line the walls. It is the fact that her mother is coming home. Eliza is like the teenager left alone for the first time, carefully covering all traces of a forbidden party. She plans to spend the rest of the weekend cleaning, tidying, sorting, finding temporary homes for things, enough to impress the occupational therapist; enough to impress her mother; maybe enough to impress herself too.

Eliza is in contemplative mood, not just due to the sorting of belongings and the talking of the past with a stranger. Eliza Carthy has moved back home to Robin Hood's Bay, the village where she grew up and where she hasn't lived for a decade or more. It must be giving her a weird sense of *déjà vu*.

At present, she and her young family are camping at Martin and Norma's whilst she looks for a more permanent home. But the popularity of the village with holiday makers means that finding a suitable property to rent is proving far from easy.

Understandably, inevitably, Eliza is taking stock of the past ten years, casting a critical eye over both her professional life and her personal life with each item she brings over the threshold and sets on the carpet. Now she is mother, as well as daughter; her new album, *Neptune*, is only weeks away from being released on her own label and is slowly doing the review rounds; a launch party complete with a David Owen set design has been planned.

Every now and then, she pauses to look at her watch. The removal men are due to be arriving with the last of her belongings which have been in storage since the move from her last home near Edinburgh. They are late: not the ideal start to the latest chapter in Eliza's eventful life.

ONE

Don't Put Your Daughter
On The Stage, Mrs Waterson

Norma was singing right up until Eliza was born.
And with that racket going on upstairs you're going to
become a musician. And what a musician.
Martin Carthy, *Eliza Carthy: My Music*, Channel 5 2008

It wasn't long after Norma Waterson returned from DJing in Montserrat in the West Indies that she and Martin Carthy were married. Lal and Mike Waterson were in the middle of writing and recording *Bright Phoebus*, and Martin had been called in to contribute arrangements. 'Martin, matter of factly, said "isn't it about time we got married?" There was no hoo-ha,' Norma acknowledged.[1]

When the Watersons were growing up in Hull, there were few cars on the road. 'It was a backwater little place,' Norma recalled, 'but by the time the '70s came along, Hull roads were chocka.' The M62 was being built and was snaking ever closer. Furthermore, boundary changes had dictated that Hull was no longer even part of Yorkshire. The Humber was now the focus, with either side of the river designated North and South Humberside respectively, though local residents were far from pleased, forming a movement to vent their spleen at being forced out of the county. They were Yorkshire folk through and through.

The Watersons were also Yorkshire people through and through, too. The increasing amount of traffic and the constant droning of the M62 did not appeal, and the siblings and their young families decided to move back to 'proper' Yorkshire, seeking out a better life in which to raise their young brood.

It wasn't difficult for the Watersons to decide which part of England's largest county would be their home. Robin Hood's Bay, the small fishing village just south along the coast from Whitby, was where the Watersons had holidayed as children. Young Mike Waterson would cycle there with his friends, whilst Lal and her new husband, George Knight, took their honeymoon in the village. They had friends, connections, there.

It was a sleepy place, where cars were replaced by walkers, maps in hand. Many of those intrepid tourists were completing the new Coast to Coast walk which had been founded by Alfred Wainwright in 1973 and which finished in the village. Couples took their children to play on its beaches. Its steep cobbled streets gave way to open fields and, rising up, the purple heather of the glorious moors.

One summer, Norma and Martin took a let in a farmhouse run by the Herbert family to spend time in the area to ensure that it really was the place for them to put down roots. They placed advertisements in all the Yorkshire newspapers, which read:

> *Large family seeks enough land*
> *for three houses and self-sufficiency*

The plan was for each of the three families, Mike and Ann, Lal and George, Norma and Martin, plus their respective offspring, to take a house in close quarters and live off the land as best they could. 'We wanted to be self-sufficient in those days but it didn't work out, in the end,' shrugged Norma.

'There was some kind of EEC [now called the European Union] directive, as it was in those days, which had been issued and suddenly people wanted to unload land,' Martin added. The couple started exploring each of the possible candidates until they found the perfect location. On top of the moors, just outside of the village, stood a big farmhouse and three enormous barns, a classic farmyard with the house at one end and the outhouses huddled together to form the shape of an 'F'. It was called St Ives Farm.

'The barns were big enough to make two houses out of,' Norma recalls, 'so that's what we did. My brother, and George, my brother-in-law, and Tom, this friend of Mike's ... Martin went out to work and got the money, we did the gigs and got the money, and they did the actual building of it. They built two houses themselves.'

'It was great,' Martin smiled, 'We couldn't have done it any other way.'

As Martin and Norma were the first couple to sell their house they were naturally the first to move in, on 1 June 1975. Coincidentally that was the same month that the BBC sitcom about self-sufficiency, *The Good Life*, finished its opening series.

'And it snowed. It was such a bad year: it had snowed at Easter and it snowed in June. We thought "Oh my God, what have we done here?" The oil had run out of the heaters and we had to go and order some more,' Norma laughed. But she was putting a brave face on things as Norma was seven months pregnant at the time and their new home was cold and secluded, almost cut-off once the first snows began to fall. They were unable to use gas, and so lugged coal, wood and oil to their homes for heating. Once Norma's siblings had also sold their houses, they too moved to the farm, bringing their children with them.

The families quickly settled in to farm life, enjoying each other's company, the cousins overjoyed at having their playmates on constant call.

Two months after the couple had moved into their new home, Norma and Martin had gone to bed after enjoying Whitby Folk Week's closing night. As Norma woke the next morning, she was horrified to discover that she was losing blood. Martin quickly awoke George and the two men padded her into the back seat of the car.

'It was nose-to-tail traffic all the way to Whitby hospital, so George drove on the wrong side of the road, his lights flashing, his hand on the horn, praying for a cop,' Martin recalls. And it was during this mad dash to the hospital that Martin experienced a communication with his soon-to-be-born child.

'I promise you this is true,' Martin begins, warily. 'I'm sitting in the front with George, Norma is lying on the back seat, and this – I have to call it a voice, but it wasn't a voice – this *thought* came to me. I distinctly heard "What the hell is going on?" and I turned round to answer Norma, thinking it was her, and I looked to where it was coming from. I realized it was coming directly from inside Norma. And I know it was Liza. She was inside wondering what the hell was going on, "let me out!"'

The close bond between Martin and his daughter, that anyone who has seen them together will have observed, must have been formed at the earliest point possible: her impending birth.

The car arrived at Whitby hospital in just thirteen minutes, at 8.30 a.m. Norma had been sent home from the hospital only two days before, but this time, she was loaded on to a trolley and rushed in. Martin was told to go home and ring at midday, though in actual fact Eliza was born just over an hour later, at 9.40 a.m. Eliza was a placenta previa, meaning the placenta had grown in the lowest part of Norma's womb, blocking the baby's exit route. She had to be delivered by emergency caesarean section and it's a sobering thought that, in years gone by, this complication could have been fatal to both mother and child.

Despite the quick and traumatic delivery though, Norma still had time for a song! The woman in the bed opposite had just had a little boy, and they soon began talking about singing, the other patient revealing her father had taught her 'Willy Went To Westerdale'. The pair sang the song, the very same which had been recorded by the Watersons almost a decade earlier, on their album *A Yorkshire Garland*.

With only one in 200 women experiencing placenta previa, a filmic race to the hospital and a song, perhaps this was the first indication that Eliza might enjoy the limelight.

She was immediately recognizable to her father. As Martin entered the maternity ward and peered into the row of incubators, he picked his daughter out straight away. Her face so obviously held something of them both, as well as their respective families. Aptly, then, it was decided that she should be named after both her great-grandmothers: Eliza was the name of Norma's grandmother, and Amy was Martin's grandmother whom he never had the chance to meet.

St Ives wasn't a working farm, though the families kept pigs, geese and chickens. There were two small woods next to a paddock and plenty of space for the children to play around in. They fashioned a swing from a tyre and rope, and the old coach that had been left behind by the previous occupants had been duly transformed into a den. They picked the bluebells that grew in the woods and, like all kids, revelled in getting covered in mud.

But, due to the age differences, it often fell to the older cousins to look after little Eliza, which, of course, didn't always go down too well.

'I remember tying her up to a ladder and leaving her there while we all went in for tea,' Oliver Knight, Lal and George's son, recalled rather sheepishly. 'She used to tell audiences that. And there was plenty of sword fighting and playing tricks on each other.'

Marry, Oliver's sister, is twelve years older than Eliza. 'I had to babysit Eliza when Martin and Norma were on the road, and I vividly remember having to take her into town one time. She had a spectacular paddy and I was desperately hoping that no one saw me. I can't remember what it was about, but it was so embarrassing.'

A calm, sweet baby, Eliza emerged into a fearsome, cheeky toddler. When Norma took her to the shops, she would secretly take things from the shelves, as Norma concentrated on filling the trolley with provisions, only to reveal her catch at the checkout where the hapless Norma had no choice but to cough up.

'That's how she got Monkey Moozle: she just grabbed him and held onto him and when we got to the checkout, there she was, holding this little monkey and I had to pay for it,' Norma shook her head, smiling. Monkey Moozle, you'll be pleased to hear, is still with us, though his little dungarees are more of a pastel pink rather than the bright red which caught the young Eliza's eye in the shop that day. Watch out for him in the video made by Marry Waterson to accompany Eliza's song, 'Monkey'.

Eliza and her cousins are thankful for the way in which they were brought up.

'I was very glad [our parents] did it, it was a great place to live. We had motorbikes; we could drive cars all over the fields. When local kids came up here from the village for birthday parties and so on, they were amazed at the freedom we all had,' Oliver recalled. 'We were known locally as the hippy commune.'

For a while, until her cousins Eleanor and Matthew came along and 'I had someone else to pick on', Eliza was the youngest on site, her cousins just that bit older. Though Oliver was like an older brother, teasing and playing pranks on her just as a brother would, Eliza was desperate for a brother of her own and regularly used to plague her parents with requests for one. This is one of the reasons, Eliza claims, her parents began fostering for around five years. Then, when she was aged eleven, a brother did walk into her life, but not in the way she had envisaged.

Both Martin and Norma had been hitched before. Martin had married Dorothy, with whom he had two daughters, Lucy and Rachel. They remain close to their father, and also to Norma and Eliza.

Norma had married Eddie young – too young and a long time ago, according to Eliza – and the marriage had soured. Tim was around three or four at the time that Norma went, and they had remained estranged ever since. That was until Eliza was eleven, and he made contact, keen to get to know his mother and her new family.

'I'd always gone on at her about having a brother,' Eliza winced, 'you know how kids do, oblivious to the fact that it was completely insensitive as I did actually have a brother and they were estranged. It wasn't something that occurred to me.' Thankfully, the reunion was an extremely happy one. 'We now have a wonderful relationship,' Eliza says proudly.

Norma made the decision to cease gigging during the week once Eliza was of school age. Gigs and festivals still happened at the weekend, but Norma wanted to ensure that Eliza was not distracted from school and routine. However, of course, if a booking arose that was too tempting to resist, Eliza could be cared for by the other members of the family. 'The house was full of people so she went to everybody. On one tour of the States we did, Tom, Mike's friend who had helped us build the houses, looked after her for the whole month,' Norma remembered.

Eliza accompanied her parents to gigs frequently, from folk clubs and festivals in the UK to lengthy tours of America, Canada, Australia and New Zealand. Many of her interviews over the years recounted how she would fall asleep under tables and stages as her parents performed. 'I grew up in pubs. For me they were a place of work,' she commented to *The Guardian* in 2005.[2]

Music and work were always sociable occasions for Martin, Norma and their extended family. During the many parties held at the farm, Eliza would readily sneak downstairs to listen to her parents singing together, often hiding under a table for good measure knowing she should have been in bed. She became accustomed to all manner of musicians and music scene folk dropping in to the house for a song, a cup of tea, a party, a chat. She became familiar with the regular rhythm of the working musician's life, a rhythm as predictable as the movement of the seasons: folk club gigs punctuated by summer festivals, perhaps an overseas tour, preparation for the recording of an album, a Christmas gig. She would recognize the label owners, the managers, booking agents and publicity officers; she would begin to grow accustomed to the regular pattern of festivals and to which summer weekend they were attributed.

In a 1996 edition of *fRoots*, editor Ian Anderson remembers a determined character, even at four years of age, at Sidmouth Folk Festival:

> The only time I set eyes on Eliza Carthy before she was in our midst as the fully fledged being she has become in the past few years was

as a particularly … er … strong willed 4-year-old giving a bunch of wilting young Kirkpatricks and other folklets their marching orders at Sidmouth Festival, whilst her somewhat frayed mum was heard to blame it on all the red meat she'd consumed on doctor's orders during gestation. Not somebody you wanted to mess with, even then.[3]

But most importantly, the young Eliza began to learn all the songs. This was not prescriptive though. Her parents did not sit her down in front of a dog-eared copy of the Child Ballads and tell her that she wouldn't be allowed pudding unless she learned 'Lucy Wan', 'Tam Lin' or 'Sir Patrick Spens'. The songs her parents sang and loved were just the soundtrack to her childhood. They were shared with other family members and friends, and they were performed. Those songs were not generally learned from record, though, the family preferring a more traditional passing down from one person to another.

And she first recalled that repertoire on stage at Fylde Festival in Fleetwood aged six. She had begged and pleaded with her dad to be allowed to join them on stage. 'I told her that she could, and she could stand next to me. I told her that if she knew the song we were singing, if she tugged on my trouser leg, I would lift her up on to my hip so she could sing in to the mic,' Martin remembered. 'The first song she knew, so I lifted her up. When the next song started, she signalled she wanted to sing that one, too. In the end, I didn't put her down. She knew the entire set.'

Derek Schofield, editor of the English Folk Dance and Song Society magazine, *English Dance and Song* (EDS), first witnessed Eliza sing when she was just eleven. Martin and Norma were frequent attendees at Will Noble's folk nights, commonly referred to as Will's Barn Concerts, which, on this particular occasion in September 1986, hosted the Copper Family, Bob Davenport and the Rakes.

'[Academic and writer] Ian Russell recorded the event and put it out as a VWML [Vaughan Williams Memorial Library] cassette, the first in a series,' Derek recalled. 'He recorded Eliza singing a single song, but it wasn't included on the cassette. Then she went out and played in the yard with Ian's son, Joe.'

The primary school Eliza attended is the main school that still serves the village today, sitting next to the Bay's tiny fire station, though she expects the school is very different now to what she experienced at the beginning of the 1980s: 'When I was there, there were probably around 115 kids. Now there's more like 45; it's all holiday homes and B&Bs in the village now.' She's right too. Every other building boasts No Vacancies and the clink of china cups on hotel verandas signify an abundance of afternoon tea for visitors.

It was a good school and Eliza enjoyed her time there. Both she and Norma hope that Eliza's children will be able to follow in their mother's footsteps and go there. However, when it was time for Eliza to move to secondary school, the local comprehensive didn't appeal. At the time, the exam results coming out of the place were poor and now Eliza had begun piano she wanted to develop her musical skills in the classroom. There was little provision for music at the local state school.

With Eliza winning a scholarship to Hunmanby Hall, near Filey, Martin had the difficult task of explaining to his father that his granddaughter would be privately educated. In Martin's mind, however, there was no question. 'Mike [Waterson] was a great mind, but he was completely let down by the education system in our country. He wasn't even allowed to take the eleven-plus. Well, it was called the Common Entrance exam then, up here, which makes it even worse! Common Entrance! Everyone should be able to take it,' Martin shakes his head, exasperated. 'Instead, only ten or twelve people in Mike's class took it, and they were selected. Naughty boys like Mike weren't allowed.'

Martin recognized in Eliza the academic gift that his brother-in-law, Mike, had. He was determined to ensure the best opportunity was available to his daughter, in the way it hadn't been for Mike.

'She's a very clever girl, an extremely clever girl,' Norma explained, without a hint of motherly bias.

However, the trip to Hunmanby Hall was a long one each morning and afternoon, involving a bus from Robin Hood's Bay to Scarborough, followed by a train to Hunmanby and then a mile or so walk to the school. This was particularly difficult in winter when the farm was known to get snowed in. Actually, the first winter of Eliza's secondary education saw Norma and Martin head off on tour, so Eliza took advantage of the boarding facilities at the school. It was quite a 'rickety old place', as Eliza remembers it, the school accommodation was cold and draughty, and the conditions aggravated her asthma. There was one particularly bad attack which saw Eliza rushed off to hospital in an ambulance.

When her parents were due to tour again in the summer, they sought out boarding closer to the family home, at Fyling Hall School, in case an attack occurred again. Eliza seemed to like Fyling Hall: her daily commute was much shorter, and she hadn't made any great friends during her first year at Hunmanby Hall anyway. As the school term edged closer, she transferred schools and started her second year as a Fyling Hall student. Which was just as well really. Hunmanby Hall, rather unexpectedly, went bust, a consequence of 'the downturn in private education' as the retrospective website explains.[4] Eliza's cousin, Emma, who was also a pupil there, had to leave the school without any qualifications.

Fyling Hall School has more than a touch of Enid Blyton's Malory Towers about it. The collection of tall, sandy buildings still quietly whisper elegant stately home rather than school, and cluster on the brow of a hill overlooking the sea. There is a peaceful, shady garden complete with topiary hedges and sundial nestling close to the main building. A chaffinch greets me at the wall near to reception; a woman tells me that the Headmaster is still at church but I'm welcome to look round.

The dorms look more like the holiday cottages which dominate the village, and the cymbals of a drum kit catch my eye, glinting out of the window of a small music room densely packed with keyboards and guitars. A notice board advertises the piano and singing lesson timetables. Past the grand main house, voices float out of dormitory windows and an indoor football match is taking place in the sports hall. Peering into a window obscured by a skeleton mannequin, the classrooms look small and homely, probably relatively unchanged from the 1920s when a local woman, Mab Harrison, founded the place. The school's horses graze in the fields and the gentle chirrup of sparrows make this a very welcome home from home.

Descending back down the meandering lane to the village, I pass a small troop of students making their way back to school. Though it's midday on a Sunday, they're neatly turned out in their burgundy blazers, pristine white shirts and striped ties. The girls sport tartan skirts and dark tights, not a scrap of makeup or a hint of a high heel. It's difficult to imagine Eliza attending school here, with her penchant for dyed, cropped hair, stonewashed dungarees, piercings and platform trainers. 'I seem to remember her trying to bend the uniform policy and having regular disagreements with the Senior Mistress and the Principal,' her former music teacher explained. 'Although I can't remember what she tried to wear, unfortunately.'

However, Eliza loved school. 'I loved learning, I loved it all, but I had a bit of an awkward relationship with my teachers as I was opinionated and stroppy. I'll never forget one of the teachers [at Hunmanby Hall] trying to explain folk music ... he never did it again. He was just talking innocently, explaining the Scotch jump ... skip ... what's it called? See, if I'd paid more attention, I'd be able to tell you! And I remember that I just said "no, it's not like that, that's not it at all."'

Cathy Hornung was the Fyling Hall music teacher for many years, though now she teaches modern languages on a part time basis. When Eliza arrived at the school, around twelve years of age, Cathy taught her. 'She could be infuriating in rehearsals,' she concurred. 'She was an active member of the choir, always taking part in concerts, singing in either the alto or seconds. But she would often improvise her own parts from time to time, making it very difficult for the singers around her to follow their parts. But she knew how to make her voice blend in with the others so never stood out.'

Music is enjoyed and encouraged at Fyling Hall School. Over half of the current students take instrumental lessons with peripatetic teachers, across piano, voice, woodwind, strings, brass and percussion; many students rise through the Associated Board and Rock School examinations. Choirs and smaller music ensembles, such as recorder and string groups, have healthy attendances and terms are interspersed by concerts, often held in local churches. A quick glance on Fyling Hall's own dedicated YouTube channel reveals some of these musical endeavours, from a choir singing Adele's 'Rolling In The Deep', a Year Ten duo's cover of the Killers' 'Mr Brightside' to the more traditional school musical fare of *Les Miserables'* 'I Dreamed A Dream'. Interestingly, one video features a performance by the Junior Folk Orchestra.

Eliza had begun to learn piano from an early age and already had a great repertoire of traditional songs. It was obvious she had a talent for music. Martin remembers a moment when he realized the depth and breadth of his daughter's burgeoning musicality. 'We were at one festival, I think it was Redcar Festival, when she came over, holding something in her hand and said "mum, dad, can I have this please?" It was an ocarina and it was expensive. So we set her a challenge. There was a tune book with it and we said "We're going to go away for half an hour and when we come back, if you can play one of those tunes, we'll buy you the ocarina.'"

You know what's coming next: 'We went away for half an hour, maybe thirty five minutes, and we came back and she played the tune book. The whole tune book! So we had to buy her the ocarina!'

Eliza had also begun violin lessons at school, though was left far from enamoured, holding little regard for Associated Board exams. 'I remember having to drive her up to St Ives one day to collect music because she was doing a grade exam on her violin; against her wishes, I suspect,' Cathy recalls. 'She had left the music at home, though I expect she could have played it perfectly well from memory.'

15

Following the common path of learning an instrument – lessons, grades, Saturday morning music schools – did not suit Eliza. An interview I did with Eliza for *FiddleOn* Magazine in 2005 reiterated this, as she said 'I find that the Associated Board way of teaching is not very motivating, where kids only have grades and exams to look forward to. You have enough exams at school as it is. They don't play you any Balkan gypsy music, Stephane Grappelli. I became quite cold towards the violin.'[5]

In the radio documentary, *A Place Called England*, which was broadcast on BBC Radio 3 in 2003, Eliza explained how she would like to work with the government and music teachers in schools to provide an alternative to the one route of music tuition which is currently on offer to UK children: largely classical music-based learning, orchestras and the steady treadmill of terrifying Associated Board exams. The documentary gave way to a discussion about Newcastle University's Folk and Traditional Music degree, a relatively new course which aims to equip its students with practical business skills required by professional musicians, alongside performance and technique coaching, ensemble work and histories of songs, contexts and cultures; Eliza welcomed formal training such as this. She felt it mapped out an alternative to conventional music tuition and could well be used as inspiration for music teaching to younger pupils.

And, she admitted, had a course like this been on offer when she was of undergraduate age, she may well have become a university student. 'But,' she said almost wistfully, 'I'm self-taught and as such there are gaps in my knowledge.'

But more of this later.

Discouraged by her early conventional training on the violin, the young Eliza instead looked to other instruments. Shying away from picking up the guitar – Eliza is the first to admit that she wouldn't dare compete with her father, or 'Dr McMBE' as she calls him on *Anglicana* – the mandolin was an early choice which neatly translated to fiddle later as they both use the same tuning.

As clichéd as the teenager stereotype is, it seems that, for Eliza, her thirteenth year was to prove pivotal for the rest of her life. It was her social life that was going to dictate how her teenage years – and beyond – would be spent.

Eliza maintains that she had difficulty in making friends, that she was the most unpopular girl in school. When you see her up on stage, laughing and joking confidently with an audience, patiently signing autographs in the foyer, assembling and leading a band, it seems impossible. In person, she is warm and sweet, greeting and leaving with kisses on cheeks; keen to laugh and to share experiences. How could this woman, who finishes every telephone conversation to her parents with a 'love you' and has a drinking story for every occasion, have been an unpopular child?

But Norma concurred with Eliza's views about her teenage self: 'She did find it hard to make friends; she was very different to her peers. She had three friends and they hung out about together, but they didn't do music so that set her apart. She and Alethea were closest but they had a big bust up when they were thirteen. She always says it ruined her life.' To make up for the devastating argument, which effectively robbed Eliza of her best friend, Norma came up with a brilliant plan. She asked Eliza to join with her and her sister Lal and Lal's daughter Marry. Thus were the Waterdaughters conceived.

'It was a natural progression, as mum and Norma always wanted to get us involved,' explained Marry. 'No excuses were needed to sing, we'd just have a singsong in the kitchen. Our first gig as the Waterdaughters was at Vancouver Folk Festival in front of 30,000 people or so. It was just a sea of faces. But it came naturally to her, we felt safe performing.'

Kit Bailey, daughter of folk singer Roy Bailey and later Eliza's agent, heard about the Waterdaughters from her enthusiastic father. 'My dad used to go to Vancouver Folk Festival quite a lot and he came back one year, telling us how Norma and Lal had got the Waterdaughters together, and I remember him raving about how fantastic it was.'

As Eliza sang, flanked either side by her relatives, she made up her mind that she, too, was going to be a performer. 'We did our bit, came off stage and Eliza said "right, I'm not going back to school, that's it. This is what I want to do for the rest of my life. Is that alright, dad?"' Martin laughed. 'I had to say that it was illegal; that she had to stay at school until she was sixteen.'

So the gaps left by lost friendships in Robin Hood's Bay were duly plugged by gigs and a furious learning of music. 'I was working as a graphic designer, then,' Marry explained. 'All my holiday was taken up with gigs and festivals. We didn't like all the songs they taught us: I remember me and Eliza putting on stupid voices when we sang one about a pear tree. Then one time, at a folk club gig, we got the giggles. Mum and Norma had to stand in front of us to block us from view.'

Eliza forced herself to go to school during the day, knowing full well that her evenings and weekends would be taken up with playing, learning and performing a growing repertoire.

And then the fiddle came back into her life; this time, on her own terms. Martin's father died and the family inherited his fiddle. It lay in the house on the table and each time she walked past it, she felt it eye her, challenging her to 'play me, play me'. Singer and fiddler Chris Wood was a great friend of Martin and Norma's, and would always call in to the house whenever he was gigging nearby. 'Chris came and saw the fiddle and found he had a spare tail piece which he put on,' Martin remembered. 'He set the bridge, strung it up and handed it to her, saying "there you go, get on with it". She always acknowledges Chris as the one who first fired her up, until she met Nancy [Kerr], of course.'

The fiddle soon became Eliza's focus. She would come home from school and work her way through the tune books belonging to her parents. Because she was now playing the music she realized she loved, she rose to the challenge and progressed quickly: 'I find the violin an argumentative instrument; I take one thing and it'll take another back. It gave me a hard time and it wasn't always enjoyable.'[6]

Often more interested in rhythm than melody, she found her right arm, her bowing arm – rather than her left, which was picking out the notes – more integral to the sound she wanted to make, the sound in her head that she aimed to replicate. She looked to the traditions from the Cotswolds and Essex, and focused on the music of the Morris, stating 'I'm interested in the rhythmic capabilities of the fiddle, the rhythmic variations. It's what I call "rocksteady", the only word I can use to describe it. Less notes, more opportunities to improvise, a lolloping sound.'[7]

It was around this time that Martin, Norma and Eliza decided to leave the farm. Lal and George had left two years previously, and Norma was finding that the onset of arthritis was making living there uncomfortable, plus the location of the farm being a little off the beaten track – three and a half miles from the village if you were to walk, six by road – meant that the parents found themselves dedicating a large amount of time to chauffeuring the kids to and from their social engagements. Though that, too, did have its uses, Norma was keen to point out. Up until then, Norma hadn't learned to drive. Needing to ferry Eliza to Scouts once a week prompted Norma to take up her driving licence, though Martin, to this day, cannot drive, instead preferring to take the train to gigs.

Martin and Norma bought a house in the village proper, the same house they live in today. It's a fairly large pile sitting just off the main thoroughfare that leads down to the water's edge. A number of guesthouses and a couple of inviting pubs sit expectantly round the corner. Most importantly, for the apprentice fiddler, was the acoustics of their new residence. A wide landing with a tall ceiling dropped down a fairytale banister, the kind Mary Poppins would have loved, to an open hall. Eliza would sit on the stairs where the sound reverberated best, sight-reading the tunes in the pile of tune books balanced precariously on the step next to her and choosing which ones she wanted to use. No doubt she sought inspiration and approval from the assortment of framed pictures of musical personalities which still dot the walls of the hall.

When the neighbours called round to speak with Martin and Norma about Eliza's music, her parents could only hold their breath and brace themselves. The farm had allowed them all to make as much noise as they liked; they weren't used to having to worry about belting out a rousing chorus or playing until late into the night. They didn't want to have to line the walls with egg boxes and mattresses. Thankfully, Martin and Norma had nothing to worry about and the eggboxes and mattresses could stay where they were. 'The man across the road, Michael, and the people next door used to love it. They absolutely loved her playing. The lady next door said "one of these days I'm going to knock a hole in the wall so I can hear her better!"' Norma recalled, proudly.

It was during her early teens that Eliza began to marry together her two loves: words and music. She had discovered the Child Ballads and was drawn in by the stories, the poetry, and the way in which the ancient tales still have a bearing on society today. 'That's when we knew we had her!' Norma chuckled, mischievously.

Eliza had been writing to amuse herself for years, and had always assumed she would be a writer. 'I wrote a couple of books when I was a teenager. Thank God they've never seen the light of day, as they're bloody awful. But that's what I wanted to be; I wanted to be a writer. I was into the heavy research and all that sort of thing. I wrote a lot of plays, too. I was really into fantasy, exploring epics, and writing books from the ballads. I was really into that; I wanted to bring it all together. And when I was mid-teens I was into people like Katherine Kerr, the big generational writing for fantasy nuts,' she recalls.

In an interview with the Musicians' Union magazine, *Musician*, Eliza mentioned her passion for writing and how it crossed over into her love and understanding of the tradition: 'I wanted to convert big ballads into massive Tolkien-esque books. It fascinated me to learn that Tolkien envisaged *Lord Of The Rings* as an English saga. He wanted to invent a mythology for England. Of course, they never think to ask English people to do the music for it. They just wheel out Enya instead.'[8]

Despite the naivety of the young writer, her writing showed great promise. Eliza would share her writing with her parents.

'I remember a composition she wrote, a piece of homework for school, a story. And I remember reading it and it was fantastic,' Martin said. 'The thing I remember about it was this description of a hall full of people, a big party going on, a banquet. And something happened and everything stopped dead and after two seconds, a dog sneezed. And it's the kind of thing that happens: there's a party going on and the dogs are there, getting all excited and when they get excited, they sneeze. And she'd spotted that, at the age of eleven or twelve. I remember shaking my head, bloody hell, what an imagination.'

'I did write songs, too,' Eliza added, 'but a lot of it was pants. I can see where I was coming from but that was about it. I heard about someone the other day who had just burned all their diaries, saying it was the best thing they'd ever done. I may yet do that. I used to keep a diary when I was thirteen and when I read it now, I think "oh dear, oh dear."'

But even as late as 2008, Eliza revealed she'd been indulging in creative writing. In *Time Out*'s article 'Ten things you didn't know about Eliza Carthy', Eliza stated that the death of her hard drive resulted in the loss of 'the first and only chapter of the book I was writing on tour. It's a story about a boy looking for his father, and part of it is set in a circus that's run by a bear with a mouse in its ear.'[9] A bear with a mouse in its ear? 'She wrote really weird things,' clarified Norma.

Finding herself without friends, particularly musical ones, Eliza didn't feel comfortable doing what most burgeoning folk musicians would do: attend a session. 'She had quite a lonely life here,' admitted Norma. 'Normally young people that want to play, they go into sessions, sitting on the outside and listening to the older musicians in the middle. They learn the tunes that way. Because there was nothing like that here, she had to do everything more or less on her own.'

The first year Martin and Norma attended the Whitsun celebrations at Bampton, Oxfordshire, was when Norma was pregnant with Eliza. Since then, it has become an annual ritual. The couple, with Eliza in tow, would travel to Bampton to watch the Morris sides dance around the village, joining in with the sessions and singarounds in the village pubs. They were mesmerized by the tunes and the ways in which the sides interpreted them through the dance, and enjoyed meeting up with friends and acquaintances to have a drink, a sing and a play.

Today, there are three Morris sides in Bampton, with only one affiliated to the Morris Ring. 'The only advantage, as far as I can see, is that it offers cheaper insurance!' smiles Tony Daniels who has been dancing at Bampton for 46 of his 52 years. For the last sixteen of those he has been squire of one of the three Bampton sides. Francis Shergold had preceded him, the well-known squire who had danced in Bampton for an astonishing 60 years and passed away in 2008, just two months before he was due to celebrate his 90th birthday. Contrary to the perpetuated stereotypes, Tony is actually one of the oldest dancers in Bampton, with the three sides dominated by local men predominantly in their twenties and thirties.

Whit celebrations take place each year over the spring bank holiday and there are festivities in the village on each day, beginning with music in the pubs on Friday night. The annual Shirt Race takes place on the Saturday, where costumed groups perform a mad dash around the village whilst pushing a pram, downing beer in one go at each allotted stop. Then there is the making and judging of the May garlands, and more sessions and singarounds. It is the bank holiday Monday when the sides tour the village and dance outside the houses. 'There's never a typical Whitsun,' Tony laughed, 'but it seems to balance out each year, one way or another!'

Whitsun in Bampton draws enthusiasts from all over the country. In the late 1970s, Tony told me, it was commonplace for the celebrations to attract an audience of anything between 2,000 and 3,000 people. Though there are certainly fewer spectators today, it remains a big weekend for the locals. 'It's so much to do with the village; it's part of village life. It's more than just a tradition, it's meeting with friends that you might only see once a year,' Tony affirms. 'But it's nice to see the regulars each year, people like Derek Schofield [editor of *English Dance And Song*] and [folklorist, academic and archivist] Doc Rowe.

'Martin [Carthy] and his family have been coming here for years; Eliza's been coming since she was a baby. They see Bampton as a holiday and make sure they come every year. I remember one year, Martin had been booked somewhere in Germany the same weekend as Whitsun and he didn't want to miss it, so he told the promoters some kind of ridiculous fee, a hell of a lot of money, thinking they'd never say yes. But they did say yes and he had to go!'

Martin remembers his introduction to Morris in Bampton and the Whitsun celebrations: 'I'd recorded a Bampton tune and Francis Shergold, who was the Bampton squire at the time, said "oh you've recorded our tune, you better come and play for the lads so you can learn how to play it properly." It transformed my playing. The tunes are there to tell people what to do and there's nothing like it, seeing six pairs of feet hit the ground as I'm playing for them. It's fantastic, and it's metronomic, it changes your whole attitude.'

'Some people think Morris dancing is strange and old-fashioned, with funny ideas about women, and so on. But we're all fired up, and it shows in our dancing,' Tony added. 'You watch those feet,' corroborated Norma, 'and it doesn't matter if it's a ceilidh or Morris dancing or whatever, you watch those feet hitting the floor and it does something to the rhythm in you. It's almost magical.'

'Liza would've heard us talking about that, she latched on to the idea,' Martin confirmed. Eliza, too, wanted to play for dancing.

The Yorkshire village of Goathland is probably best known as the location for the long-running television series, *Heartbeat*. Each year, it welcomes coachloads of visitors, keen to see the roads on which the classic cars from the show pootle along. Goathland is also home to the Goathland Plough Stots, a long sword dance team. Clad in pink and blue tunics, to represent the 19th century Whigs and Tories, and fastened by a white sash, the Plough Stots were revived in 1922 with the help of Cecil Sharp and have been dancing pretty much ever since.

Keith Thompson, then Secretary of the side, knew of Martin Carthy and Norma Waterson, but had never spoken to them. When he took a call from Norma, who explained that their daughter was keen to come along to a Plough Stots practice, he acquiesced, expecting a young girl of eight or nine to arrive:

> We don't play by the rules of the Morris, really. Not the arcane rules written by silly buggers in Oxford that say Morris is men only, anyway. So we said we didn't mind if Norma's daughter came along. I remember it was a Tuesday night, a dark November's night, the kind where you don't go wandering round the village. We were practising and the door opened and in walked this ... well, this *thing*. She had purple boots, or silver boots, I'll be damned if I can remember. No, she had Doc Martens sprayed purple, that's right. She had earrings through her nose and funny-coloured hair. She looked like nothing we'd ever seen. We all looked at each other. We'd been expecting a young girl, just learning the violin, not some punky-looking teenager. She produced a fiddle, listened to our melodeon and joined in. It was quite strange, really!

But despite her outlandish appearance, she had no trouble fitting in. Martin remembered that 'She played all the tunes and right at the end she played the Laurel and Hardy theme and they said, "right, you're in."'

Each January, much like Bampton's Whitsun festivities, the Goathland Plough Stots dominate their village for the day, dancing outside the houses and pubs, entertaining the local residents and tucking into a roast beef dinner in the evening. It's a day which begins early, always in the freezing cold morning, and the participants keep themselves warm with layered clothing and plenty of alcohol. Eliza participated that very first January after joining with the Plough Stots, and still comes back to Goathland each year to do the same, regardless of her current place of residence or the location of her current gig date. The birth of her babies, both in winter, didn't prevent her, either.

'I missed it [in 2010] because I was with the Imagined Village and we were in Glasgow one night then Newcastle the next,' Eliza said. 'I could've driven down the night after the Glasgow gig and driven back up to Newcastle the following day, but, to be honest, my family stopped me. They said "you're insane; if you fucking do that, we'll never speak to you again." I did go the year before, but obviously Florence was only a month old, so I went in the morning, played for a few dances, then went home. I haven't been that committed over the last few years and I'd really like to get back into it, but having young children makes it quite hard.'

The secretary of the Plough Stots, John Atkinson, invited me to attend their day of dance which, in 2012, fell on Saturday 14 January. I was more than happy to oblige, and keen to witness this spectacle which drew Eliza back to North Yorkshire each year.

Sadly, though, public transport was not as cooperative. Despite a meticulously planned journey – a two-hour train ride which would allow just enough time to hop on to one of only two buses which would visit the village of Goathland in winter, the second timetabled too late in the day to catch the dancing – complete power loss and signal failure between Huddersfield and Leeds meant we were corralled on to too few coaches heading for Leeds, adding an extra hour and a half on our journey. We missed the connecting bus to Goathland spectacularly, and a kindly man in Malton tourist information office found us another bus which would take us a third of the way to Goathland, before a taxi completed the final leg. We arrived in Goathland at just gone three in the afternoon, the 100 mile-or-so journey taking an incredibly frustrating six hours.

Nevertheless, and not to be defeated, we bounded down to Beck Hole, the tiny hamlet just outside the village which consists of nine cottages, a farm, and the Birch Hall Inn, the compact, whitewashed pub which sits next to the stream running through the valley and gives the hamlet its name.

Before we could see the pub, we could hear the musicians and dancers, swords gently rasping and the clatter of uniformed footsteps, in full flight. As we rounded the last corner, we saw that a small audience had gathered either side of the lane, juggling pint glasses, cameras and patters of applause. Eliza was busy sawing away with the rest of the merry band, which consisted of guitars, squeezeboxes and more fiddles. Four teams were dancing, including one junior team clad in tabards and holding slight wooden planks rather than swords. Each time they finished a dance, the triumphant pentagram of swords, called the sword lock, would be held aloft.

Thankfully, as we warmed up with hot mulled wine, we caught the last four dances before the performers, exhausted from the dance, the excess of booze and the endurance of the thick frost which had lingered all day, took over the pub and passed round the parkin, sausage rolls and flapjack, before indulging in yet more whisky. Unlike Bampton and its crowds from all over, it seemed that we were the only visitors: everyone knew everyone else, and lived nearby enough to share lifts and to save the inebriated from having to negotiate the winding roads home. Eliza was duly bundled into a car en route to Robin Hood's Bay to relieve the babysitter and bring her daughters back to the festivities.

Later, the Goathland Plough Stots and their families, friends and supporters arrived at the Village Hall transformed – hair had been tamed, red faces calmed and there were even one or two tuxedos being sported for the occasion. Guests were assigned tables, and the two spare seats at Eliza's table made obvious the absence of her parents: Norma hadn't been feeling well and wasn't up to it; Martin had forgotten he had a gig in Bridport, Dorset. 'And it was supposed to be a family outing,' Eliza lamented and shook her head, breaking up bread rolls for Florence and Izzy.

Following the three courses, and the decimation of the paper tablecloth, thanks to Izzy's enthusiastic tearing and some neat biro indentations courtesy of Florence's artistic eye and a borrowed pen from Ann Waterson, the speeches began. Master of ceremonies was John Atkinson, but the main feature of the night was remembering the members of the team who had passed away during the course of the year and the legacies they would leave behind. Keith Thompson was anointed president, a post he accepted with humility – and a rather long speech, about which John teased him for the remainder of the evening.

Looking forward to the future of the side, though, was also very much a focus. Plans for a May 2012 dance weekend were unveiled, a first for the Goathland Plough Stots and their wider sword dance tradition. For the first time, the village will be host to a day of dance for all six teams in the British Isles that practise the long and short sword dance – the Grenoside and Handsworth teams from South Yorkshire, Flamborough from the East Riding, High Spen Blue Diamond from County Durham (seemingly the only short sword team who are actually referred to as rapper dancers) and Papa Stour from the Shetland Isles. Confirming the attendance of the latter, John explained, would be a particular coup, the team having only danced on English soil on one previous occasion.

John was also keen to let the diners know that the Goathland Plough Stots would be encouraging the girls and women of the village to dance with the team, should they want to. It seemed that a number of girls had already jumped at the chance – literally! – as I had already seen a few girls joining their fellow villagers in skipping over the swords outside the Birch Hall Inn earlier that day.

'I had decided to dance girls from the village to keep the team going,' John said later, 'as we only had two or three boys, and as you know we need at least six to make a team. The senior members of the team all decided that the Plough Stots is the heritage of the village; not an individual team and we would certainly not be dictated to by someone or somebody who has no interest in the village history.'

As the team's existing constitution failed to mention whether women and girls should be permitted to dance with the team or not, John and his colleagues decided to leave the constitution untouched as it was written in 1921, amended from 1820.

Before the raffle was called, however, there was one final thing. John wielded a crude artificial pig's head in his hand, menacingly. It was placed on the head of the member who had embarrassed himself or herself most throughout the course of the day, a sort of pagan dunce cap to tease the member who had made the most mistakes. It seemed there had been a few contenders, but the overall 'winner' was a rather sheepish looking man who came and sat in front of the diners and assumed his punishment most graciously. His crime? John laughed so hard, he found it hard to tell the audience, but it appeared the man had lost control of his Plough Stot sash which had plummeted to the ground, despite fumbled attempts to keep it at his waistline, impeding his dance as he did so. One of the funniest sights he had ever seen, John snorted, his eyes watering in laughter.

No wonder Eliza had made every effort to attend the festivities each year. Not only was it great fun, dancing and playing throughout the village all day, aided by adrenalin, camaraderie and alcohol, but the attentive, supportive audience which gathered in the evening to eat together, raise money for the village reading room and share memories, jokes and plans for the future, were a really nice bunch of people. They weren't necessarily dyed-in-the-wool folk music fans or folklore enthusiasts, but people who lived in or near to Goathland and felt pride in their village – and this weird old tradition which, they repeated proudly, had been in the village's history for around five hundred years.

And it wasn't just Eliza who returned each year. The son of the owners of the B&B in which we stayed had a friend in his early twenties who was born and raised in Goathland and always returned for the annual event, despite working 100 miles away in Oldham, Greater Manchester. The first January that Eliza made an appearance with the Plough Stots on their day of dance, though, gave the assembled an insight into the teenage Eliza's musical ability.

'Steve had a new melodeon and he put it down on the table. Right away, Liza said "can I have a go?" She took a look at it, put the straps on and promptly started playing it,' Keith recalled. 'Similarly, another time, we were in a hotel room having our January dinner and there was a baby grand piano in the corner. I asked, "Can anyone play that thing?" Eliza said "I can," and sat down and started playing. I remember her playing Scott Joplin's "The Entertainer". It was peculiar as she'd never cracked on she could play the melodeon or the piano. She decided around the age of fourteen that she was going to play as a professional, but she'd never been pushed into it. And nobody would have known she'd turn out to be this international folk star, she just thought it'd be a good idea to play with the team.'

Eliza made sure she accompanied the team wherever they went. The first time the Plough Stots were invited abroad was to a festival in Antwerp, Belgium, which became more of a village trip when the extended families of the Plough Stot dancers decided to come along, making it more fun for Eliza as there were more female faces and people her own age along for the weekend. Keith remembers:

> It was the first time we appreciated how good she was, how well she could play and sing. She was bloody marvellous. We danced every hour on the hour in Antwerp Square, dancing along with the cathedral bells. We started at 7a.m. and kept going until the afternoon, when we marched down the road. That was when Eliza decided to play Nellie the bloody Elephant! That's the sort of thing she'd do! I remember, in particular, her playing and singing in the hotel. She had on silver boots and a frock, 'poshed up' as she said, and she was playing and singing away, tapping her foot. She silenced the whole room, and this was long before she went on stage. I have a video, the earliest one of her playing, which is now part of the team archive.

Keith also talked of trips to the Fools Festivals on the continent:

> Europeans tend to eat, drink and go off their trolley during their Lent Fools Festivals. But in the Czech Republic a few years ago, Eliza came along and sang in the church. It was stunning, there was not a dry eye, and we've got that on CD, too. I also remember her

and some of the other younger members of the team hiring bikes in Bruges, racing round and round the cobbled streets. And also in Belgium, she thought it'd be a good idea to let all the caged animals out in the pet shop! She was extremely shy at times, and her dress sense was odd. Red, black, purple … you never knew what colour her hair would be. But she was always lots of fun, a lovely lass.

When the Watersons performed *A Mighty River Of Song* at the Albert Hall in May 2007, the Plough Stots were invited to dance on stage. Eliza donned her pink and blue tunic and accompanied them. Keith Thompson sang the longer version of the Goathland Plough Stot song, only proffered on very special occasions:

> *Here's a host of us all*
> *From Goathland go wee*
> *We're goin a rambling*
> *The country for to see*
> *The country for to see*
> *Some passtime for to take*
> *So freely you will give to us*
> *As freely we will take*
> *So now you see us all*
> *Dressed in our fine array*
> *Think of us what you will*
> *Music strike up and play.*

Honoured to accompany the family at such a prestigious venue, the Plough Stots presented them with an ornate ploughshare which proudly sits in the Waterson Carthy home in Robin Hood's Bay.

TWO

Little Gypsy Girl

I've reached the point where I'd like to make some noise
Eliza interviewed by Ian Anderson, *fRoots* [1]

Music took Eliza away from a lonely teenage experience. Honing her burgeoning skills, she had something in which to immerse herself. The fact that it was something she could do with her parents and wider family was fine by her: she had always got on incredibly well with them all. The typical parent-hating teen stereotype didn't extend to Eliza; she and her parents were more like friends, as her bandmates and friends would later testify as they, too, found themselves accepted into the fold.

And as she became increasingly active in the folk scene, attending more festivals and gigs, accompanying her parents who were performing there, she found that there were other young people like her: children of folk revivalists who had been brought up on a diet of tune and song, where Morris dancing was respected and parents made a weekly pilgrimage to the pub for a session. Many were the children of her parents' friends and peers, and introductions were made, friendships forged.

In amongst the workshops and sessions, friendly faces would peer out, only to be recognized again the next weekend, at the next festival; names were often put to faces by Norma or Martin, recognizing the parents of the child in question. With a dwindling social life back home in Robin Hood's Bay, the teenage Eliza could start afresh with new characters from all over the country. Different ages, varying accents, but common ground in the form of an emerging passion for and understanding of folk and traditional music.

The people literally instrumental in the first tentative steps of Eliza's career were discovered on the festival field. Many of her early collaborators and band members were sourced from these newfound friendships, and would stay with her through her formative professional years, providing a refreshing change from her more solitary existence at home.

John McCusker, multi-instrumentalist and producer, known for his diverse portfolio which has seen him work with the likes of Mark Knopfler, Graham Coxon and Kate Rusby, was one of these. Having been entrenched in traditional music from a young age, he joined the Battlefield Band in his early teens. He and Eliza gravitated towards each other very quickly. 'Fantastic! There's other young people!' I remember thinking. We started hanging out at festivals, and I remember hanging out a lot in Australia. We were the cool young kids, though not that cool,' he laughed.

'My dad was a Morris dancer so that's how I got into English music. The first time I met Liza was at Sidmouth Folk Festival, maybe 1993 or something like that,' piano accordionist Martin Green remembered. 'We used to sit around the Hobgoblin stall and there was a guy who made instrument pick-ups and we'd sit around playing tunes and he'd stick pick-ups on us. I met Seth Lakeman then, too.'

Tristan Glover's parents were also folk enthusiasts who, at the time, ran the Cheltenham Folk Club. Summer each year for the Glover family meant a wealth of different festivals across the country and before long, Tristan had assembled his own rag-tag band of other 'folk children' keen to make the best of their weekends away – independent from their parents.

The Chipolatas came out of these early folk festival meet-ups. Now an international touring sideshow experience, encompassing circus, music, theatre and dance, and with an incredible CV boasting performances all over the world, the Chips' first early rehearsals and performances took place at numerous UK folk festivals. Though now best known for their theatrical expertise, early Chipolatas performances were more music-orientated. With Tristan on melodeon and Sam Thomas on drums, many performances of their 'happy tunes' saw guest appearances from emerging musician and fellow 'folk child', Eliza Carthy. Tristan and Sam, two-thirds of the Chipolatas, found in Eliza a similar mentality. 'We were from the same stable,' Tristan recalled, 'we have always worked really hard.'

An early band, which included the Chipolatas and Eliza, was King Ligger and the Bathing Boys, named after Sam Thomas' teenage reputation. 'That was my nickname when I was a kid,' he says of King Ligger, 'because I was always getting into gigs for free. Or trying to!' he laughed.

Although an informal band of young festival goers, it was an early learning curve for a number of rising stars. 'It had Kathryn Tickell, Simon Care, Liza, Gareth Turner, all the Chipolatas, Jock Tyldesley, Martin Green, Barnaby Stradling. It was a way of getting everyone together at festivals, and it became an informal session band. We did it at Sidmouth quite often, and it very much came from an organic need to just get together and play,' Sam explained. 'We did it in public because the Chipolatas have this kind of street theatre ethic and we just used to busk for beer and cigarettes at the time. And as soon as we got enough to buy a pack of twenty, whoever was old enough would nip to the offie,' he smiled, 'And it was just brilliant, and most of the people Liza would later go and work with came from this band.'

Friendships made at festivals, though, weren't just restricted to summertime. Eliza and her new-found friends would meet up regularly at weekends and in school holidays, travelling to each other's parents' homes to stay. Inevitably, these were music-based relationships, and the snatched weekends would revolve around music and the tunes they brought to the table.

Eliza was a regular contributor to the Chipolatas' material and, in return, they provided backing to Eliza's early work. 'Liza was very influential in the tunes we were playing in the Chipolatas because she was prolific in the amount of new stuff she would turn over, the amount of research she was doing. She always had an attitude of being very inquisitive, being really up for trying stuff out, and that was my energy, too,' Sam added. 'It was diplomatic, it had to be,' Tristan explained further, 'When she was our guest, she played our set lists. And when she was in charge, she wrote ours.'

The fact that Sam felt they were, to a degree, growing up in public also connected the Chipolatas and Eliza. 'Having famous parents, or known parents, was something we both shared,' he explains. 'My father, Taffy Thomas [the UK's first laureate for storytelling], had his band, the Salami Brothers, so I was second generation, like Liza. The Chipolatas used a lot of the lines and patter that my dad and the Salami Brothers used on stage and, in the same way, Liza borrowed lots of the tunes that Martin had taught her. She also sang with Norma at first until she ended up forming her own repertoire, which was just what the Chipolatas were doing. What we'd inherited from our parents gave us a foundation, but it took us until our mid twenties – or even now really – for it to become our own,' reflects Sam.

Tristan feels that Eliza's influence on the Chipolatas' early material, though, was more than just a guest slot from a young, promising talent. 'Eliza went to Australia in 1995, touring with her parents. Whilst she was out there, she got speaking to a director of a festival there. She gave us a glowing recommendation and he said "OK, I'll give them a chance", so he booked us for one gig. To make it worthwhile, going all that way, we knew we had to get more than one gig. At the time, I worked for Mrs Casey Music so I had a few contacts and managed to get ourselves a few more gigs. And actually, we're really popular in Australia now; we go out there regularly. We've moved up the levels and play major international arts festivals, and it's all thanks to Eliza,' Tristan enthused.

Eliza seemed to have been something of a lady luck figure for the Chipolatas in their early days. Tristan, during one of his many stays in Australia, made an album with Australian musician Texas T.Rex called *The Reality Check*. As Eliza happened to be in Perth at the same time, she was invited to contribute to the album and sang on one of the tracks, the old song, 'I Drew My Ship Into The Harbour'. This track was later picked to be included on *Dirt Music*, a compilation album conceived to accompany the Booker Prize-shortlisted novel of the same name by author Tim Winton. 'It's a gorgeous, beautiful song,' Tristan said, 'And Eliza essentially gave it as a gift to me, I'll always be indebted to her for that. *Dirt Music* is being made into a film at the moment, I think Colin Farrell and Hugh Jackman are going to be in it, and I'm holding out that they'll want to use that track!'

In 1997, the Chipolatas recorded and released an album, entitled *Skinless,* on which Eliza guested. Post album, the lineup had grown to five core members and so they christened themselves the Chipolata 5. But Eliza wasn't invited to be a permanent member.

'I was very hurt when they didn't ask me to be in the Chipolata 5. I put a lot of time and effort in, I'd taught them lots, lots of research into tunes that we'd end up using and when they formed and didn't ask me to join – especially as I'd been all over the album – I wrote Tristan a very stern little letter. I felt I had invested a lot,' Eliza recalled. 'I don't know [why it was], but back in those days, they were very boy-sy. I learnt to turn a blind eye, especially as Sam really was quite a ladies man, and I think it just didn't occur to them to ask me; it wasn't out of spite. It was just a case of "girls aren't in the band", you know what I mean?'

But regardless of the snub, Eliza continued to appear with the Chipolatas when their schedules collided, usually at the big festivals. In fact, one of Tristan's all-time favourite gigs was during this post-*Skinless* period. 'It was one of those amazing gigs that you are so glad you were involved in. It was 1999 at Sidmouth, I think it was a Late Night Extra, and we were playing with a big band called Honky Trash. So we had all these big drums and a DJ and there was Liza, up on stage, the one girl on stage, giving it everything. She really was a massive superstar, sawing away at her fiddle, driving the whole thing.'

In summer 2011, the Chipolatas invited Eliza up to the Stockton International Riverside Festival to accompany them during one of their gigs. It had been a while since the ensemble had played together on a public stage – probably in the region of a decade – but Eliza was delighted to be involved once again. On 6 August 2011, she tweeted 'Stockton Riverside festival tonight, in Spiegeltent with a pan-full of Chipolatas. It'll be like being 19 again, without the thinness.' Any rustiness can't have showed, as she performed the next day, too, tweeting 'Spiegeltent show with the Chips and their Argentinian friends just lovely. Beautiful and funny and gorgeous and wicked fun. Come today!' and 'Chipolatas! In a spiegeltent! In half an hour! In Stockton! Hurrah!' A tweet from 8 August simply said 'Old friends', like a satisfactory sigh summing up the past couple of days.

Though the teenage Eliza had begun to forge friendships based around music outside of school hours – friendships which would fill the positions in her band lineups for the next few years – and her evenings and weekends were beginning to fill up with gigs and festivals (not to mention practice), she still had academic commitments to fulfill and needed to succeed in the classroom. GCSEs beckoned.

An integral part of the curriculum at Fyling Hall School, music is an option for both GCSE and 'A' Level, with between two and five hours dedicated teaching time for older students. Cathy Hornung remembers Eliza's 'Little Book of G Minor', a folio of compositions she drew together for her music GCSE. 'She became entirely hooked on G minor and wrote an entire series, all for the piano, I think. I'm not sure if she was inspired by Bach or Mozart, but we had some fun putting together her work.'

Though Cathy is a classically trained musician and teacher, she knew of Eliza's background and her family's involvement in the folk scene, and was not at all surprised at her future career path: 'She talked about festivals she would perform in and where she would travel to, as well as where she had been already. I was certain she would continue the tradition.' And Eliza's fondness for folk music did occasionally creep into her activities at school. She remembers composing waltzes and singing unaccompanied in school shows and competitions, whilst Cathy has vivid memories of her GCSE music performance.

At GCSE, it is the school music teacher's duty to decide the marks for each student's instrumental or vocal performance, though performances are recorded and sent to the exam board for invigilating. As well as a solo performance, candidates must perform in an ensemble …

… Eliza drafted in her father.

Cathy remembers this unique moment with great fondness:

> The two of them played for in the region of five minutes and it was obvious they were enjoying every minute. They were certainly deserving of full marks. I sent off the tape to the moderator and the next evening, I was very surprised when he rang and asked who Eliza was, questioning our award of full marks. I duly informed him that the other performer on the tape was Martin Carthy, assuming that he thought I had over-marked the performance. He simply said that he agreed completely with our marking and wished he heard more performances in that vein! Interestingly, the tape was never returned, although the centre is supposed to retain all coursework and performance materials until the October after the publication of results.

Perhaps that tape will surface on eBay one day! Cathy Hornung's report on Eliza's musical performance that term read:

> As you well know Eliza has caused me many headaches over the last few years but I have to say that I was very honoured to be present at the marvellous performance she and her father gave for the exam. It could not be faulted and the obvious enjoyment on her face was a pleasure to see. I expect her to do very well and I'm sure that in years to come I shall still be talking about Eliza! I shall miss her, maddening though she may be, and wish her lots of luck and happiness for the future.

Eliza finished school with 10 GCSEs, including French which she completed a year early.

Despite an increased amount of musical activity outside of school hours, and a summer spent at festivals, Eliza returned to school for her 'A' Levels, this time to Scarborough Sixth Form College to study English Literature, History and Music.

However, during her first winter at Sixth Form, she contracted pneumonia and spent much time convalescing at home, meaning she fell behind in her studies. A tour with Waterson:Carthy and a romantic relationship also helped to distract her further from her academic work. 'She was courting at that time, a lad called Adrian, they were very much in love, young love like that,' Norma began. 'And I think he wanted her out of school.'

Martin recalled a phone call and a conversation he'd never forget. 'I was in America and I got this phone call. I picked up the phone and said "hello love, everything alright?" There was this little pause and Norma said "you need to have a word with your daughter". Those dread words: "*your* daughter"'.

'She went out to school in the morning and she was fine,' Norma remembered. 'But when she walked in at night time, she announced that she wasn't going to go back tomorrow.'

'Eliza came on the phone to me and I just didn't know what to say to her,' Martin shook his head. 'I had left school at the end of spring term in 1959 because I'd taken my 'A' Levels the year before, because that's how my school had worked, and I failed every one of them. The only thing I'd got out of it was an 'O' Level pass in Greek. I did a great Greek verse paper, the rest was hopeless, and I left school because I was going to fail my re-sits. She was doing precisely what I did, so I told her "I don't know what your mother thinks I'm going to say to you." It was just a case of trying to make the best of it.'

'My mum really took a deep breath when I left college, she wasn't happy about it at all,' Eliza explained. But surely it was a comfort that Eliza looked likely to enter the family business, taking the baton for the next generation? 'Yes, that's what she was worried about! You have to remember that she didn't think it was worth it. She's always loved the music, but as a career, she wasn't into all that. The Watersons found touring so stressful that they packed it in;

they actually retired. My uncle Michael had a proper job, George had a proper job, Lal was busy bringing up Olly and Marry and it wasn't until they were grown up that she made her own albums. Mam wasn't interested in pursuing a career; all they cared about was the music. She was very worried about me and rightly so.'

But Eliza wasn't interested in her maternal side of the family's choices: 'I wanted to be my dad.' It was then Eliza told her mother her plan: she would sign on whilst working out her next musical endeavour. Norma was beside herself with rage. 'I said "you sign on the dole and you're out of this house." I told her that she has…' At this point Martin chimed in, as though this was a story told many times before: '…two good arms and two good legs.' 'I told her that the dole is for people who can't work or people who are ill: "you are strong and healthy, get off your arse and do something."'

So Eliza took her music to the streets, busking first in Scarborough and then further afield as her confidence – and takings – increased. It was a quick way to try out new material, to practise projecting her voice over the throb of the town centre, to take the songs and tunes she knew to a potentially cold audience. If she made a mistake, it rang out into the cold air and was instantly forgotten; if she impressed, she made a quid or two. And she certainly did impress, enough to earn 'bloody good money', as her father put it.

That was until a local photographer took a snap of her mid-tune and placed it in the Scarborough Evening News. 'The very next day, she's busted,' Martin shakes his head in disgust. 'She was busking on the pedestrian precinct and some copper, to get his average up, got her busted. It didn't stop her busking but she was more circumspect. She started going to York and other places.'

Nancy Kerr opens the door to her home with a big, breezy smile. The purple delphiniums I have brought her match the colour of her top, which stretches across her pregnant belly. I follow her in and instantly recognized the familiar features of the folk musician's home: polished floorboards, brightly painted walls and a piano piled high with sheet music and songbooks. As she makes the tea, she laughs. 'We're still getting used to having a kitchen,' she tells me. 'What tea would you like?'

Nancy and her partner, James Fagan – a partnership of both romance and music – have only recently bought their house, a large mid-terrace in Sheffield. Before that, they lived on the canals for twelve years, predominantly on a narrowboat in Bath where Nancy completed her Masters in music therapy.

It is no overstatement to claim that Nancy and James are quiet favourites of the British folk scene. They have been gigging through Britain's networks of folk clubs for around fifteen years, their summers always booked out with festivals, and the duo boast a healthy back catalogue, a number of Folk Awards (the Horizon Award in 2000 and for Best Duo in 2003 and 2011) and a loyal following in James' homeland, Australia.

However, it was with Eliza Carthy that their respective careers began, very much interlaced during their mid to late teens, before disagreements sent them along different paths.

Though Nancy Kerr was born in North London, where her mother, folk singer Sandra Kerr, was a member of Ewan MacColl's Critics Group, she spent her formative years in Northumberland. 'I started [fiddle] at five and my parents were both instrumentalists, as well as mum being a singer. Dad was a Northumbrian Piper and they definitely decided I was going to play fiddle, and I was fine with that,' she says, nonchalantly.

Classical lessons were begun in earnest, but the folk influence was there from the very beginning. In Colin Irwin's *fRoots* article 'Young Arise', he mentions that she was 'subjected to the dual attack of Willie Hunter albums being systematically injected into her brain while she slept'[2], and very much like Liza, she was soon singing with her mother, adding to her increasing mental repertoire of English and Irish songs.

But it was the fiddle where she really excelled, studying the Northumbrian style with vigour. Each year, she would visit fiddler

Will Taylor and listen to him play, entranced by his approach and panache, and allowing him to influence her own learning. 'He wasn't really a teacher of mine; he was more like a guru. I would go there every year and sit and watch him, talk to him. But he never really gave me technical advice so, in that respect, I did pick it up myself, though I was classically trained and so I had the technique which I found really helpful.'

It wasn't long before Sandra Kerr and Norma Waterson, contemporaries and friends, hatched a plan. Their daughters, with only a month in age difference between them, should meet and play together. Nancy remembers meeting Eliza at Sidmouth Folk Festival aged around thirteen or fourteen, but the plan didn't come to fruition until a couple of years later, probably to coincide with Eliza's burgeoning interest in the fiddle from the age of fifteen onwards.

In 'Young Arise', Eliza is frank:

> … me and Nance didn't get on at all. We had tunes in common but nothing else. I used to go to Nancy's on the train, get there fairly late in the evening and have some food and we'd kind of sit there and look at each other sideways across the room and say 'Do you want to play some tunes then?' We'd get the fiddles out and play till the birds started to sing and then go to bed without having said a word to one another. In the morning we'd get up, have some breakfast, watch some telly, look at each other across the room and say 'Do you want to play some tunes then?' and we'd start again.[3]

As funny as it sounds, this wasn't a ploy to get the collective folk press' tongues wagging: there really was no immediate rapport between the two teenagers.

'But I don't think I would've clicked with anyone particularly at that time,' Nancy explains, describing a character that seems so far removed from the talkative, amicable woman in front of me. 'When you're fourteen or fifteen and you meet your exact contemporary… well, you can't fake that. You've got fewer of the social graces you have when you're older. We weren't hostile but we were surly teenage girls. But actually, in hindsight, I think that's a nice way to start as it means the links that you do build up are for real. They were genuine and they developed due to time spent together, rather than some ideal that because we both sing or play, we're going to have something in common.

'We are really different people, though,' she adds, 'and already [at that age] we were really different people.'

By the time the duo came together, Eliza had only recently picked up the fiddle, whilst Nancy had been playing for almost a decade. Though Eliza was quick to learn, she soon felt inferior, commenting 'I was insecure anyway as she was a much better fiddle player and I pretty much thought she didn't like me, so I was very nervous around her.' On relaying that sentiment back to Nancy, some twenty years after those emotions had first surfaced, Nancy couldn't help but laugh. She felt there was never a real, obvious difference in the standards of their playing. 'Audiences would never have noticed as we played in such a different style anyway. I mean, in Northumberland, without bigging it up too much, there is a tradition of ... well, a different sound to what became the other-English way of playing.

'To me, Liza, from the start, summed up a very different sound: [it was] very earthy, approachable, and a quick way of playing English tunes, and it was quite different to how I was playing. I was playing really smoothly and everything was about flow and intonation. We were just different, so it wasn't obvious. Audiences would've said she had flair, you know? Which maybe makes up for perhaps not having all the technique early on. I never felt superior, I just felt that I could pick up the fiddle by then and be completely confident on it. I'd spent so many years doing very little else, whereas she'd done different things. She probably felt like that about being a singer. And I felt like that about the fiddle: by that point, the fiddle never let me down. It does take years for it to feel like that.'

But Eliza felt indebted to Nancy. It was Nancy who had opened her eyes to the possibilities with the fiddle: the sounds they could produce together, the material they could cover. Later, she would tell Max Reinhardt, for BBC Radio 3, 'I'd been playing the fiddle for four years and never gotten anywhere, then I met her and within eighteen months we'd recorded an album together and I was touring professionally.'[4]

The fact that the young women chose to play predominantly English music too was an advantage: they had few immediate contemporaries, and there had been few players to set an English traditional standard. 'It was different back then, because there wasn't such an aesthetic of English playing. Really, we were all looking to people like Chris Wood, who was pretty avant garde anyway because he was a smooth player but he was going for something really earthy; just different, pushing it in different ways. It wasn't just about making a sweet sound. We were picking up on that and I think that suited Liza fine.'

Their decision to focus on a largely English repertoire was an easy one. 'It just really suited us and where we were at: I was really into Northumbrian stuff which was English but just off-to-the-side, and had a different kind of vibe. I also think we were partly guided by the books that we picked up. Liza had *The Sussex Tune Book* and a fiddle book called *A Northern Lass*.[5]

'Quite quickly it became our plan to find and play English tunes. They weren't very familiar to me, those tunes, because, like I say, I played Northumbrian, but now when I look at them again I think a lot of them were probably Morris tunes, plus a fair few from Yorkshire which, of course, Liza was interested in. I don't remember it being a mission statement, as such, but I think we did have a definite aim to show off English music.'

Nancy and Eliza found themselves embroiled in a fact-finding quest. 'I wanted to create a new English fiddle style based on the existing tunes, the surviving players, the obscure and neglected manuscripts I found wherever I went,' Eliza explained.

I started this huge collection, which included the music I had heard from around the world that related to English music through the travels of Empire and discovery: the Appalachian stuff and New England square-dance I heard from my early visits to the States, and Quebecois music which I heard from Lisa Ornstein and Chris Wood and Andy Cutting.

I wanted to know what the fiddle tradition would have sounded like had the Great War, in particular, not knocked a great hole in our instrumental and dancing traditions. I wondered what it would have sounded like if it had been influenced by all the places it had travelled, by the mainly young men who took it there. I thought it would be good to create something influenced by where it had been since it had been here; bringing it back home if you like, completing a circle.

But at the same time, I didn't want to sound like anyone else, I wanted to start something, or restart it. Pretentious, possibly, and pointlessly idealistic and hopeful! But it was fun.

Following on from their early gigs at Folkworks, during the first years of the acclaimed folk development agency, the duo were booked for their initial gig at the Black Swan Arts Centre, the venue where Folkworks was originally based. And it couldn't have been a more poignant debut for their new venture: a support slot for their aforementioned music heroes, Chris Wood and Andy Cutting. 'They had just brought out their album, the first one, the eponymous one with the fiddle and the box on the front, and we all sat there and folded up the tape inlay things just before the gig. I think Liza played mandolin for quite a lot of that set we got together, which can't have been more than half an hour,' Nancy remembers.

More gig offers followed, and they began to play regularly, acquiring an income which supplemented their studies. And, in the beginning, their audiences were largely the same that their parents played to.

'I actually remember my mum warning me and saying "look, you do know that Liza's parents have this fantastically huge profile and she's going to be very focused on in that respect. Are you OK with that?" But I actually felt the scene was pretty open to both of us, probably because there wasn't a glut of young players at that time so people were ready for us. And to be honest, we'd seen it done by our folks which makes it not just possible, but gives you an opening. They can do it, they're doing it now and from watching them I know the pitfalls, the difficulties.'

The two girls' parents, as can be expected given the circumstances, were keen to give feedback to their daughters as they drove them to and from gigs. With this, though, came a certain pressure, Nancy recalls. 'I think I felt that both sets of parents had an attitude of "OK, if you're going to do this, you really are going to have to do it well" which was fine; apart from a couple of times when I knew we hadn't delivered a great gig. That was a hard thing to feel because it was a bit like slipping from unconditional love to professional expectation – from your parents. I don't blame either set of parents for that, though; I think it's a really good ethic, a work ethic.'

What a pressure to have to shoulder and conceal, though, at a tender age; an age when their peers would have taken rebellion by the gritted teeth, living life by the age-old teenage standard of trying your very best *not* to impress your parents – in fact, to shock, where possible. Instead, here were Nancy and Eliza, two strong-willed, conscientious, talented young women, hoping to win over their respective parents – considered giants in their sphere – with their take on the music by which their parents had largely made their living and their reputation.

It wasn't sufficient for Eliza and Nancy to simply make a nice sound together, singing and playing in tune; here was a music that needed an understanding, a kind of respect but with a game plan. They would discover where the music had come from, how it had lived on in players and singers since its birth, and they would need to work out exactly how they were going to make a mark on it in the twentieth century.

It makes the tasks of Zak Starkey, Sean and Julian Lennon, Jason Bonham, Coco Sumner, and the musical progeny of other superstar musicians, look easy by comparison. Their parents might have had bigger profiles than the parents of Nancy and Eliza, but second generation pop stars essentially just had to sound good and look cool and the world would be forgiving. They had little hope of living up to their parents' legacies, anyway. But, undoubtedly, it was hoped that Nancy and Eliza would further the tradition, by wielding their fiddles and taking gigs in the folk clubs in front of the audiences their parents would also court. The two young women, then, had greater feats to live up to, and their parents would no doubt prove their toughest critics.

But don't assume that it was a silent car, wending its way over the moors and back to Whitby after a more lacklustre performance. No, instead imagine a heated discussion, Eliza gesticulating wildly with her animated parents; her mother singing a line to reinforce her own interpretation, her dad bringing forth an example from one of the old singers who first captured his eyes and ears on the club circuit in London back in the day. All the while, Nancy quietly listens and looks out of the window, the lights reflecting on the sea.

None of this parental influence really worried Nancy, having grown up with music and all its trappings. She knew that she would make her mistakes in public, that she would need time to develop a stage craft, to find her own voice and fiddle style. Her mum would have imparted that knowledge an age ago, and though her family had high expectations, it wasn't unpleasant pressure. In fact, it was rather exciting. Here they were, with all this music; it was theirs. She very much subscribed to the mantra of her new collaborator's father: the only way in which to damage a song, to break it, is not to sing it at all.

But, in retrospect, Nancy is far less forgiving about the ways in which she felt her first musical endeavours were received by her early audiences and reviewers. Today, the British folk scene is always waiting to champion the Next Big Thing: as the University of Newcastle's Folk and Traditional Music degree unleashes a wealth of eager musicians each summer; as Folkworks continues to deliver its action-packed courses with guest tutors; as projects combining street dance and Morris dance, and hip hop and folk music take to the country's schools; as Cecil Sharp House continues to run Folk

Rising showcases. Each year, there is a new crop of young singers and instrumentalists, perhaps raised on an annual diet of festival workshops or simply having stumbled into a local folk club and discovered it for themselves, ready to make the tradition their own.

Nowadays the scene looks on excitedly, raising its collective notepad to record young outfits' influences: keen to spot from whom they'd gleaned that version or which bowing arm had been held in high regard during the recording of that particular tune. There's the Radio 2 Young Folk Award and BBC Scotland's Young Traditional Musician of the Year; there's young folk musicians presenting documentaries on the television; folk clubs geared towards younger listeners and even a dedicated website, *Bright Young Folk*.

Back in the early 1990s, however, the folk scene was a rather different landscape.

'I don't think the folk scene was as generous to us as it is now to young instrumentalists and singers, especially to female singers,' Nancy comments. 'There was a lot of expectation for female singers to be certain things that is very hard for young musicians to be, simply because there wasn't such a culture of young musicianhood. Not that I'm saying that young musicians now aren't great – they're amazing – but there's a lot of them and there's such an excitement and a glee that there are people doing this. Are they going to push it, or are they going to keep the old things going? When we did it, I think there was a faction of people who were like "OK, are you really taking this seriously? Are you going to do this properly?" That was a definite pressure: there was an expectation to be mature players and performers when actually we were really young. Gee, I wish reviewers or people we met at gigs or audiences had been a bit more generous, that they'd allowed us to make mistakes.'

Regardless of this pressure, Nancy and Eliza had certainly made an impression.

'Liza and Nancy were completely unique in that they were young women playing traditional music, music with just fiddles and voices, and there hadn't been any other young women doing that,' Kit Bailey remembers. 'There was Kathryn Tickell, but she was doing something quite different with pipes and fiddle, and a different kind of music altogether. And the sound that Liza and Nancy made was just lovely, they were a lovely duo.'

Kit had grown up entrenched in folk music and the scene. Following a degree in anthropology, she became an agent at specialist folk and roots agency, Adastra, before leaving to establish her own, Brass Tacks, with John Eeles. Already representing Eliza's father and his duo with Dave Swarbrick, as well as Andy Cutting, Karen Tweed and Ian Carr, Eliza and Nancy soon found themselves on the books of Brass Tacks:

> I sent them all round the country doing festivals. They were very independent and confident, but quite different in their musical styles … and sometimes they put a different band around them for ceilidhs, and there they were, creating this scene. They were drop dead gorgeous, the pair of them, and they were happy to be going off places: I sent them off to a festival in the Azores, in Portugal, when they were quite young. Because they were confident, I felt like they knew what they were doing. And because of their parents – our parents – there was this feeling within the UK folk scene, in particular, that you were looked after, it felt safe, and when I sent them off to Portugal, I didn't realize how out on a limb they were. They were still quite young and I was quite young. Now, when I think back, I think I was a bit naïve sending them out there on their own. I should've gone with them. They were uncomfortable with some of the people they'd met. They'd travelled out there with a lot of other musicians that we'd organized to send with them from Britain and Ireland, but as young women on their own and abroad, I think they probably got hit on quite a lot. They came back feeling quite uncomfortable even though they were quite a hit musically. But it shows how confident they were, though, that I thought about sending them in the first place.

Eliza laughs at the memory of this particular festival. 'It wasn't that we didn't have a good time; we had a great time!' she assures me. 'All I really remember was the fact that Ron Kavanagh was playing there and he stood on an anemone on the beach and really hurt his foot. I was trying to help him out and he was yelling at me in pain, a huge Irish bloke yelling at me. It was quite frightening! And I also remember that Karen Tweed and Ian Carr were there and I had a massive crush on Ian Carr at the time.'

Kit felt that it wasn't long before Eliza and Nancy's family names were secondary to their reputations as great players. 'There was a lot of interest in them because of who their parents were, but I think they very quickly blew that away because they weren't carbon copies of their parents, they were always original,' she adds.

And, thankfully for Kit, they were willing to work hard - *very* hard:

> Liza and Nancy definitely did have a younger following, especially the festival gigs. They were just funny, they'd waffle on onstage. Their stagecraft at first was either genius or a bit 'oh God ...' ... not cringeworthy, as such, but surreal; you'd wonder where it was going. They very quickly got better at that! They toured ever such a lot, and they were also partying. There was one time when I was working at Towersey Festival, I was stage managing, and I got a phone call from Liza saying that they'd had a car accident. It wasn't anything serious but it was just because they were so tired and they'd ended up driving into a ditch. They were both fine, but it was those stresses you can get while you're on tour: they were young and partying, staying up for drinks. I think they burnt themselves out; they were exhausted.

'That was pretty classic for us at that point: we were desperate to get home, get on to the next thing and were really exhausted. It was daft. We were really lucky,' Nancy acknowledges.

The crash has also remained a poignant memory for Eliza: 'I had a little red car that me and Nancy used to tour in and I was such a bad driver. I drove to Towersey and we all wanted to stay and watch the fireworks at the end. So we did, but, of course, fireworks start at midnight. We set off to come back up [to Yorkshire] and I remember having a sleep at Meadowhall. From there to junction 34 is only fifteen minutes' drive but I just fell asleep at the wheel.'

49

It wasn't long before the duo's workload affected their health. Kit remembers Eliza suffering particularly from her asthma at this point and having regular attacks, whilst Nancy was driven to consult a homeopath due to her constant exhaustion. 'The homeopath asked what I did when I came off stage, and I told her nothing; that I tended to go straight to bed as I was so exhausted. She actually encouraged me to party, saying it was a really good outlet for winding down. I actually wondered if I partly got sick because I wasn't very sociable and I wasn't very good at being with lots of people and so didn't party.'

The differences in personality between Eliza and Nancy were beginning to become exacerbated post-gig, off stage. 'I was never fully involved like Liza was; she's much more sociable than me. There was always a bit of a tension that I wasn't a party person and she was. I think that might have made me a bit poorlier because I wasn't winding down, I was having gigs and lots of adrenalin but no real social way of getting it out of my system. I just felt the life was really exhausting and I wasn't even driving: Liza did all the driving!'

But the constant touring did mean that they had well-rehearsed, well-crafted, tried-and-tested sets. So when Steve Heap, director of Mrs Casey Records, approached them with the opportunity of recording an album, Nancy and Eliza knew exactly what elements of their repertoire would form the basis of their debut. Nancy recalls:

We had a meeting at Sidmouth up on the arena hill. He sat us down and showed us the proposed recording schedule. Neither of us had done our own recording before, but I think we'd both recorded with other people at that point, with parents and stuff like that. Steve was really sweet, he said 'Don't worry if nothing happens the first day, we might just be trying out the sounds and the equipment. It might not work so don't feel pressured.' What actually happened was that by the end of the first day, we had every single track on the album recorded: we did everything in the first or second take. It was amazing, brilliant! And it actually set the standard for how I like to make records now, which is asking a lot of yourself, but I do like first and second takes. I like that freshness. It's a warts and all album, that first one, the green one, but that's how we did it. And we were so pleased with ourselves!

It soon became clear that music was a distraction for Nancy's academic studies. Having missed a substantial amount of schooling during her 'A' Levels due to illness – she had contracted glandular fever – she decided to leave school and enrol on a Performing Arts BTEC at college, a course which she hoped would teach her a few more tricks for her burgeoning musical trade.

A move mirroring Eliza's decision to leave school, academia seemed irrelevant now she and Eliza had a full tour diary, a car, an income, a recording contract.

'I seem to remember [Eliza] passed her test the day I got my distinction in my BTEC, so we were really pleased. I remember setting off on tour for the summer after that, and that was the end of my [formal] education,' Nancy explains.

Eliza bought a house in Whitby and invited Nancy to move down from Northumberland and in with her. It made a lot of sense: they were good friends, they were working together and needing the physical space in which to practise, write and arrange. In fact, Nancy was so eager to move to Whitby that she arrived prior to the house being ready for inhabiting and was kindly put up in the top room at Martin and Norma's, down the road in Robin Hood's Bay.

Neither young woman was deterred by the thought of living and working in close quarters. 'I've never been phobic of the living together and working together thing and I wonder if it's because I worked with my family from a young age,' Nancy muses. 'Liza's the same, James [Fagan] is the same. We don't idealize working with your family, it's got its toughness, but it does train you that if something becomes difficult in your working environment, you still share that living environment. It will need to be resolved. Our problem was that we didn't give ourselves breaks, I didn't seem to rest. Not that we were partying exactly, but we were always on the go. The knock on was that we always had the freedom to play whenever we wanted. Are we going to get a song together? And we'd do it, no matter what crazy hour of the day or night it was.'

The consequence of having so few young musicians on the folk scene at that time was that they formed a very close knit group. The music press – both folk-orientated and the nationals – cottoned on to the idea of a 'folk brat pack', symbolizing, not long after the American 'Brat Pack' films of the 1980s, the same young faces in a myriad of revolving lineups and musical outlets. Like-minded friends soon became band mates and house mates, and now there was more music to be played, more influences to be added to the mix – and more fun to be had.

'We were on a bus in London and we developed a plan to get a ceilidh band together; that's what Kings of Calicutt was going to be to start with, or at least that's how I remember it … that's how I learnt to play, playing for dances, but I wasn't massively confident about doing it in public. But we did the Walthamstow Ceilidh one year, which is just huge, it's massive. Whenever I drive past Walthamstow Town Hall I always think how audacious we were; we ran a ceilidh there when we were eighteen or nineteen. I called it, as well; I'd never called a ceilidh before or since! I wouldn't do that now, and I know so much more about music. We were just brave, I think,' smiles Nancy.

Saul Rose began to learn the melodeon at his father's suggestion when a broken leg confined him indoors for a lengthy period when he was eleven years old. He first came to recognition in 1991 when he made it to the finals of the Young Tradition Award, now the BBC Radio 2 Young Folk Award, and three years later, he attended a Waterson:Carthy gig at a folk club in Watford, opening for them with a few tunes.

'We glanced at each other appreciatively,' Saul explained, 'we liked each other's playing. At the end of the gig, Eliza just came over and asked me to join her band! She was so forward, even then!'

As the son of two enormous Martin Carthy fans, Saul must have enjoyed telling his parents about his new friend and her proposition.

Eliza introduced Nancy and Saul one year at Sidmouth, and the three of them decided to play together as a trio, forming the very first incarnation of Kings of Calicutt.

'I remember the first time I was invited to Robin Hood's Bay to rehearse with Eliza and Nancy. My mum and dad were such big fans of Martin's that he knew me and my family, but I thought that here, rehearsing with his daughter, that he might see me almost on equal terms, or something. But the very first thing he said to me as he strolled through the dining room and into the kitchen, where we were rehearsing, was "yeah, that's the thing with melodeons: when you make a mistake, it's really public,"' Saul laughed.

As a trio, Saul felt the material they tackled initially was gentle and sensitive, of which Saul had previous little experience having primarily played for dance. He found his knowledge and repertoire growing, his capabilities stretching and he was grateful for the opportunity to play with two fellow young enthusiasts. Back then, he wasn't a confident singer, occasionally breaking out a bit of backing, and left the song choices to Eliza and Nancy, instead bringing tunes to the table including some of his own compositions.

'I didn't have an agenda about English music then – I do now! – but I did play what I enjoyed, which was mainly Morris and Southern English tunes, which obviously Eliza liked, too,' he said.

Eliza and Saul also formed a duo, which continues – on and off, and when other commitments allow – to this day. When Nancy contracted glandular fever and was compelled to pull out of a tour she had booked with Eliza, Saul was asked if he could take her place.

'I had a job in Harrow at the time, and I'd end up finishing at 5.15p.m., jumping in the car and getting to Redditch, or somewhere, for soundcheck at 7p.m. I managed to do the whole tour like that; getting back after the gig, having a couple hours' sleep and then going in to work again. I might have pulled one sicky, and maybe used a little bit of holiday, but it was absolutely mad!' he remembered.

Saul and Eliza refer to each other as 'musical soulmates'. 'The simple explanation is that it's just easy, effortless; we understand where we're each going to go,' Saul illustrated. 'I could play with Eliza all day long. In fact, I went to stay one Christmas and I'd decided not to take any instruments; that I was going to have a Christmas off. But Eliza managed to find a one-row melodeon, with only ten buttons, and even with its limitations, we found that it was really good for playing French Canadian reels. So we ended up playing French Canadian reels solidly for three days.

'But the less simple explanation is what happened during one gig. We were playing the 'Zycanthos Jig' set [from *Rice*] and we'd had a pretty good set up until that point, but then we played in unison, then Eliza went off into the harmony. But I thought it was me playing the harmony, so close were our harmonies that I fell off the tune. That'd never happened to me before!'

It wasn't long before the Kings of Calicutt trio called on their new-found friends, the Chipolatas, Maclaine Colston and Dan Plews. It became a fluid outfit which could expand and contract as and when the occasion demanded.

'This is boys, you see,' Saul explained. 'Two attractive girls in the band and they all wanted to join!'

As the friendships strengthened, romantic unions were fostered, too. Nancy and Saul soon became an item. Eliza, meanwhile, was continuing to work with her parents and, whilst on tour in Australia in 1995 for a month, met James Fagan. James was a medical student and a talented folk musician from a well-known Australian folk dynasty, easily comparable to her own.

'We started going out, though it wasn't for long, to be honest,' Eliza explains. 'We got on, hung out for a few festivals and then he told me he'd be coming to England in seven months. It was a will-you-be-waiting-for-me kind of thing, and I told him that yes, I'd be single when he arrived. We wrote to each other over the seven months, and although technically I was single when he got here, I'd been going out with Dan Plews for a little bit. We were all living in the same house and it was just really incestuous, to be honest. When James arrived, we realized it wasn't what we wanted, so that was that.'

But still the expanded lineup of Kings of Calicutt lived and worked together, despite the romantic frictions. Saul and Nancy had a painful break up, which, according to Eliza, resulted in a fight on stage at Sidmouth. James was initiated into the band, joining them on the road for a winter tour.

'We did some gigs in the winter of 95,' Nancy remembers, 'which was a bitterly cold, crazy winter, and we had a short pre-Christmas tour. James had come over just having qualified as a doctor, and he was having his big post-university blast in the UK and Ireland. Of course, he'd known Liza and they'd been involved and he'd come over to visit her, so he was at our house and he joined Kings of Calicutt; it seemed a logical thing to do. I'd never seen a guitar-shaped bouzouki thing before, and it had this really cool bass resonance to it and it really seemed to work, musically it was really funky.'

When putting the set together, James and Nancy realized they had a shared love of Irish music and used the forthcoming gigs as impetus to learn a couple of Irish tunes which they could showcase in the middle of the evening. 'It was really nice as it was a chance for me to play how I wanted to play, that kind of smooth thing that I used to go for. And it was an opportunity for me to play the tune, as, of course, I was always a harmony person; Liza mostly played the tune and did improvisations and embellishments, whilst I'd do the harmony. So when James came along, there was an accompanist for me to play the tune, and I hadn't had that before. We had a musical meeting long before we had a romantic one, and it was all in there with the Kings of Calicutt stuff, it was all mixed up.'

The tour made for a tense time. Alongside the emotional tensions and blossomings, as well as the poor weather, the car that Martin and Norma had lent James broke down outside Bristol and had to be towed some 250 miles, all the way back to Robin Hood's Bay. 'And,' Nancy added, 'unless I'm making this up to be more dramatic, I think Saul's car was pinched after that gig in Bristol, too. James and I were a bit lost in each other by then, so we had no idea what was going on. So there was romance here and there, beginnings and nigglings, and a car being stolen and a car breaking down.

'It's awful as it sounds really tawdry but it was just circumstance. We were moving in this particularly intense artistic group, without sounding really wanky about it, and I really liked all of those people, I found them all so interesting … Liza was much more gelled in with those guys, she always seemed to gel better,' Nancy adds, again describing herself so differently to the warm, charismatic personality I was experiencing.

When I questioned her further about why she was so keen to criticize her own social skills at that time, she replied simply: 'I had a tough teens, and I'm sure Liza would say she had a tough teens, too. So we did have issues. I wasn't very good at being a sociable person, but I've spent years trying to mend myself since!' The friendship stumbled on, but was deteriorating rapidly. Nancy remembers a trip to Australia, her first visit to the country, around Easter time in 1996 where her relationship with Eliza was so uncomfortable, so up and down, that she decided that when she returned to England, she would move out of their shared house in Whitby. She and James moved to Sheffield and lodged with Kit Bailey for six months whilst they plotted their next move.

It was a shame that a friendship which had started so frostily came full circle to end much as it had begun. As a duo, they had their first taste of professional musical life: recording, touring, playing festivals both in the UK and abroad. They had a shared heritage in that they were children from folk music-loving families and their parents were peers during the folk revival of the 1950s and 1960s. Together they had picked up the baton from their parents, starting with their parents' audiences before finding their own, and recorded two albums and formed the basis of the Kings of Calicutt, which Nancy left before the ensemble recorded their only album.

And then it ended, just as romance came in to the frame. Nancy is keen to stop me there, to disagree:

We talk about the romantic things that happened, but they were really just blips. They were straws that broke the camel's back. I think what was at the root of it was, and I don't mean this with any antagonism at all, but when you get two young women who do something very similar, going for a similar thing at a similar level, it does assault your sense of self. Especially if people – not to put too fine a point on it – are comparing you constantly, *constantly*. And for me, I found that I was nowhere near her standard of being a performer, of being a public person, or anything, and that was more at the root of it than any of the other stuff, which probably didn't help, either. I'm a feminist and I don't like the idea of competition between women, but when you're that age, and you're ambitious and in the public eye, you want to do well. It's going to go either way: you're either going to be totally in love with each other forever, or it'll assault you. And I think we both felt that.

It seems that this wasn't simply the case of two teenage girls each armed with talent and passion, wanting to succeed in a tough field when only a very slim few can and do. With a duo founded on such different personalities, it is likely that each would look to the other and envy the perceived qualities the individual felt she herself lacked; whether it be the stage presence and amiability that Nancy believed Eliza possessed, or the exceptional confidence and skill with the fiddle, which Nancy radiated according to Eliza.

The very fact that Nancy and Eliza felt competitive towards each other indicates, however, that they believed the scene, at the time, could only accommodate one or the other – that there were few places available to young, female professional musicians. Nancy's comments regarding how little generosity the scene afforded them – not allowing them to learn and make mistakes in public – makes it all the more poignant, accentuating how few young women were succeeding as professional musicians within the folk scene then. The subsequent labelling of Eliza as 'folk babe' only goes further to illustrate this.

At the time I met Nancy, she had recently seen Eliza, at Spiers and Boden's tenth anniversary celebration concert which took place at Shepherd's Bush Empire. Nancy had met Eliza's youngest baby, Izzy, for the first time, and I couldn't help but raise the point that Nancy and Eliza had both decided to have two children, almost at exactly the same time.

'I know,' Nancy smiled, 'and I always thought I'd never have kids.' Which was exactly what Eliza had said when I asked about her decision to have children.

Though they see each other from time to time, Eliza and Nancy don't spend time together. Nancy wonders whether they might one day be closer, but feels that, at the moment, the arenas in which they work and socialize are just that bit too different. 'James and I don't get a lot of attention or anything, but we do play lots of music and that's great. Our worlds don't cross, really. But when they do, it's fine, it's really nice.'

THREE

'The Future Of British Folk Music'

I don't like the idea of English traditional music as a nerds club.
Eliza interviewed by Colin Irwin, *fRoots*[1]

Independent folk label Topic Records has recently celebrated its seventieth birthday, making it the oldest independent record label in Britain. Home to some of the biggest names in folk, from A.L. Lloyd and Ewan MacColl right through to Nic Jones, Anne Briggs, the Copper Family and June Tabor, it began as an outlet for British folk song rooted in urban and industrial interests as the recording arm of the Workers' Music Association. It was also the label for which the Watersons and Martin Carthy had been recording since the 1960s and 1970s.

With the departure of Nancy, Eliza became the focal point – her new musician friends were looking to her to see what musical journey they would be taken on next. Topic Records' Tony Engle had an inkling that Eliza was going to be around for a few years; that she'd garnered interest from the press and wooed the gig-going audiences, that they, collectively, were also anticipating her next move.

In 1995, Tony Engle approached Eliza with the view to putting out a solo album. 'But I didn't perform solo or have any solo material,' Eliza explained, rather unexpectedly. 'So I told them that I wanted to put something together, but what I wanted to do was have a band and that if I was going to do that, then I want to do it a certain way.'

Despite never having made an album under her name alone, Eliza didn't baulk: she would relish the chance to put together her own repertoire, but more importantly, would use the opportunity to achieve some of the fundamental things she had always aimed to do. 'First, I said I'm going to want an agent. And I wanted to have decent photos on [the album]; I didn't want pictures of me stood on a mountain, or anything. I went in there quite opinionated, saying I didn't see the point in doing it any other way. So, early on, I forced the issue of having a band and having a say in the way the photos looked. And I don't want to blow my own trumpet or anything, but I think we really did start something.'

Eliza was determined that any album she would put her name to would look as good as it sounded. She felt that the musicians working within her genre didn't always take themselves seriously, with jokey album titles and clichéd, sometimes even downright cheesy, album covers. Eliza wanted to employ some of the slickness, the polish, she felt was a given in the genres to which she listened outside of work. With Topic's blessing, Eliza assembled her band, unsurprisingly consisting of many of her Chipolata, King Ligger and Calicutt bandmates, including James Fagan, Dan Plews, Barnaby Stradling, Sam Thomas and Jock Tyldesley.

As Topic Records could never afford to stump up enormous recording costs in luxurious studios, albums tended to be conceived by 'travelling around with the company Revox in the back of a Morris Traveller and setting it up in someone's house.'[2]

So, as was to be expected, the recording of Eliza's debut solo album was a home-grown affair. Her cousin, Oliver Knight, had been learning the art of sound engineering outside his full time occupation as a landscape gardener, acting as a kind of informal apprentice to Ray Williams in his studio, PA North Dalton Associates (PANDA) Sound. In 1996, Williams sold PANDA Sound to Olly who relocated it to the top floor of his parents' house, conveniently a stone's throw from Martin and Norma's.

'Heat, Light And Sound [as Eliza's first solo album became known] was one of the first sessions where I was fully in charge within the mobile studio in the house. They muddled in, tuned up and did their bit. It was a real learning curve for all of us. Eliza had all the

material, she'd been gigging it for a while, and had all the musicians ready,' Olly acknowledged.

'She never said "Sam, I'm going to employ you",' Sam Thomas remembered, 'we were always just in the same pot. With *Heat, Light And Sound*, it was a case of "I'm going to make a solo album, there's four or five tracks here with you and Barnaby on them so when you're free, let's record them". Olly had his recording equipment in one room and we were recording the instruments in the other rooms in the attic. It was really grassroots stuff, proper old studio. We were learning arrangements and recording them very raw, as they came out of us, really.'

Barnaby Stradling felt that the contributing musicians were asked to be involved simply because they were Eliza's friends and could bring a wealth of different influences to the table, rather than a focussed, folk ethic. 'She liked what I brought to the mix. I'd played a lot more reggae and rock, as I'd grown up thinking folk was unhip and unfashionable, what my parents were into. I knew that if she was after ideas from outside of the folk scene, then I could help her out. And though Liza had most of the melodies sorted, we wrote and arranged stuff together, all of us. It was a democratic arrangement. We're a good writing team, me and Liza; we can push it and pull it in different directions.'

And it was these different directions by which reviewers were preoccupied, clamouring to dub Eliza as 'The future of British folk music'*[Mojo]* with her 'nice wah-wah fiddle over a "Shaft"-type funky guitar line. Welcome to the new brand of folk.'[3]

But contrary to the contributing musicians' reports, *Heat, Light And Sound* does not hint at a studio learning curve. Instead, the album exudes confidence: here is a young woman enjoying her talent, presenting arrangements of a number of tracks which will remain in her set for years to come, most notably 'Cold, Wet And Rainy Night', which she will later revisit with the Imagined Village, and '10,000 Miles'. There's the sauntering rhythm section underneath a Bampton Morris jig; the space and time dedicated to the unaccompanied rendition of 'Clark Saunders', but most importantly, there's the fiddle playing.

This does not sound like the fiddle playing of someone who had picked up the fiddle in earnest only six years or so previously; this is a confident, skilled musician with a realization of style, both the style she admires and the sound she's aiming to produce. It's not always a pretty sound, as evidenced by the creaking and crashing in the self-penned tune 'Stamps For The Dog', for example, but then her voice is not 'pretty', either: Eliza's emphasis is on the plaintive, the earthy, the real.

And her album did look as good as it sounded. The images and artwork reflected her idiosyncrasies: on the front and back cover, it is her short hair which is the focus, a flash of fiddle for good measure. Inside, she is balancing the fiddle, scroll downwards, on her chin. This is inevitably acknowledging the lasting influence of the Chipolatas, but it also represents her desire to do things differently: her approach to the tradition would be to turn it on its head; her fiddle – and the tradition – would not be placed on a pedestal, but used, experimented with, played with. A healthy kind of disrespect.

The outtakes from the promo shoot for the album further demonstrates Eliza's playfulness. A series of shots record her attempts at trying to get the fiddle to balance. She laughs as it falls before - thankfully – it is caught. Wearing a long, open trench coat over baggy trousers and boots, a cropped top reveals a pierced belly button, and a beaded braid swings from her temple. In one shot she is sultry, leaning back against the wall, one foot propped up behind her, her violin held down at her side. She looks calm and self-assured. In another, she is holding her violin away from her, and looking in the opposite direction. It's a stance of defiance, one that conveys that she will not be compromising her attitude and her approach.

As with all women in the public eye, commentary on Eliza's appearance was never too far away from the critique of her debut. In fact, praise for the album seemed to come hand in hand with praise for her appearance. As Ian Anderson's interview with Eliza in *fRoots* observed: 'If the column inches devoted to Eliza Carthy in the national press and mainstream music media in the wake of her recent Topic solo debut, *Heat, Light And Sound*, are anything to go by, we have a new star in our midst.'[4]

And just as the 'folk brat pack' phrase began to wane, Eliza was christened the 'folk babe'. With her penchant for Doc Martens, piercings, short hair and sporting a very North Easterly pale complexion, though – not to mention her enviable musical talent – Eliza wasn't a likely 'babe' candidate. However, perhaps the 'folk babe' tag was there to insinuate more about the genre of music than the 'babe' herself. Folk music has always suffered from a negative stereotype, all Aran jumpers, beards, socks with sandals, silver tankards and fingers firmly plunged in ears.

In the BBC Radio 3 documentary *A Place Called England*, Fiona Talkington asked her guests about the persistent, unshakeable folky connotations. Martin Carthy replied, exasperatedly explaining how, in his experience, the media interact with folk music, stating 'it's the finger in the ear hoop, the pewter tankard hoop, the Aran sweater hoop and the Morris dancing hoop. Stereotypical images that the media love. It's all about "eccentrics"; you don't even get to talk about the music, you don't get to sing the damn stuff, it's just "'go through that hoop, that hoop, that hoop, oh we don't have time for any more. Goodbye." It's really upsetting.'

Norma's irritation was evident, too, patiently explaining that the only Aran jumpers she had seen in the folk world were worn by one or two Irish groups such as the Clancy Brothers. How it had become synonymous with English traditional music was anybody's guess. The finger in the ear derision was also unfair – singers throughout history, regardless of style and genre, have cupped an ear to hear better (the Bee Gees were even satirized by the late Kenny Everett for doing this incessantly); why this has been found to be a particularly 'folk' trait is peculiar, and why it arouses such scorn is also perplexing.

Of course, there is a grain of truth in the stereotype: head to a typical folk festival and you will see an uncanny amount of beards, tankards and jumpers, Aran or otherwise. And as for the age of its followers, Eliza is only too aware, stating 'I became fond of saying that we get everyone in the end, because everyone turns 40. That's not entirely fair to folk music, obviously.'⁵

Frankly – who cares? No doubt a metal festival will attract copious amounts of black hair dye, leather boots and pentagrams; reggae will have its fair share of dreadlocks and tams. There is no need to deride and sideline a musical form due to the appearance of its performers and followers, or revert back to the stereotypes to such a degree that any valid discussion about the music is lost. But, I would argue, no other genre has continued to suffer such sustained mockery and ridicule as folk music.

But Eliza Carthy, as the mainstream media rubbed its hands together with glee, presented a new, more 'acceptable' face to the genre: young, attractive, striking. She had multiple piercings and dyed her hair, the cut and colour of which changed from one tour to the next. The fact that she wasn't a true 'babe' in the Baywatch sense of the word didn't matter too much: this was *folk music*, after all. Add 'elfin' to the tag to explain the androgynous haircut and the angular features of the early Eliza, and here was the perfect package. 'And why not?' Marry Waterson smiled. 'She does make it sexy with her lovely publicity photos. I can see why journalists will do it and she does look the part.'

Now that Eliza's older and there's a younger crop of women on the scene – and young female folk musicians are more visible in number – the tag isn't bandied about as frequently as it once was. In an interview with *Musician* in 2005, she was asked 'You've been referred to as a folk veteran. How does that feel at the age of 29?' Eliza replied 'A folk veteran, really? I'm not sure if that's better or worse than "folk babe". At least now there are no unreal expectations I suppose.'⁶

Ash Green was raised by folk music enthusiasts and was even named after Fairport Convention and Albion Band maestro, Ashley Hutchings. He first heard Eliza when she and her band were touring the *Heat, Light And Sound* album and supporting Oysterband:

It was December 1996. I was hitchhiking round the country watching Oysterband; we used to hitchhike a lot watching New Model Army, Levellers, Chumbawamba, all that kind of world, and there was this support that I'd never heard of before. We'd got there early and heard this music strike up. I'd recognized the name, the Carthy name, my parents being into Steeleye and so on. I was just blown away. It was the first tour she'd done with a band, but not the first gig. I thought it was absolutely superb, so I watched three or four dates of her with those guys, the *Heat, Light And Sound* album with the Eliza Carthy Band. Eliza and I are the same age, so she must have been 21 then. I was so impressed that I bought the CD which had a flyer advertising all the other gigs coming up. So a month or two later, I went to watch her in this hole of a venue, in Stoke I think. Only forty people or so turned up and it was a reasonably large venue. After the gig, I realized I'd lost my hat, my big stripy hat with a pom-pom on top that I always took to gigs. A few days later, she was playing another gig so I went along and, lo and behold, she had my hat and handed it back to me.

A friendship was born. As it was only Eliza and her band on the road at that point, Ash offered to take care of her merchandise, making sure that cash was safe during performances. It was one less job for Eliza to do, and she welcomed the respite. For Ash, it was a great way to get to know his new hero, and get in to her gigs for free. He was present at most gigs for the best part of twelve years.

But as a self-proclaimed 'techy nerd', it was his computer skills which proved the most use. 'Around 1997 or 1998, I started up the Elizanet website. The internet was still pretty new back then, so I thought I could be some help. In fact, I think I *told* her I was going to do it. It was just basic biographies back then. It was mostly other people [who supplied the photos]. I only really updated the gig list; I kept in touch with promoters and just added them as they came up.'

Although his site is now several years out of date, it is still online [at http://elizanet.org.uk/] and still provides comprehensive – and often rather subjective! – information about Eliza and her early projects. A discography put together by Ash demonstrates all of her strands of activity and plots them against a timescale, highlighting when they came to fruition through album release, whilst a database allows web visitors to track which band members had contributed to which albums. User-generated content was provided in the form of photographs, video and audio clips, and one page still promises forthcoming tutorials for fiddle players wanting to learn Eliza's repertoire.

The most active part of the site, when it was current, was the forum. 'The ones that contacted me were mostly female, early twenties. The forums were quite a sociable thing. "Anyone going to this gig?" "What are the lyrics to this song?" There were some people who wanted to find out about the music, but mostly, people wanted to know about her. Certainly, at the beginning, the majority of the audiences were older, middle class people who had been beard-wearing, pipe-smoking kids in the 1960s, but there was a growing younger undercurrent, particularly at festivals. I used to go down to Sidmouth a lot and there were a lot of kids there, trying to take up the fiddle and so on because they'd been inspired. The Carthy family were always there because they would be performing in one guise or another.'

Ash feels that the Kings of Calicutt were one of the best projects Eliza had going, deeming them 'The bestest band ever to have existed – dance like you've never danced before! Seeing her play with the Kings of Calicutt were some of the best nights of my life, but I found that very few people went,' he added, sadly.

The Kings of Calicutt album came out in 1997, a year after *Heat, Light And Sound.* 'The Kings of Calicutt existed before I joined it,' Barnaby explained, 'after they'd been working as a three- and then a four-piece. It had been driven by Liza and Nancy as they had the back catalogue to choose from, but then Nancy left. We gigged quite a lot for ceilidhs.'

And though the material they were playing was mainly English, it was a Scot, Eliza's old friend John McCusker, whom she approached for production duties: 'We recorded that up in Edinburgh and helping on that record was the first time I'd properly worked with her, really. It really struck me how confident she was, so driven. She was so easy to work with, inspiring, because she just gets out there and does it. Even when she was a little kid with spiky hair, singing with her mum and dad, she was great, it was unreal. But then, she's always singing so it's very natural. But I knew, producing that album, that the Kings of Calicutt wasn't going to be the band she'd be in forever, just because she has so many interests. She will keep on doing different things because you need to keep yourself excited. You want it to be as exciting as it was when you first started.'

John, of course, was right, and the Kings disbanded, though a reunion has recently been touted. Watch this space.

FOUR

Where's My Fiddle?

*I want to be current. I can't just play traditional music
and not connect with people my age as well.*
Eliza interviewed by Joe Lost, *fRoots* [1]

'It became more professional when we did *Red Rice*,' Sam Thomas remembered. Eliza and her circle of musician friends were drawn to Edinburgh. Having recorded the only Chipolatas album in the Scottish capital, Sam felt that the scene there was 'a hub,' one they could mine for musicians, experience and inspiration. 'Mystery Juice, Shooglenifty, Peatbog Faeries ... there was a massive amount of good stuff going on there so I decided we'd record up there. We used a flat where Angus from Shooglenifty lived at the time, and we were recording in the Stone Roses' studio. We were residential and someone was cooking for us, always a sign you're doing well,' he laughed.

Martin Green was impressed with Eliza's set up, too. 'Up until Liza had called me to do *Red Rice*, I was playing in an Irish pub band. We wrote our own music, we were conscientious, really into it, but it wasn't nationally successful. Liza, though, was able to go to proper studios for a length of time; there were people in place to solve problems, and so on.'

Eliza had decided that this was her opportunity to experiment: that she would demonstrate her commitment to, and respect for, the tradition by a healthy dose of reinvigoration. She hoped she could prove that traditional music could weave current musical influences and other sounds she liked – electronica, drum and bass or simply the piano accordion – and be successful, possibly even appealing to a younger audience. She adhered to her parents' mantra, that 'a substantial part of the tradition is getting your hands dirty, falling flat on your face, making mistakes, being dangerous', as her father Martin put it.[2] Eliza had begun an intense period of research. A 'Billy no mates', she took to Cecil Sharp House, poring over the collection, absorbing *The Penguin Book Of English Folk Songs* and revisiting some of the tune books she and Nancy had previously digested. Her father directed her to 'Billy Boy' and hearing '10,000 Miles' on a Nic Jones record encouraged her to come up with her own interpretation.

'Liza had a sketch of stuff she wanted us to do, which was a mix of tunes and songs. There was this idea that she'd do a double album: one [CD] would be acoustic, so to speak, and one would be electric,' Sam illustrated. 'I can remember being really fired up, having that energy that was youthful, very optimistic, and not overly self-conscious.'

Red Rice was initially released as a double album, later deleted, but its conception was very much separatist – and the two halves of the initial album went on to be released as two separate albums. Eliza wanted to hammer home the different atmospheres and approaches contained within each album so chose to reflect this in the choice of hair colour and style: angelic blonde hair on *Red* and fiery scarlet tendrils on *Rice*. 'I just had too much going on in my head,' Eliza explained, as to why she chose to give life to two albums in one go, despite it still being the early stages of her professional career. 'I had my band, but then I had this working relationship with Saul [Rose] which I wanted to explore, too.'

Topic's Tony Engle didn't seem too perturbed by Eliza's latest venture, either. 'He had a big laugh and heaved a big sigh, probably rolled his eyes, too, but he's nearly always fine with my ideas. He has lots of patience, and lots of ideas, too,' she confirmed.

It was *Red* which began north of the border, with her old friends Sam, Barnaby and Martin forming the core band. She slept on the sofa at the house of her producer, Niall Macauley, the two of them engaging in 'big, spirited discussions' when the other residents had gone to bed.

Once the ideas were down, the actual recording took place at a big estate in Flintshire, now used for bottling and selling water. At the time, though, it was inhabited by a man who made weapons for films. The grounds were used for archery and in between takes and sessions, Eliza and her band found themselves 'swinging swords around' and practising their shots on target. 'There was also an incredible network of arches, like railway arches, but it was in the middle of nowhere.' she remembers.

'By the time Liza asked me to do it,' Martin Green said, 'she had all the songs. Some of them had been gigged, some had been demoed, but they were pretty fixed. A third of them were pretty loosely arranged… maybe it's easier for me as I was there, but it always seems to me that you can hear the difference between the ones that were fixed and the ones which weren't so certain in their arrangements.'

And right from the outset, it is no surprise that *Red* attracted the media attention it did. Opening with an 'accidental Saturday night kitchen mix', 'Accordion Song' features the one-row accordion alongside Martin Green's deft jazz noodlings on the piano keyboard. The drums are allowed to echo, given chance for more of a timbre akin to the leading kit in the samba band, and the bass is not reminiscent of the 1970s folk-rock oompah, as is probably to be expected from a contemporary folk record, but is softer, neater and more like the bass found in reggae and dub. It is the bass that continues to surprise, particularly in the transition between '10,000 Miles', sweetly augmented since its last outing on *Heat, Light And Sound*, and 'Billy Boy', with its ability to reincarnate the late-night ambience of chill-out tents at festivals.

Then the fun really begins. Eliza invited two friends, simply known as 'Shack and Paul', in to the studio to contribute electronica: waves of sound, programmed beats. In the dying days of rave culture, and the crossover appeal of jungle and drum and bass, this was Eliza responding to her surroundings, the influences of the time – and, no doubt, the music to which her peers would be dancing in clubs across the UK: 'They were putting stuff under a track we were making, and we got to sit with them and their cool synthesisers and a copy of Cubase, though I seem to remember having difficulties in getting Cubase to work,' Martin smiled. 'The [track] that we had most fun with in the studio for me was "Russia (Call Waiting)" when I got to do some programming which I hadn't expected to do. I was into it, but I wasn't really expecting the chance to do that on Liza's record.'

It is towards the end of the record where the programming comes to real prominence, with 'Russia (Call Waiting)' seeping in and out of electronic consciousness, before the title track closes the album with the energy of a fiddle tune fuelled by robotic beats and doused in consuming soundscape sweeps. And, to me, it immediately evokes childhood nights spent listening to specialist dance music shows on Radio 1 before falling asleep.

In retrospect, though, Eliza wished she hadn't included 'Red Rice', the final track on *Red*. 'It was all a little bit piecemeal. Half the beats were missing; I shouldn't have let it go on the album. It had some unkind comparisons; someone said it sounded like "Cotton Eye Joe" [released by Rednex in 1994],' she said.

It was obvious that though Eliza was keen to integrate sounds and technologies typically found outside the folk world, how it was to be incorporated and by whom was pretty much left to the organic process of writing, recording and producing the record. Niall Macauley had also been the producer for the Chipolatas' album, *Skinless*, and Eliza and her band enjoyed entrusting him with what they came up with, encouraging him to shape the material, chopping and splicing as he saw fit. 'I really like that way of working,' she said.

And though the concept of *Red Rice* was premeditated – that Eliza's take on traditional music was not going to be simply regurgitation, preservation, but a modern reinterpretation – this was not experiment for experiment's sake. 'I was using the traditional material as a template, and trying loads of other stuff with that,' Eliza explained on the Channel 5 documentary,

71

My Music: 'We tried to do what came naturally; it wasn't a case of shoehorning a ballad into a 4 by 4 type of a beat.' Listeners agreed, with Stewart Lee proclaiming 'when she uses a programmed beat, it's only like using clog dancing for a rhythm. It doesn't feel like desperate attempts to appeal.'[3]

'It was an experimental time, and we loved it,' Barnaby said.

Rice, in contrast, was recorded at Olly's PANDA Sound in Robin Hood's Bay with a smaller contingent of contributors, including her then brother-in-law, Saul Rose [who had married Eliza's half-sister; they are now divorced] on melodeon and Ed Boyd on guitar and bouzouki. Whereas *Red* defiantly proclaimed 'The traditional music on this album, with the exception of "Billy Boy", is all English and out there. Not to exclude anyone or anything, but just because we can', *Rice* took the time to explain and thank the source material: a wealth of different tune and song books, 'the book of pipe tunes and the long afternoon that went with it', and a number of different source singers.

However, Eliza is keen to emphasize the fun that she has had in researching, arranging and treating the material; that though she respects the singers and musicians before her, her process does not involve kid gloves, dusty tomes placed on pedestals, a wrinkled brow and a hushed silence. She acknowledges her twentieth century outlook and revels in the wealth of technology, new sounds and information that being a twentieth century person brings. She is having a laugh with us when, in her liner notes, she writes, 'Robert Rowlands of Shipley in Sussex in about 1908 – *I remember it well*, Cecil Sharp, Maud Karpeles, Bill Bailey of Cannington in Somerset in 1906 - *I think he was at home at the time*.'

And though its first iteration was as a double album, the difference between *Red* and *Rice* was apparent, with the media apparently holding preference for *Red*.

'Put crudely, *Red* is for clubbers and *Rice* for crusties,' Tony Hendry stated bluntly in his review in *The Living Tradition*.[4] A rather overstated claim, but, after a fashion, he was right. The term that Hendry used to describe the audience for *Rice*, 'crusty', was itself a moniker of its time, a 1990s term to describe a culture so scorned by the mainstream – the tattooed, dreadlocked New Age travellers with a penchant for folk-tinged punk music like Levellers and New Model Army. This subculture, with its political, anti-consumerist and wholly unfashionable outlook, was never fully embraced by the mainstream music press, unlike many other musical subcultures which are adamantly adopted, indulged and perpetuated through the likes of *NME* and, previously, *Melody Maker* (which folded two years after the release of *Red Rice* in 2000). Though *Rice* was an energetic, refreshing take on English traditional music, it was deemed 'too stereotypically "trad" for all but the most austere folk adept'[5] and it was with *Red* that the music press was preoccupied.

'The press was very interested in the fact there was drum and bass on it,' Martin Green remembered, 'which was a sign of the times, as that now wouldn't seem like a radical idea. That aspect caught a load of media attention outside the folk world, which has actually stayed with their impressions of Eliza ever since – that innovative edge is still something that people outside of the folk press will continue to associate with her.'

For all the talk of experimentation, though, Eliza sees *Red Rice* more simply. For her, it was an album where she handed English traditional music to her musician friends, friends who weren't primarily playing English traditional music and thus didn't approach it in a 'we-must-do-it-this-way-because-of-what's-gone-before' fashion. She wanted fresh ears to these age-old songs, players who would perform them as they saw fit. They were largely songs and tunes they hadn't heard before and so didn't have a prescribed way to play them – or a definite instrument on which they should be played, or accompanied. She hoped that Barnaby would bring some of his punk and reggae influences to the table; that Martin Green would add some of his Irish inflections or his Eastern European nuances.

She also disagreed vehemently with the critical response to the double album. To her, *Rice* was the contemporary album: though it had been largely acoustic, it combined fiddle, accordion and foot percussion, the latter which had inspired Eliza whilst she was on tour in the States. Eliza felt this was the modern, the contemporary, experimental, take on the traditional material. 'I felt that the fiddle and the accordion together was a very modern thing; whilst *Red* was expressing traditional music in the traditional way: the source material came to me generationally, I was playing the music with whoever was around at the time using whatever sounds were around at the time. But everyone called *Red* the contemporary album because it had drum and bass on it, and so on. I was in a real fighting mood back then,' Eliza confirmed.

'I know exactly what she means,' Saul corroborated. 'There were some really experimental bits to that album. The step clogging at the end, the fact that Ed just wanted to play the basslines that I'd come up with – I'd never heard that from a guitarist before! Some of our key choices were deliberately mental, and the way that 'Mons Meg' bounces into 'Tuesday Morning' into what is then essentially a solo fiddle piece … well, you can just tell we were having a blast.'

Eliza also viewed *Red Rice* as a breakup album. The BBC Radio 3 show *The Verb* sees presenter and poet Ian McMillan invite a wealth of guests to the studio to discuss and perform their work with a focus on their words. On Friday 13 January 2012, Eliza was one such guest and though her interview and performance was largely centred on her original songwriting, her approach to traditional music was also a topic of interest. 'Though *Red Rice*, the album I made in 1998, was actually 99.9% traditional material, I consider it to be a breakup album. I had just broken up with my boyfriend and the material I chose and what I did with them reflected that … Writing about your life is very exposing and I'd always looked down on it a little bit [before she made purely songwriting albums], but it's a difficult thing to do well.'

Later she told me, '"Russia (Call Waiting)" was about Conrad [the boyfriend she had recently split from] as he'd had a girlfriend when we started going out, not that I knew. She was living in Russia, and I'd had no idea. Then "The Snows They Melt The Soonest", that was *really* about him! I imagined myself sat on the stile, lamenting about the whole thing.'

For Eliza, traditional music – however ancient the lyrics or tune – should be used in the now, to reflect the spoils of the moment. Whilst pop stars sing a cover version to pay homage to a particular person, or to add variety and scope to their existing repertoire, perhaps even in a crude attempt to show off their musical knowledge of other genres or eras, Eliza's performance of traditional songs and tunes is to enhance her understanding of her own situation and emotions, as well those of others who are also operating in her world.

Red Rice, then, is a perfect example of this. It not only uses styles and instrumentation of the late 1990s – ambient dance, drum and bass – but the words, musicians and the material showcased exactly how life was like for Eliza in 1998: the people she was associating with, the sounds she was enjoying, and the feelings she was experiencing. The surprise media attention for *Red Rice* culminated in a nomination for the 1998 Mercury Prize.

'Everything was surprising to me at the time,' Martin recalled. 'Perhaps I hadn't realized what a big deal it was because that was the first proper record I'd made, or played on, that had a record company involved. And then I went to HMV and there were big posters with Eliza's face on it and it was hard to know whether that was normal or not.'

Eliza and her bandmates were beside themselves with excitement. 'It felt like we were doing what Liza had set out to do: put English folk music in the mainstream, wake people up to the idea that we have some sort of a cultural identity, the music we had been left by our ancestors,' Sam enthused, 'that felt very realized and really strong.'

'I felt shy, out of my comfort zone,' Barnaby admitted. 'We had to play one of our tunes at the awards ceremony and when we went to sit back down at our little round table, suddenly Jarvis Cocker and Cerys Matthews were there. Jarvis has always been a fan of Norma and the Watersons, and there he was, chatting away with Norma on one side; on the other, there was Eliza and Cerys talking. I remember just thinking "wow"! And Eliza really enjoyed the attention – that comes from her dad!'

Jarvis Cocker was there with his band, Pulp, opening the evening's ceremony in celebration of their nomination for *This Is Hardcore*. They had previously won the Mercury in 1996. Eliza was also up against a feast of other names including Cerys Matthews' Catatonia, Massive Attack, Cornershop, Robbie Williams, Asian Dub Foundation, and the album for which the Verve will be ultimately remembered, *Urban Hymns*.

However, it was Gomez's debut album, *Bring It On*, which went on to win the Prize, stealing it from under her nose, or so the twenty-three year old Eliza thought. 'I got so monumentally pissed that I was just off my face on champagne,' Eliza stated matter-of-factly, without so much as a hint of remorse. 'I remember rampaging around the back of the Shepherd's Bush Empire, and being in the dressing room where it had those tall windows with the top bit that flaps out. I leant out the top of one of those, watching Gomez get in to their cars to go home after the ceremony. And I remember yelling – in a friendly, joshing manner,' she concedes, 'various things at them, as they'd just won my £20,000 as far as I was concerned. I was screaming at them! It was friendly abuse, though, of course.'

Some kindly souls, obviously realizing the rather tired and emotional state that Eliza was in, took care of her fiddle and the award she had received in recognition of her nomination to ensure they weren't abandoned to the general post-event, booze-sodden detritus with which the Shepherd's Bush Empire was likely to be plagued. But Eliza and her band hadn't a clue.

As the venue emptied, the doors of carefully polished hire cars closing on their famous musician residents, preparing to whisk them away to after-show parties in the company of an excess of notable names from the British cultural scene, Eliza and her merry party were gently escorted out of the building by the stage manager, and pushed out into the night.

'Where's my fiddle and where's my fucking award?' Eliza shouted at the stage manager, at the building, at any other person who happened to be nearby. She was still clutching an empty bottle of champagne. The door was closed and locked behind her.

'Where's my fiddle and where's my fucking award?,' Eliza repeated again, this time in 2011, with a 'What was I like?' expression, smiling and shaking her head.

As the Mercury Prize tends to do for musicians of a lesser mainstream status, often those working within the more niche genres, the nomination opened a door or two, one being to the main Pyramid stage at Glastonbury in June 1999 where Eliza and her band played probably to their largest ever audience – certainly to their largest cold audience, without a doubt. The ratio of self-confessed fans of English traditional music was sure to be lower here than any of the other stages she had graced in her career to date.

They were sandwiched between Billy Bragg and Beth Orton on the Pyramid stage's Saturday bill, which would later be headlined by the Manic Street Preachers. 'Playing on the main stage at Glastonbury is like a golden memory,' Sam recalled. 'I can remember giving my water bottle to Beth Orton and I was like "Beth Orton just asked me for my water!" We were giddy with it, we were having fun.'

Lucy Adams had contributed 'incidental singing' and clogs to *Red Rice* having become Eliza's best friend when they had met in their late teens. Daughter of a folk musician and clog teacher and also based in Yorkshire, Eliza had visited Lucy's mother for a few clog lessons before the two young women began to 'live in each other's pockets.' They met frequently at festivals, staying at each other's houses so often that Lucy came to regard Eliza's parents as 'Uncle Martin and Auntie Norma'. And, no doubt thanks to a healthier budget due to the success of *Red Rice*, Lucy was brought on board as a member of the touring band, along with Heather McLeod of the Bevvy Sisters.

'I just remember touring solidly between 1997 and 1999, well, for two and a half years really, and it was just a fantastic, crazy adventure,' recalls Lucy. 'We had been supporting Billy Bragg and the Blokes around the UK and then ended up on the main stage at Glastonbury. After a little while, though, I needed to do something for myself so I went off and did my degree. I'd come back and do bits and pieces, though, hop up on stage when I was needed. I really loved it, both the closeness with Eliza and her music.' Now a carpenter designing and building sets and scenery for theatre, Lucy remembered the late 1990s as a period of festivals and jokes shared on the tour bus. 'And lots of drum and bass,' she laughed, 'we listened to a lot of that on tour. Though we were all pretty much the kids of folk fans and folk musicians – the next generation – and were playing a lot of folk music, we listened to all kinds of things, and we all liked such different music.'

'*Red Rice* was when it was most fun,' Sam stated. 'We played all the kind of sticky-floor rock 'n' roll venues, and I remember Liza bought this Volkswagen minibus kind of thing to drive us all round. It felt like we were proper musicians, really, and we toured with Billy Bragg which, I remember thinking at the time, what a privilege it was. He was a childhood hero of mine and it was almost like our dreams had come true. The pinnacle of that was being at the Mercury and meeting Roni Size and Jarvis Cocker and it was amazing.'

Sadly, though, the year 1998 brought with it tragedy. Lal Waterson, Norma's younger sister by four years, died of cancer on 4 September; her illness had only been detected ten days previously. This fiercely private woman had long given up touring and singing publicly, but the songs Lal had written – on acclaimed albums such as *Bright Phoebus*, recorded with her brother Mike in 1972, and *Once In A Blue Moon*, made with her son Olly in 1996 – continued to have a lasting impact on the folk scene and beyond, with her songs being covered by a range of different artists such as the Unthanks and James Yorkston.

Marry Waterson felt that Eliza's aptitude for songwriting was inevitably honed through the exposure to the writing of her auntie Lal, stating 'Liza will have listened to mum's work. It was so different and so well-crafted that it would definitely have an effect on any songwriter.'

Lal's singing style and unusual melodies also appealed. In November 2010, folk music journalist Robin Denselow presented a BBC Radio 4 documentary about the life and legacy of Lal

Waterson, entitled *Once In A Blue Moon*. In it, Eliza said: '[Lal] had quite a throaty voice and I was always amazed by the notes she could hit and the tone ... for someone who had smoked for so long, you wouldn't have thought she'd be able to sing and yet she had the most gorgeous tone to her voice. I liked the awkwardness and the non-prettiness of it, the real gravity to it.'[6]

But it seemed that Lal was also appreciative of her niece's talent. 'Mum was knocked out when she heard "10,000 Miles" so up to date,' Marry smiled, 'and Eliza as a writer ... well, she was amazed at the bare honesty conveyed in her lyrics.' The year in which Lal died, Eliza had earned the prestigious nomination for her album *Red Rice* – an album which contained a song of her auntie's, 'Stumbling On'.

At the Mercury Music Prize awards ceremony though, there was more to celebrate. Eliza had made a double album of which she and her contributors were immensely proud, which successfully introduced a different way of thinking, of sounding, for traditional music. Sam Thomas did overhear someone in the audience at the awards ceremony comment that Eliza and her band 'sounded like Captain Pugwash', but, he reassured me, they laughed it off. Eliza and her band also treated Jo Whiley's comments on BBC Radio 1 in good humour, too. 'She said that she thought I was "irrelevant",' she smiles, 'I've always loved that quote.'

The album sold well, in excess of 50,000 copies, which Eliza thinks may well mean that it continues to be her biggest seller to date. As a result, the night that *Red Rice* was awarded the kudos of nomination for the Mercury was also the night that Eliza signed to Warner Brothers USA. She, her band and her family deservedly celebrated with champagne.

It was a coup: a major label liked what they heard, and they were keen for her to produce more. Though this time, it'd be different. Warner Brothers USA stipulated that this album would be a move away from Eliza's back catalogue, 'their main proviso: no traditional music.'[7]

Andrew Wickham, an A&R man for the best part of 40 years, modestly claimed to me that he 'had some fairly big successes' – when, in actual fact, he is responsible for the discovery of Joni Mitchell and was tasked with setting up Warners' Nashville office which still thrives to this day. A Brit working for Warner Brothers America, he was a disciple of Mo Ostin, the label executive who 'revolutionized the music industry.' 'He created the concept of artist rights and artistic freedom,' Wickham explained. 'He told us that the artist is always right, even if they're wrong. We can advise them, but they must do as they please, they can say what they like.'

Wickham was posted back to England in the 1980s with the purpose of finding new European talent which would sit comfortably with an American audience. He found success with Norwegians a-ha, but after that, little else. 'a-ha had a singer with a three-octave range! Colossal! And they looked beautiful; it was perfect for Smash Hits. But after that, I had difficulty finding anything for the US. English pop music at that time was a very strange scene; there was lots of cross-dressing, and most of it didn't translate to American audiences,' he said.

Andrew Wickham wouldn't sign any old artist, or a fad he knew would fade: he had to have good singers. 'Your ear becomes used to great pipes; you can't have poor singing, whatever you think of [the music or the artist's image].' So he was drawn to the British folk scene, lured by his long-term love of the Watersons. He was also an admirer of Topic Records and its forthright managing director Tony Engle, claiming 'he is responsible for some of the greatest music I've ever heard'.

'Unlike American folk music, British folk music will not enter the mainstream. In England, the folk world is a niche,' Andrew believed. 'But I wanted to hear Eliza Carthy. I liked the way she looked, so two of us – myself and my assistant – went to see her in an upstairs room in a pub in Highbury. She just came on with her fiddle, and I thought she was great. I wanted to sign her, but my assistant told me not to. She said, "she won't translate, we can't sell this, it will be totally unnatural."

'So I didn't. But there was nothing else I wanted to sign. I needed good singing. So I did approach her and I seem to remember her father being there, too. We had a great meeting with Tony Engle and it wasn't like talking to rock agents; we had different economic apparatus for one thing, but we made a deal for two albums.'

She would no longer be redressing, reinterpreting, re-inventing the songs that she grew up with, the songs that she found in her family songbooks or researched in the library at Cecil Sharp House, or the songs she learned from her peers and her parents' peers. She would be producing her first collection of entirely self-penned tracks, original music that, the label hoped, would appeal to American music lovers, regardless of their level of knowledge of the British folk canon and of Eliza's famous family.

Eliza was absolutely delighted with the prospect. The opportunity meant reaching newer, potentially bigger audiences, at venues she hadn't visited, venues that weren't necessarily reserved for 'folk' performers. There would be money, too: not just for Eliza herself, to make a decent living, but more money for promotion and publicity, to better pay contributing artists, to produce a more lavish package once the CD was finished: a CD which people might pick from the shelves in HMV and Virgin Megastore because it looked interesting, or because they'd heard a track on the radio, rather than a seasoned fan who bought it at a folk festival or one of her gigs. This was a natural next-step from the glittering prestige that the Mercury brought; this was the kind of thing that happened to pop stars, *real musicians*, not singers from Robin Hood's Bay.

Mostly, though, Eliza was excited that this was exactly the break she needed in her quest for traditional music. 'I've written poetry and songs since I was a kid,' she told me, 'and [signing to Warners] was part of the crusade for me, part of the mission. I felt that by making contemporary music and bringing people to it, they'd hear the traditional music I'd done before. I hate the ghettoisation of traditional music, I hate the ghettoisation of all music, and coming from a traditional music background shouldn't stop you from writing your own material.'

But she didn't stop there. The original music she planned to write also had a *raison d'être*; it simply wouldn't be a case of laying down the first melodies that entered her head. 'I wanted to know what pop music would sound like if it hadn't travelled to America and had the journey that it has. I wondered what it would sound like if it had stayed here, how it would have been affected by the people that came here in the 1940s and 1950s: people of Jamaican descent, for example. I suppose I'm just more interested in the music of the people that make up this island. I was interested in the process, and the fruits of the process.'

She also wanted to make clear that she didn't think that popular, contemporary music was the evolutionary step from interpreting traditional music. 'I felt like what I was doing with traditional music was worthwhile – I was singing unaccompanied folksongs over DJs in Brixton and stuff; *Red Rice* didn't sell millions of records, it didn't get in the charts like Kate Rusby's album did, but it did pretty well. It wasn't that, it was that I wanted to see what another step was.'

And then there was the difficulty of how to refer to this music. 'I mean, not calling the traditional music that I am making now "contemporary" is a misnomer, isn't it? It's a *contemporary interpretation*. But the singer songwriter stuff is somehow always labelled contemporary, despite the fact that I was writing with the British Isles' musical traditions in mind.'

From the conversations I had with Eliza about her writing and arranging processes, I had never realized that writing and arranging music – whether 'contemporary' or 'traditional' – could torment so. Like all musicians, Eliza has reasons for why she chooses to write and the goals she hopes to achieve, but she is always aware of her place within her music, and her music's place within the tradition and within music as a whole.

Most alarmingly, Eliza seems to write her music with her audience's – and critics' – questions and interpretations in mind. Whereas many musicians will wonder whether their work will garner a two-star or five-star review, Eliza seems to have to work harder: why has she chosen this particular song and interpreted it in this particular fashion? How is this impacting on or contributing to the furthering of the British tradition? She knows her audience – and her critics – well; she understands what might wind them up, what might get their toes tapping, so she writes with retaliations, rebuttals, explanations, at the ready. It is this perfectionism and attention to detail that makes her such a fascinating musician to follow.

My understanding of the writing processes of the 'popular music' band, through being in one myself, couldn't be further from this. The common-or-garden indie band musician is likely to be motivated to write a song because a riff has come to the guitarist whilst she or he is noodling one evening before band practice, a lyric has formed in the mind after reading a news story, or the drummer has shamelessly stolen a beat from their biggest influence's latest single.

There may have been an hour-long jam around a chord progression that turned into a song about which, for once, all members are enthusiastic. Or it may be as practical as *we need a slow one as all the rest on our debut are speedy three-minuters*. And the interview questions the common-or-garden indie band is likely to have to consider aren't particularly taxing, only those Steve Lamacq can throw at them in the allotted ten minutes on his 6Music show: Where does the band name come from? Who are your influences? What is the song about? And isn't that drum beat from …?

Jumping ahead in Eliza's story and giving away the game a little, when Eliza returned to Topic after her time at Warners, the reactions of the folk fans, the interrogations she had anticipated, made themselves known. The contemporary versus the traditional, the major label versus the specialist, became the subject her fans – or the self-proclaimed fans of the genre which claimed Eliza as their own – wanted to bring up. She found herself cross-examined in the face of selling out.

'I was very annoyed by the people who kept coming up to me and saying "Welcome back! This is where you belong!" I used to be like "what are you talking about?" and then I realized that they meant welcome back to traditional music. I remember being at the

Big Session, one of the first ones, 2003. I remember coming down the steps and someone going "oh, welcome back!" I turned round and they were wearing an Oysterband t-shirt. And as much as I love the Oysterband – and I do – they're not fucking traditional music. What the hell is someone saying "Welcome back" to me at the Big Session, wearing an Oysterband t-shirt? What does that mean? What is that?'

Once the deal was inked, and Sam Thomas and Barnaby Stradling were signed up for another tour of duty with the Eliza Carthy Band, the writing process began. She filled her notebooks. She knew the kind of material she wanted on this album, her first for a major label, and wrote avidly, writing with her new audience in mind. To Eliza, lyrics are the easy part – after all, this is a woman with much to say.

What she did request, however, was a writing partner; someone to act as sound board to those lyrics, mood board to the atmosphere and ambience, and someone who would help flesh out her compositions. 'Ben [Ivitsky] used to say that I wrote these horrible, monotonal tunes with two chords in them,' Eliza laughed. 'And to a certain extent, he was right: I really am a singer, I'm not a musician.

'Because I don't write chords, I restricted myself and did it all upside down – I think, right, I'll come up with a melody and a beautiful song, and then I'll apply the musician head and try and take steps forward.'

A co-writer, Eliza hoped, would take her notes, her intentions, and build on it, making it easier for the contributing musicians to step in and play their part. With enough advance from Warners for a two-week writing session at the Riverside, a studio just outside Glasgow in East Kilbride, she asked Niall Macauley to join her as co-writer. She had enjoyed working with him on the *Red Rice* album, and found his blend of innovative pragmatism to be just what she was looking for.

Above: Waiting for fish and chips in Whitby - the best there is.
Left: A sleepy looking Eliza with her head on her dad's shoulder.
Below: Eliza looking very cheeky.

Above: L-R Leathy, Eliza and cousin Emma.
Left: 'Meet Me In St Louis'
Below: The family that plays together, stays together.

Top: Eliza's first group, the Waterdaughters L-R Norma, Eliza, Marry, Lal.
Bottom: Christmas Watersons' style. The late Mike Waterson with trademark flat cap. Jill Pidd stood in for an ill Lal.

Left: Eliza busking it. Martin & Norma like this so much it is framed on their wall at home.

Below: King Ligger And The Bathing Boys busking in Sidmouth. They were named after Sam 'King of the Liggers' Thomas.

Bottom: Eliza and the Chips - rockin' out.

Busker Eliza riding high in the charts!

ORMER Scarborough stu-
dent Eliza Carthy is fitting in
a bit of busking between promoting her hit record.

The 18-year-old, who used
to go to Scarborough Sixth
Form College, has shot to
number five in the folk music
charts.

The record, *Eliza Carthy
and Nancy Kerr*, is available
countrywide in top stores
like Virgin.

Eliza (pictured), who lives
in Robin Hood's Bay, has a
musical background.

Top: Eliza and Nancy clogging. You'll believe a girl can fly.
Chris Wood and Andy Cutting supply the music. © Saffron Summerfield
Bottom: Kings of Calicutt at Towersey Village Festival. L-R Saul, Nancy,
Eliza, Dan Plews. © Ron Hill (HillPhotographic)

Above and right: The
Chips are not only
great musicians, but
great entertainers, too.

Above: Eliza eating a bag of crisps - *HL&S* tour, supporting Oysterband. Phil Udell behind her. Ben Stone (former Oysterband manager) in the background.
Left: No prizes for guessing who got Eliza's vote. Possibly taken at the Mean Fiddler.
Below: Lucy Adams puckers up for Barn Stradling, possibly en route for Jersey.

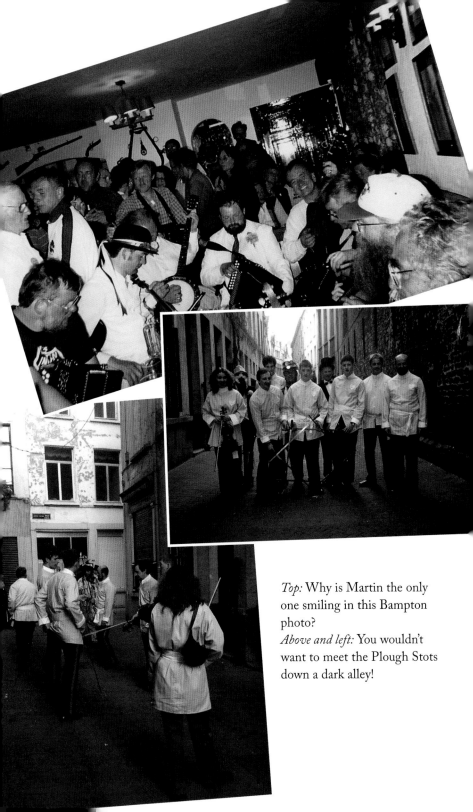

Top: Why is Martin the only one smiling in this Bampton photo?
Above and left: You wouldn't want to meet the Plough Stots down a dark alley!

When she turned up at the Riverside, however, his enthusiasm quickly waned. 'He said "OK, where are your songs?" so I brought out my notebooks and he was just horrified. He was expecting songs. He just sat there and looked at me. He said "I thought you wanted me to produce your album?" and I replied "no, I said I wanted someone to write with; what I need is a co-writer".' And having realized he hadn't understood Eliza's intentions, he said he wouldn't do it. 'He said it wasn't what we'd agreed, and we had a bit of a falling out,' Eliza explains, glumly. He left, and Eliza was resigned to an empty studio, a full-to-bursting notepad, and little else.

Thankfully, Dave, the sound engineer booked for the sessions, rose to the challenge. Though his job description meant he wasn't required to get involved in the writing and arranging of the album he was to record, he happened to be an enthusiastic keyboardist and jumped in to help. Between them, they coerced some of the musicians from Shooglenifty to join them, and much to Eliza's relief, it wasn't long before the lines in her notebooks started to come to life.

Eliza remembers vividly the impromptu ensemble coming up with an Afro Pop inspired tune which she carried into live performances with the Angels And Cigarettes Band, despite it not making the final record. It was also this rather uncertain, ramshackle session where 'Poor Little Me' was born, Shooglenifty's Quee Macarthur putting down a solid bass line for Eliza so she could write the melodies and harmonies over the top.

As the two weeks drew to a close, Eliza had four or five songs down, perfect for a demo to send to Warners for their approval for the next stage. Given the disastrous start, this was a pretty miraculous turnaround, especially when the label called to say that they were impressed with what they had heard. They were happy for Eliza to proceed.

With a little more money from Warners, Eliza procured some recording equipment so that she could write at home with her then boyfriend, Ben Ivitsky. When the offer of an Australasian tour with her parents and with Saul came about soon afterwards, she and Ben packaged up the new mics, keyboard and digital recording station and took it with them to use for recording and demoing in the evenings and days off that the gigs permitted. Once the tour was over, Eliza and Ben hired a campervan and travelled around the country, writing as they went, her parents accompanying them on and off along the way. Their travels proved fruitful, laying down a further seven songs ready for Warners' approval.

Here, Eliza nonchalantly added, 'We had some time off in the Blue Mountains and went and stayed in the Clarendon Hotel in Katoomba where I wrote "Company Of Men" with my dad.' How lovely, the unsuspecting reader might think, combining holiday, creativity and family all in one go. How refreshing, how sweet to include her father in her creative process. But that's where the discerning Eliza fan would stop, hesitate, check the tracklisting of the album which became known as *Angels And Cigarettes*. 'Company Of Men' is also lovingly known as 'The Blowjob Song', the song which opens with very soft but plaintive singing of the words:

> *I've given blowjobs on couches*
> *To men who didn't want me any more*
> *Why they didn't tell me before*
> *I have never been sure*

Eliza even has a photograph of her father writing and recording the melody, depicting him hunched over his guitar, his face a picture of concentration: there is not a hint of laughter, or a speck of a squirm in his body language. He is taking this song – and its blatant, unavoidable sentiment – every bit as seriously as he would any other.

Whilst Eliza was away, sightseeing, singing and writing, Warners secured a producer for the album, and arranged for Eliza and her band to move to Brighton for recording sessions at the Levellers' Metway Studios. Al Scott is probably best known for his work with the Levellers, producing their number one album, *Zeitgeist*, alongside their platinum album, *Levelling The Land*, which was toured in its entirety by the band in spring 2011, twenty years after it was first released.

Before Eliza and her band travelled to Brighton for the sessions, Al Scott decided first to pay the band a visit, to see how the project was coming along and get to grips with what exactly he was letting himself in for. It made sense for him to have Warners pack up his equipment so that he could travel up to Edinburgh to meet with Eliza and her musicians, planning to stay for two weeks. He was hoping to get a head start so that they could better use their more costly time in Brighton.

Scott told me that he was hired on the basis that he was able to work well with 'difficult people'. Though Eliza is opinionated and headstrong, and the first to admit so, she welcomes the input of others and cherishes the contributions of her band members and producers as much as her own. She, at twenty five years old and with her first major label contract in hand, wasn't about to make Al Scott, an experienced producer with results and reputation, regret his decision to work with her.

But Warners anticipated that Eliza might find the transition from independent specialist label to major, global conglomerate challenging. Al Scott would be there to toe the company line, whilst gently encouraging, mediating and stretching the artist. And from the moment that Al arrived in Edinburgh, it was soon clear that the problems dogging the first writing session weren't going to disappear.

"'Why don't you play me a song?" I'd asked Eliza. She just brought out these notepads of lyrics; no melodies. I remember saying "but you must have something!'" Al Scott laughed now, safely on the telephone more than a decade on in 2011, but just from his voice, it was all too apparent that this was a man who would not take no for an answer. Not a soul would have wanted to step into Eliza's platform trainers during this altercation.

Eliza could recall Al's response in an instant: it was just a big, horrified intake of breath. Al thought Eliza had nothing but notepads. He knew that she had previous writing and recording sessions scheduled, but, judging by the notepads she had presented to him, he assumed the sessions hadn't amounted to anything. Eliza was going to be more of a 'difficult person' than he had initially thought.

Eliza was a little perplexed by her new producer's reaction. Why was he perturbed by the sight of her notepads, when she had a pretty solid foundation in her initial demo and the seven songs she'd brought back from Australia and New Zealand? Surely he should have been pleased that she wasn't resting on her laurels, that she was continuing to write, record, redraft, re-assemble, prior to her arrival in Brighton?

Then it clicked. Al hadn't heard the demo. He didn't even know it existed.

It materialized that Warner Brothers hadn't sent it, the first experience of poor management and administration which was to recur throughout Eliza's time with the label. 'Someone wasn't arsed to send them over; it was down to bad management, at the end of the day, it wasn't really anyone's fault. It wasn't down to opposing visions [that there was a clunky beginning to the relationship]: they wanted me to be the next Judy Garland, *I* wanted to be the next Judy Garland, I would've enjoyed that very much,' Eliza laughed. 'They thought I was a cross between Joni Mitchell and Judy Garland and I thought "yeah, that'll do! I'd be up for that!" and then every tier of another person in another office got in the way of that.'

However, it did seem there were opposing visions for Eliza's trajectory. Al Scott felt that Andrew Wickham's ambition for Eliza was completely unrealistic. Scott understood that Wickham was imagining her at a grand piano, ball gown-clad and shimmering under a spotlight. Scott remembers being told '"What I don't want is a folk album", and I thought to myself "Great! You've just signed a folk artist!" I realized quite early on that she wasn't going to make a pop album, she wasn't going to play ball, but I don't think Warners had ever had that discussion with Eliza. I was there to pick up the pieces.'

'I didn't realize what demands I'd made,' Wickham explained, thinking back to his hopes for his new signing. 'It didn't occur to me that I was asking her to do something that perhaps she couldn't. I've since come to think that folk artists can't cross over. For example, I think that June Tabor is the greatest singer in the whole world, but she made a pop record which I found lifeless. I think her heart wasn't in it.'

In all her previous recording experience, Eliza had been accustomed to working directly with the label's director. She would take her aspirations, exactly what she wanted to achieve with the record, straight to Tony Engle at Topic who would make that happen. Or at least scale down her expectations and make the realistic happen, in accordance to budget restraints. Here, at Warners, she seemed to be speaking to a different member of staff each time she raised her hand. She recalled: 'Warners was being amalgamated all over the place and there was a continual reshuffle. I mean, you never spoke to the same secretary twice. People were being hired and fired, and it was a very stressful time.'

Early on in the process, Eliza was introduced to an enthusiastic young graphic designer who was going to be working on her album cover and inlay. Encouraged by his gusto, she invited him to Robin Hood's Bay and she gave him a full tour of the village where she grew up. She took him to St Ives farm where she and her extended family had lived in close quarters; they discussed her favourite colours and the kind of images she wanted to shy away from, the 'folk singers on top of a mountain' syndrome. They went for a walk in the woods, and finished up at the pub, discussing Eliza's hopes for the record and the kind of imagery she thought would suit. With her previous records, she had aimed for ambitious artwork and photography which reflected her interests and outlook, as well as her passion for the music. She wanted a package which looked the part. And now that her music was to be given a bigger stage, she hoped her expectations could be scaled accordingly. This was her chance to make a real impact.

Sadly, though, the designer with whom she had spent the day wasn't assigned to work on the final product. In fact, it wasn't even his successor, with whom Eliza had also had discussions later. 'It was the third or fourth person down the line and I ended up with this stupid barefoot-on-a-staircase bollocks that I hated,' she said, the disappointment still very much evident.

I was surprised to learn that this photo shoot, used as the basis for the final CD inlay, wasn't to Eliza's taste. *Angels And Cigarettes* was actually the first of Eliza's albums that I purchased (for £16.99 from WH Smith using birthday vouchers, I might add), having seen it in a brochure advertising the latest releases from the Metway. As a violin-playing Levellers fan, I had spotted this unusual CD cover and immediately thought – without having heard so much as a note – that this was for me. Here was a cool looking woman; surely her music would sound just as cool? She had long blue hair with the teeniest, tiny fringe and a labret piercing. A strange violin sat next to her, shaped rather like a silhouette of the number eight than a traditional violin, all flourishes and corners. (One that I have since learned comes from luthier Tim Phillips, from a range he calls the Infidel).

And best of all? Eliza was not smiling sweetly, or bedecked in a PVC catsuit. She was not posing in a suggestive manner, all rumps and bumps. She had her arms folded over her in self-defence and she looked thoroughly pissed off. Of course, I now know that this may be because she was engaged in 'barefoot-on-a-staircase bollocks', but for me, at the time, this was a revelation.

Inside was even better. There were close-ups of that blue hair, which I realized was not just one shade all over, but two-tone: a kind of royal blue offset by an aquamarine. There were big, military goth boots dangling over ornate stonework or peeping out from underneath a skirt that just had to be from Camden Lock market. She had mermaid eye shadow to match *and* she had a nose ring. *I* had a nose ring! And, for me, Eliza's mission worked: I did go and buy her back catalogue, and I did become entranced by her renditions of English folksongs. Before long, I was hooked; not just on Eliza's music, but the genre as a whole. She had succeeded in her quest with at least one – fifteen-year-old, rather impressionable – music fan.

Eliza remembers a time when she was called in to a meeting with Warner Brothers and the speaker, who had gathered the team together, asked the floor 'what shall we do with this Eliza McCartney [sic], then?' Incensed, enraged, she called Andrew Wickham who, she recalls, told her to 'go away and write me a number one single'.

Eliza's relationship with Warners also frustrated her parents. Martin Carthy recalled an occasion when she demanded a meeting to address some of her concerns. When she was turned down, she persevered to the point where she pulled Warners staff out of a funeral. 'And bloody right she was, too,' Martin added.

There were certainly occasions when Eliza found Warners typical to the major label cliché; the cliché that Andrew Wickham found so hurtful given the label's beginnings and Mo Ostin's approach. But in some ways, though, Warners did not adhere to this stereotype. Eliza, although making a pop album, was not remodelled into the pop star jelly mould. Stylists didn't begin to turn up unannounced at her house; she wasn't given a makeover and a punishing personal trainer. In fact, her image seemed to be of no real interest or concern to the label whatsoever.

'To begin with I was like "oh you're not going to want me to lose weight, are you?" and they said no. I actually gained a lot of weight doing the Warners thing because I'd been very ill with my asthma. In 1996, I was in hospital five times in seven months; I was very, very ill. I had steroid course after steroid course. Over the next few years, my weight went crazy. I absolutely ballooned, and nobody would deal with it: I went to the doctor and said that I had a real problem with the steroids, that I was just eating uncontrollably and getting depressed, but he said "it's called willpower, dear" and nobody would talk to me about it.'

As Eliza became more dependent on steroids, her appetite increased and increased. Her body became familiar with eating more, which in turn fuelled her appetite, but her musician lifestyle was fairly sedentary. There was much sitting around and listening to demos, staying up all night to give her reaction to new mixes and then lying in to sleep it off. And, inevitably, given the social, all-hours nature to the work, there was a great wealth of alcohol and convenience food.

'I begged them to send me to a fat farm and they wouldn't do it. By the time I went on the road with Joan Baez, I think I weighed twelve or thirteen stones but they wouldn't send me to a fat farm. They said "we'll spend all that money on you and you'd just get fat again,"' she laughed, before sourly adding, 'bastards'.

'Of course, now, there's reality shows for that kind of thing: lose weight, get paid for it. Every agent's dream!' she smiled.

On paper, Eliza had made it. Through her own hard graft, through talent and through good friendships with other skilled musicians, she had chalked up enough kudos to sign with one of the biggest labels in the world, a label which was going to focus on making her a hit with their home audience. But almost immediately it seemed like the fun had been sucked out. With all the meetings and contracts and new faces and plans and schedules came an added pressure. If Eliza and her band didn't come up with good songs, good arrangements, they knew there would be consequences this time: it wasn't just something they could laugh about in the car on the way home and try better next time.

Sam Thomas felt this rapidly: 'We'd been given a flat by Warner Brothers, we were in the studio owned by the Levellers, so all the things were in place, but any sort of emotional understanding of the artist … well, she was going through something that was like a pressure, a business pressure from this world we didn't really recognize.

'One minute we were playing at Whitby and Sidmouth [folk festivals], drinking tequila sunrises and making our own cocktails,' he said, 'and then all of a sudden, it became really serious and business-like.

'We were sending versions of songs to them and they were sending them back saying "that's no good"; they even wanted different parts. I couldn't believe it when they asked a session bass player to come in. For me, Barnaby's one of the best bass players that ever lived, and they wanted to replace him! I thought "now they're just fucking around!"'

This is something that Eliza remains bitter about today; something even her parents brought up in conversation, with Martin telling me, 'They started messing around with her musicians. They put a new bass player in and he played Barnaby's parts. He was heartbroken.'

Leland Sklar, bass player to an incredible number of names including James Taylor, Carole King, Leonard Cohen, Dolly Parton, and, relevant here, Van Dyke Parks, was secretly drafted in. Though resident in Paris at the time, he was sent Barnaby's parts and asked to re-record them, which, in hiring such an experienced musician to record in a Parisian studio, must have cost a fortune. Eliza and her band were clueless until the deed was done and revealed. Eliza's manager at the time, Nigel Morton, had been all too aware, she later found out, but had decided to keep quiet, knowing full well the kind of reaction the move would make, she told me.

Eliza was no longer in control. Though she and her band had written the album, they had little say in how the material was developed and showcased. Suddenly, things seemed to be happening without their say-so. 'The old rock 'n' roll subterfuge, that the artist mustn't know and someone else holds the purse strings, was a real anathema to the way I was used to working with Topic,' Eliza recalled. 'The pride I had in myself, the pride I had that I could organize a project of £30,000 - £40,000 and see it through to completion on budget and have a bit spare, was something I was very proud of. My mum had taught me how to do it, she taught me how to organize receipts, and all of that.

'Having a manager and a big label meant that the control was taken from me and I've never quite got that back. I look at my old accounts that I used to do myself and I was much more organized [than she felt her manager and label were]. For someone like me, who prided themselves on being a woman in charge, a young woman in charge, it really knocked my confidence.'

Sam felt that without the fun, Eliza began to close up, which, in turn, made getting the songs out of her even more troublesome: 'The process [of making *Angels And Cigarettes*] was not as enjoyable as we'd been used to and the project didn't feel like ours. From my point of view, there was a lot of talk about contracts and getting a single for the project because we were signed to an American branch of Warner Brothers and they wanted something that would be good for Middle America ... which seems like a crazy idea. To think that someone from Robin Hood's Bay could come up with a song that could work on radio stations in places we'd never been to!

'I felt like the Eliza Carthy Band as it stood had started to become a victim of its own success. There was so much pressure on Liza that she couldn't enjoy writing or making music anymore because she was having to turn herself into a young businesswoman and she didn't really know what she was doing.'

Sam recalled a vivid scene which he felt summed up the whole experience: 'I've got this image of her sat on the sofa and reading magazines, eating this soup to lose weight that was just basically vegetables and nothing else, whilst me, Barnaby and Ben, her writing team, were just bombarding her with ideas: "maybe we could do it like this?" or "what if we did it this way?"or "what about the way Portishead did that?" You know, using the influences of the time to come up with something cool, something that Warner Brothers might like.'

Barnaby also felt the frustration. He had always been Eliza's writing partner in the past, and he felt that, musically, they were a great team. However, this time, the focus was more on what Warners would like, what an American audience might enjoy, and he felt it had no real direction: 'The whole process was guided by Warners. There was a very good producer on board but Liza got really stressed out. Sam and I, we just got on with it as it was our job, but I just didn't like the musical direction it was going in.'

Sam agreed. 'It wasn't really very true to what Liza had done, or any of us had done, before. Liza used to make jokes about it. She used to say "we are working for Bugs Bunny, so what do you expect?"'

Perhaps surprisingly, Al Scott also felt a real pressure to perform, and to get out of Eliza exactly what the label, and Andrew Wickham, wanted. Warners' intentions were passed on to the producer, in the hope that he might persuade Eliza and the band to do as they were told.

Al recalls: 'Eliza didn't like the song "Perfect" and didn't want it on the record. It was the same with Paul Weller's song, "Wild Wood". She said "I don't feel it, I don't want to do it", but we were short of songs, and it came down the line to me, to tell her that was what was going to happen. When big labels like Warners get on your back, they're very good at it.'

Eliza was required to have one cover on the album and when 'Wild Wood' was suggested, she was not initially keen. However, in retrospect, it has become one of her favourite tracks on the album.

'I remember really falling in love with the song. I was on the road with Waterson:Carthy and we were in a B&B in New England. I'd had a few glasses of wine, went to bed and listened to it, really identifying with it. I don't know what it means to Paul, but at that time, it really fitted with me and everything which was going on,' she said. 'I am slow, it takes a while for me to get things and I was so glad I was encouraged to do it, it really expanded my horizons.'

'Eliza is the truest artist I have ever worked with; she's see-through. If she's into it, she's great; if she's not, she's terrible. Some musicians are very good at pulling off "professional performances" if they're not into it, but Eliza isn't. And there are some instances on that album where I think the vocals are awful: she's an honest artist and not good at blagging,' Al confirmed.

One person who seemed oblivious to the brooding antipathy, the skirmishes and frustration, was the composer and arranger, Van Dyke Parks. Known to the older generation as Brian Wilson's cohort, responsible for the lyrics for the infamous album *Smile*, and to the younger as the arranger of the sumptuous strings in Joanna Newsom's *Ys*, Parks had been introduced to Eliza at Hal Willner's Harry Smith Project in which they were both participating.

'I had met Eliza on a stage on which I was a piece of confetti,' he began, his soft American accent immediately bringing to mind the fine dining, aesthetically-sensitive psychiatrists, Frasier and Niles Crane, from NBC sitcom, *Frasier*. 'The entire endeavour was overpopulated. Of all these people on the stage, and I don't remember their names but some were quite famous, of all those people, the one person who shone above all the others in her talent, her attitude, her modesty, her ability, was Eliza Carthy.'

A fan of her parents from across the Atlantic, Parks knew of her existence, but hadn't had the chance to hear her play. So following the Harry Smith Project introduction, Van Dyke Parks was delighted to be offered the opportunity to work with her, courtesy of Andrew Wickham who was overseeing the *Angels And Cigarettes* album.

Parks warned me with a caveat: 'Now, I cannot say that I was a fan of Fairport Convention. I did not approve – in fact, I disdained – adding drums to folk music. I disdained electronica with folk music; folk rock, I thought, was a very thin and unfurnished area of thought. What I really liked was the strength and muscularity, the athletic endeavour it took to bring pre-industrial British music to post-industrial audiences.'

That was where Eliza, and her parents, came in. 'They searched to preserve and invigorate beautifully the rhythms of an England which is now beyond third person experience. We have lost contact with the generation that lived in this musical environment that Waterson and Carthy, and now Eliza herself, are able to bring to our attention so I was very impressed with her.'

Van Dyke's involvement with Eliza began curiously, but the telling of the following story is best left to the teller himself, one of the most eloquent men I have ever had the pleasure of listening to:

I got down to Brighton with a string quartet, the Mondrian string quartet, and we were very interested in the bastard son and the royals who used to cavort there and we went into a converted chapel there, unconsecrated, and tried to bring it back to its holy state with this one arrangement. And they played and I got to the control room, where priests probably once put on their robes, and I saw a box that said 'blowjob'. And I said 'What is that?' and they said 'Oh nothing, never mind.' And I said 'Wait a minute, what is that?' so they told me a story: a girl, Eliza Carthy, had written an unabashed confessional as a warning, I think, to others who might have suffered the same sense of degradation almost as a consolation. I was floored to hear that her father wrote some music for it. I thought immediately that that was one of the healthiest parental relationships that I had ever heard of. For a man to step up to the plate and ally himself with his daughter's candour in such a dignified and sacrificial way, well, I thought, I want to hang out with these people. I told these people in the studio that I'd do an arrangement for that piece for nothing, 'Please let me do that', and when we got to the dinner afterwards, to celebrate the fact that they all played the notes correctly, and they said 'Mr Wickham, that Mr Parks said he'd do that Blowjob for nothing!' And [Andrew Wickham] looked at me, in a state of irritation, and said 'We'll see about that.' A couple of weeks later, I got the phone call. Mr Wickham said 'What do you want to do to that number, "Blowjob"?' I said 'Well, I'd give it some court sensibility; I'd dress it up and make it more elegant.' That's my history with Eliza and it represents a first blush and I hope that I have another chance to serve her. And that's my story and I'm sticking to it.

Andrew Wickham did not find the song as entertaining: 'I thought it was coarse, vulgar, and that it violated pop success. Pop should give people a dream, but no one wants to be like a woman who gives blowjobs to men who don't want her. I think, given the circumstances, it was actually a big "fuck you" to the corporate world. I saw this as a challenge and delivered Van Dyke Parks. She was impressed by his lightning wit.'

Though Eliza and her family had played in the US and Canada frequently over the years, part of the Warner master plan for Eliza was to showcase her and her music to an audience which wouldn't necessarily know anything about British folk music.

In stepped *grande dame*, Joan Baez.

Keen to lend her name and knowledge to further the careers of younger, emerging artists with an obvious folk and roots influence,

Baez signed herself up as 'co-mentor', inviting them to come on tour with her and her band, playing a set each night to her audiences, and living on the road in her bus. (Though having seen Eliza's photographs of the bus in question, 'mobile home', in the full sense of the word, is most definitely a better moniker – it is an enormous vehicle, and would tower over any traditional tour bus.)

Eliza was invited to participate in Joan Baez's initiative once the recording of *Angels And Cigarettes* came to an end, and Eliza duly accepted – but the tour didn't get off to the best start. 'Though I had a duo with Saul and a trio with Saul and Martin [Green], she insisted I bring only Martin, which was actually pretty difficult as we didn't have any material together, just the two of us,' Eliza began.

'It wasn't quite a support slot,' Martin added. 'She had us in her band and then we did a bit on our own in the middle of the evening. We did a couple of months of that, two months across America, but we had to play songs that Eliza had written for Warner Brothers so we made sure we played a lot of tunes on the bus.'

'But it emerged after a while that she basically just wanted Martin,' Eliza scowled. 'We got there, nine weeks on a tour bus with loads of people I didn't know, and she monopolized him, took him off to a room at the back of a bus and wouldn't let me spend any time with him.'

Joan Baez is the reason Martin's hair is short now, Eliza told me. His long, shaggy mop, as featured in early shots of the Eliza Carthy Band, came to a bitter, shorn end when he met Joan Baez. 'She refused to tour with him [with his unkempt hair]. At Lawrence in Kansas, she basically shaved him! When we got to Chicago, she took him out and bought all these loungey, velvet suits and that's how [his] look started,' Eliza explained.

As the tour progressed, Martin became the sole focus of Baez's mentoring eye as Eliza felt increasingly isolated. When Eliza took a deep breath and told herself to go out of her way to make an effort with Joan and her band, she felt she was always rebuffed. 'One time we went shopping in Chicago. I came back with some new clothes and I was showing them to Carol, the percussionist, before putting them all back in my bunk and going into the venue to do something.

'Anyway, when I got back, Joan was dressed in all the new clothes I had just bought and was dancing up and down the bus going "look at me, I'm Liza! Look at me, I'm Liza!"' Eliza was stunned. She cannot remember how she reacted. Though when Eliza later found herself in receipt of some of Joan Baez's socks, along with a pair belonging to Evan Dando, she did consider beginning a celebrity sock collection. 'Sadly, it didn't stretch beyond those two people, though,' she said, grinning.

Despite some of the more disappointing aspects of the tour, Eliza and Martin had plenty of travel time to assemble their own repertoire in the gaps between shows. Consequently, on their return, Eliza and Martin recorded their only album as a duo, entitled *Dinner*, and released it on Eliza's own label, Heroes of Edible Music (HEM), in December 2001.

Knowing both Eliza and Martin's penchant for the more experimental – take a listen to *The Martin Green Machine* album – it could be expected that *Dinner* would be a tune-based collection of weirdness, impossible to compartmentalize and perhaps only appealing to the nichiest of niches. But instead, Eliza and Martin used the time to learn from each other's repertoire, only embellishing with the unexpected when it came naturally.

'[*Dinner* is] actually 70% straight ahead fiddle and box, although there's a bit of improvisation, but we spent a lot of time jamming on the bus so we thought it'd be nice to do that,' Martin explains. 'There were a couple of experiments: there was a beatboxer, a guy called JC001 who came in and did some stuff for us, and I did some samples.

'There was a whole load of music that Liza knew about that I wasn't really familiar with at the time; Northern English music, mainly. I found that all very exciting, the Lancashire and Yorkshire music that she introduced me to, it's quite ballsy music so there's a fair bit of that on *Dinner*, 3/2 hornpipes and so on.

'The piano box is a funny instrument, it's got no place in English traditional music … it hasn't really got a place in any traditional music. So one of the noises we really liked was Liza playing the octave fiddle, which she was doing a lot then, and me on the piano box which has a low octave and I was playing a really big box at the time. We were experimenting a lot with the left hand.'

As the tour progressed to New York, Ben Ivitsky flew out to see Eliza, bringing with him the newly mixed Warner Brothers record, now officially titled *Angels And Cigarettes*. The couple sat listening to the freshly mixed tracks in a horse and carriage in Central Park, the thud of the horse's hooves gently overwhelmed by Eliza's voice singing exactly what she wanted to get out there, 'the wrong blokes, the inadequacies, jealousies.'[8]

Angels And Cigarettes was finished, duplicated, sent out. Between the moment she had signed for Warners, in 1997, and the album coming out in 2000, Warners had discouraged her from scheduling any major tours across Britain, in the hope that she would be weaned from the folk scene, allowing the new album to bring forth those sought after new audiences in their prestigious venues, the kind not immediately associated with the English folk scene.

But the album didn't perform as well as hoped, even though Eliza was reported as having the same PR person that worked with Madonna. Having signed to an American arm of the label, publicity in the UK – where, of course, Eliza was known best – seemed to be minimal and *Angels And Cigarettes* sold around 9,000 copies, a significant drop from her previous double album, the Mercury-nominated *Red Rice*.

fRoots' Joe Lost stated in 2002 that '*Angels And Cigarettes* appeared to sink without a trace in the UK, falling between the cracks of the way the music business is organised here. Most people never heard it.'[9] In Carol McDaid's article in the *Observer*, from September 2000, she focuses on Eliza's 'secret' pop project:

For the past three years, the fiddle player and singer has been writing a pop album on the quiet ... 'It's been a secret, my little thing,' she says. [10]

Perhaps it was this secrecy and lack of live activity which did her a disservice. In a world where Eliza's fans would have been able to speak to her at gigs, catch up with her over a beer at a festival, they inevitably felt distanced from this project due to her relative silence. In 2000, pre-Facebook, pre-Twitter, maybe it was simply that they hadn't known that there was a new album on its way until they had heard a track on the radio, realized it was quite different to what they were accustomed to, and thought it not for them.

But Al Scott clarified the situation. There was no mystery for the album to shroud itself within. It was simple: 'Before the week of release, Warners sacked the entire promotions team. There had been big plans, everyone was ready for it, but they got rid of everyone, some of whom had been there for twenty years or so. It was a turbulent time for Warners, yes, but it was a disaster for the album: no press, no airplay. It was a great shame, pure major label stuff.'

And Eliza and her team – musicians, producer, manager, label representatives – were forced to sit back and watch the album flop.

'I was very unhappy at that time … they'd taken me off the road, so I went from playing full rooms everywhere else to, when they did let me gig, playing to almost nobody for whatever reason. Maybe [the fans] thought I was selling out, or maybe it was because I hadn't been on the scene for a year or so. I had no money. I put my caravan full of stuff at the end of Ben's garden and lived on his charity for a while,' Eliza explained.

Another tour to America – *sans* La Baez – was touted, this time to showcase the album, but the proposed dates clashed with a Chipolatas tour and Sam Thomas had to decide between the two. Despite his friendship with Eliza and the rest of the band, and regardless of having had the opportunity to experience the finer end of the professional musician's lifestyle – paid-for accommodation, top producers, better fees – it wasn't a difficult decision for him to make.

'I'd always had the Chipolatas running on a parallel line and it was always quite a sobering thing to go back and work with Jasper and Tristan and recount my experiences of this starry world, playing with pop stars in big venues, and then just go and do a street show or go into a school and do a workshop for kids.

'When *Angels And Cigarettes* had been done and there was a possibility of going to America to tour it, it was at that point that I had to make a choice. I wanted to go with the Chipolatas and do what it is that I love doing. And that's when Willy Molleson came in and played drums, and I stepped out.'

Eliza regularly states in interviews how she loathes the moments when members of the band decide to leave, even when the split is genuinely amicable, when it is just a case of moving on to something new. This must come from her work with her family; that her assembled musicians become extended family. Sam was not just a musician for hire, but a friend for around a decade, whose parents were also contemporaries of Eliza's parents, and so his departure was a blow to Eliza. It signified that the disappointment of the performance of *Angels And Cigarettes* was actually felt in others; that some of her friends who had been around for earlier albums, excited by their combined idiosyncratic take on folk and traditional music that was thoroughly enjoyable to play, write and arrange, did not have that same enthusiasm for the future.

'It wasn't a shame that we were nominated for the Mercury,' Sam said nervously, 'but in a way, it kind of ruined it … We got the chance to play on TV, on the main stage of Glastonbury, but that sort of spotlight made it into something that it wasn't. It lost its roots there, because we transplanted it into a world where it wasn't recognized or wasn't appreciated for what it was.'

Willy Molleson was soon a fully-fledged member of the band, and continues to be today. His lack of enthusiasm for rising from bed in the morning, though, soon gave way to some innovative tricks and ploys from the other members of the band. 'One method that was employed involved running at him and holding a double mattress, falling on to his sleeping body full-weight, and then running away, leaving him pinned underneath. This worked only once as he was so furious that he was horrible to work with all day,' Eliza remembers. 'Ben was fond of blowing coffee aromas through his bedroom door which was gentler, but again didn't always work.

'When we were staying at the Magic Hotel in Hollywood, during promo for *Angels And Cigarettes*, we hit on the perfect solution: we would tell him that there was a limo waiting outside. Somehow, he managed to get out of bed, into a suit and was waiting in the sunshine in the back of the limo with his sunglasses on when the rest of us got to the pavement. A lovely day out in Santa Monica followed which no doubt I am still paying for ... but it was worth it.'

After Sam's decision to leave and Willy's subsequent arrival, Eliza was called in to see Andrew Wickham. She didn't anticipate the kind of conversation that was had. He asked her if she would do another record.

'I think Andrew knew he was going to be let go [from Warner Brothers during the continuing overhaul] and he basically asked for my help. He sat me down in his office and said "look, I know things haven't been ideal between us but I actually think you're really, really good". What he wanted to do was the old-style nurturing that Warner Brothers was actually really very famous for ... He said that he thought that this might be the last thing he did at the company, but he wanted to be vindicated as he thought I was a good artist.'

Eliza deliberated. She hadn't enjoyed her experience with the label so far, but she had been happy with the final record. Though it hadn't performed well, she was pleased with what she heard; it was her first self-penned record and it would be a good foundation on which to build. 'Andrew Wickham, this guy who had been so unreachable, was just sat there, asking me for help. He had discovered Joni Mitchell and Ry Cooder, and managed the Grateful Dead!' she said, incredulous at her fortune and the surprise turn her path had taken.

Eliza hoped that a second shot, with 'less bureaucracy in the way, fewer tiers of short-term people missing and disrupting things', would make for a better album, and would ultimately meet Andrew's goals. 'I do think we made a very good album under very difficult circumstances, for the company and for me,' she said, 'and I don't blame him for its failure; I blame the takeovers and the mess that had been made of a once-proud institution. Under different circumstances, I think we would have been successful and I am grateful he wanted to keep me on and try again.'

It was an offer she couldn't refuse and Eliza duly received the invitation 'to take up the option on your second album' on Warner Brothers' headed notepaper. The band was once again assembled and some tentative jamming took place, a couple of demos laid down.

But Andrew's suspicions had been confirmed, and he was made redundant from the company. 'He rode off into the sunset with his severance package and Warners promptly dropped me but had to buy me out, which is what bought me my house. That was a good day,' Eliza smiled, matter-of-factly. 'Of course, I had a massive tax bill afterwards, but I did manage to spend some of it on a house.'

'It was an unfortunate experience, a miserable experience,' Andrew concluded. 'I don't even own the record: if things aren't successful I move on. But at least she bought a house and wrote some great songs.

'I wouldn't have dropped Eliza for anything. I thought we could have made a different kind of record, but when she was dropped, I could see that she was thrilled. *Anglicana* was exactly the image I wanted to put into the pop world.'

FIVE

This Fiddle Kills Fascists

People underestimate culture in this country,
and they overestimate other people's cultures.
Eliza interviewed by Ian Anderson, *fRoots*[1]

Eliza Carthy loomed large next to the stacked CDs, or at least a promotional cardboard cut-out of her did in amongst the other persuasive promotional paraphernalia. Jon Boden, then a second-year Medieval History student at the University of Durham, raced in and plucked *Red Rice* from the shelves. He had taken a trip to Newcastle especially to visit the city's Virgin Megastore and buy himself a copy of the new album.

Of course, Jon Boden is now well known for his folk singing and musical prowess in his own right. Frontman to Bellowhead, the eleven-piece menagerie which combines traditional music with theatrics and brass, he has developed a striking persona: a circus ringmaster, he flails his arms as the musicians in his ranks spring to life. Voted Folk Singer of the Year in 2010, he began an ambitious project in June of that same year to record a different folk song each day for 365 days, highlighting the enormous wealth and variety of material available as well as accentuating the steady decline of the social singing of traditional song – something he deplores.

But unlike many of the practising musicians on Britain's current folk scene, including Eliza and her compatriots, Jon Boden was not the offspring of folk revivalists. He had grown up idolizing rock musicians, particularly Led Zeppelin, which had introduced him to

Sandy Denny, via her vocals on 'The Battle of Evermore' on 1971's *Led Zeppelin IV*, and Fairport Convention. An interest in folk music soon developed and by the time his dad brought home the second Eliza and Nancy album, purchased on the basis of an excellent review in the paper, Jon was hooked.

He remained a fan of the genre until composing for theatre led him to Oxford and a chance meeting with melodeon player John Spiers. In John Spiers' household, folk music had always been on the stereo, 'not cutting-edge stuff, but 1960s and 1970s. I didn't grow up on the scene as such, and I wasn't really a big fan until I learnt an instrument'. As his melodeon playing improved, John took to busking around the city, enjoying the freedom of performing to a moving crowd who would stop and listen should they hear something that took their fancy. And with so many tourists in Oxford, it was undoubtedly a lucrative pastime, too.

His busking caught the eye of Eliza and when she arrived in the city with her band to promote *Red Rice*, he was asked to open for her. 'It was just me and the melodeon, a lot of my friends were there and then I realized how friendly the scene was. It was the first time I'd seen her live; I didn't have the album so it was brand new to me, and I thought it was massively different to anything else I'd heard.'

When he met Jon Boden, they formed a duo and began gigging before releasing their first album, *Through And Through*, on Fellside in 2001. And it was with John Spiers that Jon Boden first encountered Eliza Carthy. 'John dragged me along to Bampton one year as I didn't know much about Morris dancing and he thought I ought to learn. Liza was there, as usual, and of course John wasn't starstruck but I was like "Oh my God, it's Eliza Carthy, I can't possibly talk to her!"

'Because I wasn't a folkie, I didn't grow up within the folk scene, I didn't have that thing as seeing folk musicians as quite accessible – which of course they are if you're on the scene, but if you don't know that, you see them as pop stars, really. I didn't distinguish between people like Eliza and Paul Weller, or someone like that.'

For someone who is now so at ease on stage, it is impossible to imagine Jon Boden tentatively taking out his fiddle, taking a large swig of beer for courage and meekly joining in the session in which Eliza, too, was participating. But, due to the participatory nature of the folk scene, and the calendar chocked full of events and occasions in which to get involved, Jon Boden and John Spiers began to bump into Eliza on a frequent basis.

Jock Tyldesley, one of the many young musicians Eliza would meet with at festivals during the Chipolata and King Ligger years and who went on to contribute to *Heat, Light And Sound*, remembers introducing Jon Boden to Eliza. 'He used to meet me in Southampton, where I used to live, and we'd go to a few different sessions together. He used to sing really loud, he was brilliant! He was so into English traditional music. I remember there was a time when Eliza was staying at mine for a few days and we went down to a session. Jon came in, saw Eliza there and actually made his excuses and left! Then he ended up being in her band! I like to remind him of that.' Jock's passion is actually Cajun and Old Time music. 'I never listened to English music; Morris dancing never did it for me. But hanging round with that slightly younger crowd, with lots of box players like Gareth Turner and Simon Care, I saw that English music was actually really exciting.'

Martin Carthy, too, had told his daughter about Jon Boden. 'Dad kept saying "there's this lad in Lewes who keeps turning up and singing and you'd really like him" and I kind of brushed him aside because I was busy being existential and depressed and I didn't want to listen,' she winked. 'I don't really listen to most people; it's one of my failings. I'm just slow: it goes in, I think "ok, I've stored that in the back of my mind", now what I need to do is see if my thing works, and then my thing, because I'm convinced it's going to work, could take ten years, and then ten years later, I go "no, actually, you were right" and then everything will be fine. But Dad was right, I did love him. I do, he's great.'

Eventually, though, it was the internet that brought Eliza, John and Jon together. 'She was posting on early incarnations of internet chatrooms about folk music and I stuck my tongue out at her in an internet way,' John laughs. 'She then replied with a massive long email and said she liked our album, particularly because we were playing English music.'

It was obvious that Spiers and Boden had impressed Eliza and she was simply waiting for an opportunity to come along to get them involved in her music.

The Warners episode had dealt Eliza a hearty, hefty blow to the stomach. It wasn't so much the poor reception to the album or the subsequent abandonment by the label – in some ways, she was pleased to be free – but it was more the sour impact it had on other aspects of her career, aspects that she had spent such time honing; this was what most unseated her and knocked her confidence.

Though she had continued to play with her family throughout the Warner period, she felt that the audience who had enjoyed her and her band's material had all but disappeared, distracted by her long periods of absence from the live circuit. She felt that her grasp of the business side of her work had lapsed, and she was now reliant on her manager's sums and relationships with promoters. Eliza explains: 'Nigel [Morton, her manager] had come into this situation with Warners, thinking he was probably going to make a buck from a young singer songwriter, but suddenly he was left with this person who wanted to go back to traditional music. He had no idea how to cope with that.'

Eliza began to question the path her career had taken:

It's my own fault in some ways; I should've stayed at home and listened to my mother. But in some ways it's her fault as well because I was brought up to think that the easy path isn't necessarily always the good one! I was always taught that you should try what other people don't do; try something different and don't be like the 'folk scene'. Otherwise you'll end up singing through your nose, those weird vocal decorations that people do that don't mean anything and don't have anything to do with traditional music. But seriously, mum always told me to try for other things and I thought it was important to step outside the family unit and try something else.

Then, suddenly, the opportunity arose to get John and Jon involved. Eliza was due to go off on her autumn 2002 tour, a small run of gigs across the country, when band member Martin Green was offered a longer, more financially rewarding tour with Linda Thompson. It was something he had to do, Eliza understood, but it meant she was left without a rather irreplaceable member.

Eliza's agent called John whilst he was at work in an Oxford music shop to ask him and Jon Boden to join the band. 'The brief was essentially, "can you two together be Martin Green?"' John Spiers laughed. 'We hadn't got enough hands, for one thing!'

Coincidentally, when John breathlessly rang Jon to tell him the good news, Jon Boden was stood outside the very Virgin Megastore in which he had purchased *Red Rice* only a handful of years previously. Spiers and Boden had three days in which to prepare for Eliza's tour, to learn the full set which included a few new tracks she had been working up with Ben. 'We had one rehearsal, at Barn Stradling's dad's house, and two days later, we were playing. [We] had started gigging at folk club level in 2001, so it wasn't our first taste of gigging, but this was a big stage. Our first with Eliza was Hereford Courtyard Theatre and there were easily 250 people. It felt like a football stadium in comparison to what we knew and it was so nerve-wracking with so little time to prepare,' John said.

Spiers and Boden played the full run of gigs that autumn. 'It appeared very quickly that we were in the band,' John explained. 'It was the old band, but it was quite anarchic, fluid. Sometimes there'd be a drummer, sometimes not. Sometimes Barn, sometimes not. Sometimes we got musicians in, but soon it turned into being just me, Jon, Ben and Eliza, when Barn dropped out.'

Eliza had not spent her post-Warners six month break watching daytime television. Instead, she had used the time for herself, furthering her knowledge and researching songs. She had come up with a concept she wanted to explore; she found a thread, she had ideas, and she had followed them, fleshing them out. She took them to her partner, Ben Ivitsky, for his thoughts.

And as it became apparent that John and Jon were not only proficient musicians but shared with her a passion for English traditional music and, most importantly, a determination for it to be noticed, to be heard, she had a hunch that her new, rather serendipitous lineup would be the very band to carry off her new idea. By the time John and Jon were officially in the band, Eliza and Ben had already prepared a demo of the next record.

She swallowed any sense of self-doubt, ignored the building resentment at the lack of gigs and was fired up once again.

Immersed in *The Voice Of The People* series which was released on Topic in 1999, an anthology of almost 500 recordings of folk songs and singers from across the British Isles, Eliza used this as a foundation for her material. 'I wanted to make an all-English album, because I think that English music needs a media-visible performer, and I want to be that person,' she told interviewer James Turner. 'I whittled the songs down to a three CD set and then chose my favourites. Getting them down to 10 tracks was difficult.'

She further elucidates:

I wanted to do it like how I'd done *Heat, Light And Sound*, which was to get my peeps in, but by that time, Sam was off doing other things and I wanted to work with a more feely drummer. Sam's a great feel good drummer, he's good at the funk and the disco, breakbeat type stuff, but I developed this philosophy, well, a theory if you like, about folk rock drumming. The problem with folk rock drumming is that all the folk music serves the beat, when actually it should work the other way round: the beat should serve the strangeness of the music, because only that way are you going to amplify the thing you love. To amplify what you love, you need to start with what you love about it. And what I love about it is the odd time signatures, the way it stretches and breathes, the way a traditional singer pauses in the middle of a rhythm and then continues, like a hold and release thing, it's lovely. I wanted that and Ben suggested I talk to Donald Hay, one of my favourite drummers anyway, the drummer from Mystery Juice. We had several very satisfying conversations about that, about how to serve the song.

110

To Eliza, John and Jon seemed to be just a little bit different, too, and that enticed her very much: 'I wanted to be part of John and Jon's thing so much, because Jon Boden wasn't a part of the folk scene and though John Spiers was part of the dance scene, he had grown up not as a folkie, but as a genius who just wanted to be good at what he did, which just so happened to be the melodeon. And he's a fucking genius. That's how the world should work, as far as I'm concerned.

'People are very safe on the folk scene and they can get by with being shit, which is actually unforgiveable. I wanted to be a part of a band with musicians that I thought were better than I was and had more of a handle on things. I really felt lost at the time and I was happy that I felt that they were teaching me,' Eliza explained.

The folk scene had really begun to bother Eliza. As someone who wanted to make the music that she enjoyed – be it traditional music or her own, original material – she felt that the folk scene restricted and confined her. With her time at Warners over, she found herself 'welcomed back' to the scene – despite the fact that she had never given up singing and playing traditional music, that she was still performing with her parents and playing for the Plough Stots.

'I may well have been wrong to have tried the Warners thing; it was a musical adventure, I wanted to do it and why shouldn't I? I don't know whether it served the cause of traditional music particularly well, and admittedly that's what I wanted it to do. But if someone [welcomes me back to traditional music], if someone says that to me, I'm going to be angry, I'm going to want to slap them and put poo in their tea.

'I'm very suspicious of scenes in general, and without wanting to dob either of my parents in, neither of my parents can stand the folk scene either: because it's a ghetto and because it attracts weirdoes. Any scene does. Have you ever seen any drum and bass freaks? Drum and bass freaks are just as weird as folkies. You pack human beings into a small space and they're just going to get weirder and weirder,' Eliza added, never one to mince her words.

To Eliza, folk music is a continuum – it doesn't start and stop with the old songs, and 'the old way'. Her new album, she hoped, would explain this. When John and Jon arrived at Eliza and Ben's home, ready to rehearse and lay down demos for *Anglicana*, the duo continued to impress. 'They really showed me up, actually, in a really good way. They turned up at nine o'clock in the morning, when Ben was still in bed. I tried to coax Ben into getting up but he wouldn't, saying "I don't play music before dark." I told him that he didn't have to play music, just press play.

'He rolled out of bed just before midday. And from the point when they arrived, from nine o'clock, to the point where Ben actually pressed record, at around midday, they played non-stop. Absolutely constantly,' Eliza shook her head at the memory, smiling.

John and Jon had been given a demo of the record for practising and arrangement purposes. 'It's actually one of my most treasured CDs,' Jon Boden claimed:

> To be honest, I think her demo of *Anglicana* is actually better [than the final product], for my tastes anyway. It's just her on the fiddle, Ben on a bit of guitar; it's fantastic playing. I listened to it loads and loved it, and then went up and did two or three tracks. I was told I could pretty much do what I liked and then we'd come up with some riffs to go over her fiddle lines, it was quite open to arrangement. The only thing was that we put our parts independently to Barn, who was doing his bass separately, and you can just notice a few strange clashes now and then ... nothing wrong, but something that probably wouldn't have made it if we'd all been rehearsing at the same time. Sometimes it's good to do it like that; it stops it from becoming too clinical.

There were other mishaps in the studio.

'Something happened when it went from mixing to mastering, some plug-in or other, some reverb plug in, and everything reverted to zero,' Eliza remembered. 'I had gone to Tony Engle's place to listen to the mastering and my jaw just hit the floor. It was awful, absolutely awful. It was Cambridge [Folk Festival] weekend and I ended up having to remix "Worcester City", "Willow Tree" and

"Pretty Ploughboy". We slept under the desk, burnt the midnight oil and got it down.'

An album initially conceived as a solo album, *Anglicana* went on to have twenty or so musical contributors, including an array of unusual items employed for their percussive potential, such as hammers and girders. As ever, Eliza was hoping to demonstrate the full force of English traditional music, exposing its exoticness and bringing it back to the fore by updating and modernizing the English fiddle and song repertoire, ensuring English music was back on the menu. Of course, this had been her mission from her earliest days, back with Nancy Kerr when she had first picked up *The Sussex Tune Book* and researched Yorkshire tunes and dances.

Eliza had the English material she wanted to revitalize, and she had the musicians to do it – two of which had also been making their mark on their own collections of English traditional music. But this time, she had more anger: it wasn't just about putting English traditional music on the map; *Anglicana* sought to address – redress – English identity and culture. She wanted to define a sound for musicians that were making decidedly English music – whether that was derived from the old, or geographically located in the new England – a home much like American music has in Americana: something which can encompass traditional music and original songwriting.

'The title's a word of her own invention,' Tim Cummings wrote in *The Independent*, 'an expression of the arcane, mysterious power of English folk music, a call-and-response to the culture of Americana.'[2]

She welcomed other interviews as a chance to spout her manifesto: 'It's like we have to emulate other cultures in order to be progressive, like pretending to have a café society. It's a shame all these girl bands have to sing like they come from New York or somewhere […] No wonder we throw our crap all over the streets and people get pissed and fight. Nobody's being proud of here.'[3]

For Eliza, English identity shouldn't be something that only appears when the England football team are on the pitch, when

'Three Lions' is on the radio, the foreign lager is on offer next to the flags of St George in Tesco. It always ends in tears anyway, with the team playing poorly, the fans behaving badly and the media condemning the whole desperate affair, despite overhyping it in the first place.

Aside from this pseudo-identity forged when international football is on the telly, there is the constant ridicule of the real English tradition – Morris dancing being the obvious example – along with the belief of many that regard for English heritage and culture must equate to sympathy for the age of empire or the present-day far-right.

In the Channel 5 documentary *My Music*, Stewart Lee equated Eliza's approach to English identity through music to that of Billy Bragg's, saying: 'Whilst the English, as a race, have always been able to reach out to other countries and take what they want from them, there wasn't as much at stake in defending our identity … but you have to be careful as the English identity is always changing and evolving, and lots of cultures have passed through. What I think is great about Eliza's music is that she has always been able to take on board the different influences that have come over.'[4]

In conversation with me, he elaborated: 'English folk music has a logical problem – what should it be now? It was simple in Vaughan Williams' time because it was songs of the disenfranchised. But who are those people now? And that's what I mean by her having a Billy Bragg approach to English traditional music – [Eliza and Billy] mix it up, combine it with other influences, make it work today. He'd sell folk music when everyone is expecting a punk rock gig.'

Understandably, Billy Bragg also agreed. 'She's not afraid to say that she's proud of her traditions,' he began. 'For a long time, people who had a left wing sensibility tended to look at folk music as being very parochial, insular; in some ways, possibly nationalistic.

'People like the Watersons and Martin Carthy were always able to see within our tradition the influence of other races, other ethnicities, other ideas, and that rings right through anything they've ever done, and of course, Eliza has inherited that. Finding herself as the person who came to define a new folk sensibility in the 1990s, *Anglicana* [showed Eliza to be] trying to put forward a different idea about what it means to be English.'

Though many reviewers at that time tended to spend a good deal of their word allocation discussing Eliza's return to Topic and the ostensible failure of the Warners deal, *Anglicana* seemed to be just what the folk scene needed: fans, critics and peers appeared to be in thrall. *The Guardian* gave it four stars, closing with the question 'And you thought you didn't like folk music?'[5], *fRoots* dubbed it 'her most majestic and mature solo album yet'[6] and placed it a runner-up in their 2002 Critics Poll. Retrospectively, *The Guardian*'s Alex Petridis dubbed *Anglicana* 'her masterpiece'.[7]

A plethora of awards followed. At the 2003 BBC Radio 2 Folk Awards, Eliza was crowned Folk Singer of the Year, *Anglicana* was named Best Album and her rendition of 'Worcester City' voted Best Traditional Track.

Anglo-Japanese author, Kazuo Ishiguro, presented Eliza with one of her awards. He offered his thoughts on the apparent resurgence of English traditional music:

> There's this kind of treasure chest sitting in front of you, and if you were American or Irish, you might have opened it by now. But because you live here, it probably hasn't occurred to you to do so yet. Well, I would urge you to open that thing up, delve inside it, because I believe you will find a sublime vision of life in the British Isles as it has been lived over the last few centuries. It's the kind of vision that you can't readily get from Dickens, or Shakespeare, or Elgar, or Sir Christopher Wren. I think that if you don't open that treasure box, I think you're going to miss a whole dimension of cultural life in this country. So I urge you to do it.

He finished to whoops and cheers, evident that he – someone who was born in Japan but came to England as a child – had touched upon something that people did care deeply about. It seemed that the audience present agreed that Eliza had opened this treasure box, examined and handled the jewels that she had found and presented them as she saw fit: not as dusty relics from a bygone age, but showing off their inherent worth and beauty.

Anglicana also earned Eliza a second Mercury Music Prize nomination – though this time, she wasn't surprised. 'I knew it was good, it was a good piece of work,' Eliza said, nonchalantly.

But she was excited by the accolade because it was a sign she was healing, that the Warners period had not detracted from her reputation and the gravitas and quality of her musical output. The six months respite she had decided to take had been time well spent: she had loved every minute of the research, from her initial concept of the title right through to fruition.

Up against such mainstream radio fodder as Athlete, Coldplay, the Darkness and the Thrills, Eliza and *Anglicana* grudgingly lost out to Dizzee Rascal's debut album, *Boy In Da Corner*, though not before performing 'Worcester City' at the ceremony. Her aftershow antics were also more restrained than at her first Mercury experience.

But *Anglicana* signified more than excellent reviews and accolades. It became a landmark in the World Music story. In a four-part radio documentary Eliza presented for BBC Radio 2, entitled *'Eliza Carthy's Anglicana: the rise of British folk music from 1960s to present day'* in summer 2004, she explained the reasoning behind the coining of the phrase 'Anglicana', before going on to describe and interview key players in the English folk scene from the 1960s until the present day, highlighting the big names and those artists who influenced her most.

In episode three Eliza explains the rise in popularity, in 1980s and 1990s Britain, of traditional musics of other nations and cultures which, in turn, sought to redefine English traditional music's place in a wider context. However, as producer and writer Joe Boyd recalled:

'There was tremendous resistance from the world music community to folk music as such, tango, samba, reggae, Eastern European ... it had to be exotic, sexy. But Eliza went to WOMEX [the annual world music conference] ten or twelve years ago, at the end of the last century, and it became a key moment in interest in the English revival. She just went in there, stamped her foot and said don't be so silly. If you can listen to a Sardinian shepherd singing, you can listen to an English shepherd singing.'

Boyd was present at the 1999 conference himself, facilitating a workshop entitled 'Treasure Island Cuba? No End?' and recalls a dynamic, whirlwind of a character who wouldn't take no for an answer. 'Kate Rusby is as cute as a button, Kathryn Tickell has been key, but Eliza is a very outspoken, forthright, take-no-nonsense sort. Kathryn is articulate but is not a wave-a-flag-in-your-face kind of person – Eliza is.'

Joe Boyd cites Eliza's lobbying at WOMEX as a 'tipping point' for English traditional music stating that 'English traditional music is now invited to world music festivals, and I think it was then she began to shake off its fusty, square, sexless image.'

Eliza's campaign for English traditional music to be seen, heard and accepted paid off for her reputation, too: in 2003, *Anglicana* was nominated for the BBC Radio 3 Award for World Music, and in 2005, she hosted the BBC Awards for World Music Poll Winners' Concert along with Benjamin Zephaniah.

And she received what could be perceived as ultimate recognition for her work just a few years later in 2007: a gold badge from the English Folk Dance and Song Society (EFDSS). Gold badges are awarded to those who the society feel have made 'unique or outstanding contributions to folk music, dance or song, distinguished service to the Society and/or exceptional contributions to the Society's work.' In being awarded the gold badge, Eliza was joining a hall of fame which included her family (awarded in 1982) as well as luminaries from the English folk story such as Cecil Sharp (1923), Maud Karpeles (1928), Ralph Vaughan Williams (1943), A.L. Lloyd (1975) and Ewan MacColl and Peggy Seeger (1987).

But Eliza's gold badge marked her out: she was the youngest person to have ever been awarded it. The presentation of the award, made by Deputy Chair of the National Council, Mike Norris, took place at the Watersons' Mighty River of Song concert at the Royal Albert Hall on 12 May 2007. Joe Boyd was present and later wrote the citation which appeared in the summer 2007 edition of *English Dance And Song*.

For Boyd, Eliza's youth was important to the genre. But it was her campaigning for English traditional music to be recognized alongside the music of other cultures which he felt made her such a deserving recipient of the EFDSS gold badge, claiming 'She went to conferences and made her point and hammered at the door until World Music festivals began booking her and her band to perform alongside Cuban and African artists.'

Of course, though, Boyd wanted to make sure the reader knew just how important Eliza's own musical approach was, that her own musical outputs have contributed greatly to furthering the genre, stating 'All the talk in the world won't have an effect if there isn't the music to back it up. And what music pours from this wonderful singer and player!'[8] In conversation with me he added, 'I saw her at the Topic birthday concert at the Barbican. She came out with a band and they had a reggae, ska kind of feel which you would think would be hideous with English traditional music over the top, but she pulled it off. It was intriguing, unusual, and the musicianship was brilliant. She can pull off combinations and approaches to recording that I wouldn't trust in the hands of somebody else. She has such good taste that I trust what she does.'

And it seems that the EFDSS agreed, voting in Eliza as the Society's Vice-President a year after the gold badge award was made. The new President was to be Shirley Collins, the Sussex singer instrumental in the mid-20th century folk revival, and she felt that she and Eliza were a formidable duo, despite their different musical approaches and the years and geography between them:

> I imagine that the EFDSS believes that Eliza and I make a good team, as between us we represent much of what's current in the folk music scene. She is a modern singer, writing many of her own songs; she is also a fine singer of traditional songs with a love and respect for the tradition, as well as a real understanding of where and who the songs came from. I only ever sang traditional songs, but although totally immersed in

that tradition, I was ready to experiment with how the songs could be accompanied. So in brief, we are both willing to look forward as well as back, and I trust that all generations feel secure with us both.

But despite the praise heaped on Eliza and her album, *Anglicana*, and the recognition of her work not just within the genre in which she was closely associated but outside of it, too, she and her band continued to suffer from a lack of acknowledgement on the UK's stages. In short, she was still finding it tough to get bookings:

'When *Anglicana* came out, I'd just had six months off. I'd really worked my balls off on *Anglicana*, I absolutely loved it. The music was fabulous; I had really started to get something back through having met Jon and John.

'But when the album came out, I went to Oz for six weeks and did the scene out there, and when I came back, I had fifteen gigs that year. Fifteen. It was supposed to be my big comeback year, and it just crushed me. I have to admit that my work with Waterson:Carthy at that time was really under par and I didn't contribute at all. I was just lost, completely lost. I was floundering.'

Instead, she decided to focus on cementing the band. It wasn't going to be about her; it was going to be about the band. 'Liza has always liked being in bands,' Jon Boden explained, 'and she wanted us to be a band rather than her and a backing band.' John and Jon had amalgamated into the Eliza Carthy Band, until the idea of a name arose. Between *Angels And Cigarettes* and *Anglicana*, Eliza's ensemble had been fluid: members had come and gone, depending on availability, commitment and what they felt they could contribute musically.

But the success of *Anglicana* had compounded Eliza's belief that the four main components – herself, her partner Ben Ivitsky, and John and Jon – were worth holding on to. They were not just her band, they were *a* band. And giving them a singular name, Eliza hoped, would keep them together, ensure their ongoing commitment, almost like the receipt of a new surname upon marriage. *They weren't going anywhere.*

'The Ratcatchers' was chosen to summarize their fiddle-heavy sound, though Eliza's name still preceded it. 'She was very generous with our [album] deal,' Jon explained. 'She basically split the deal with the band as well, and I'm not sure we quite earned it really, insofar as most of the arrangements were led by her.'

'Choosing material was her prerogative,' John Spiers agreed, 'but I think we spent too much time rehearsing, really. You can overdo it sometimes, and I think we took it too deep. The music became harder to listen to.'

'Yes, the way Liza rehearses is to play it a lot,' Jon confirmed.

The Ratcatchers rehearsal schedule was intense. The musicians would descend on Eliza's house – then the house she owned with Ben in the Scottish borders – and catch up during the day, enjoying each other's company, perhaps going for a walk in the surrounding countryside. After the evening meal, the tunes and songs would commence around the kitchen table and would continue, usually well lubricated with some kind of alcohol, until four o'clock in the morning.

'The problem we had was pinning it down. It'd be three in the morning and we'd be drunk, and though it'd be sounding brilliant, we'd forget where we got up to. This is in the days before iPhones for rough recordings and we never really recorded anything,' Jon explained. 'Rehearsal was always informal and tended to be a question of what we were doing that excited her or the rest of us. There was probably a lot that was forgotten about, but I suppose that's part of the process and it made it more organic. We definitely played a lot more music that way.

'But then there would be times when she would go "no, I'm not doing that, let's try this" and everyone would respect that. No one would argue, we'd never push the point as it was her band.' Eliza was still very much the bandleader, despite the new band name, but the musicians were happy with the arrangement.

'I've always thought I'm good at being in the background and being told what to do *or* being in charge; one or the other. What I'm less good at is negotiating committees. If there were tensions in the Ratcatchers it was generally through a desire to be democratic. Which is all very laudable, but it does end up creating arguments,' Jon illustrated. 'There wasn't a lot of that, but I felt more comfortable not getting involved in any kind of musical direction role because I was comfortable doing what Eliza wanted to get out of the band. We did that pretty well. You don't want to push ideas on people because you don't want them to do it out of politeness.'

Martin and Norma were particularly fond of the Ratcatchers. 'I think it was the best band she's ever had," Norma stated, 'it was such an exciting, energetic sound.'

But when Eliza told her father about a new addition to the ensemble, he wasn't convinced. 'She called me up to tell me she was getting a tuba player in and I thought she was making a big mistake; I couldn't imagine how it would work,' Martin confessed, 'but she's fearless and brave, always has been. Of course, it sounded brilliant, it worked wonderfully.' Gideon Juckes' tuba stoutly underpinned the three fiddles and melodeon, and the band was complete.

Touring with Eliza became the first taste of full-time musicianhood for Spiers and Boden, having performed their duo gigs in time set aside from other money-making commitments up until that point. John and Jon lapped up the touring life. 'She had nice hotels. I still look back with fondness on the luxury and the stress of touring when you're not responsible for whether the audience turn up or whether you lose your voice,' Jon explained. 'And touring with Liza meant there was none of that stress, it was all on her. I don't think I quite realized how much stress that can be until I had my own band. It's really rewarding, but a lot more stress.'

But Eliza was approaching thirty years of age: her musical career had so far spanned fourteen years – seventeen, if we're counting her first festival appearance as one of the Waterdaughters aged thirteen. As John and Jon's musical careers were beginning, Eliza had already experienced the extreme peaks and troughs of the professional musician's lifestyle: she knew how to pick herself up after a poorly attended gig or a scathing review, she could sense a dodgy promoter from a distance, she knew the tell-tale signs of an unhappy band member. She had also been nominated for the Mercury Prize twice, won a whole host of other awards and played across the globe. But yet, funnily enough, Jon doesn't remember any occasions when the stress of being a self-reliant, independent musician burdened Eliza.

'She was permanently laughing and telling dirty jokes,' Jon laughed. 'It would always amuse me how we'd have a couple of days off each tour for her to rest her voice but she'd spend the day just laughing so much. And actually, if you have a day laughing and getting drunk, then you'd probably be better off playing a gig. But it was great fun.'

'She's quite rude,' John asserted. 'It was the first time I was in a professional band with a woman and she was more laddy than anyone else I'd worked with! I was actually more uncomfortable than I thought I'd be!'

The band enjoyed gigging, especially when offers to play came from overseas.

'I remember being taken for a meal after a gig in Barcelona. We were all so excited, and it was April, it was hot, we'd just played a great gig,' John recalled. 'There was an exciting seafood menu, and so many dishes to choose from. I ordered rabbit and aioli, but Jon didn't know what to order. He was getting literal translations of everything and then ordered several different dishes. When they arrived, we realized his order had basically amounted to being sausages, beans and chips from the children's menu. It was hilarious; we laughed about it for days.'

In John and Jon, Eliza had found excellent musicians who were as motivated as she was to ensure that English traditional music was being played and revitalized, that it wouldn't be overshadowed by Irish and Scottish music as it had been for decades.

However, this message, this mission, soon garnered some unwanted media attention.

Nick Griffin, the chairman of the British National Party and currently serving as Member of the European Parliament for North West England, claimed to be a fan of Kate Rusby, waxing lyrical about her on his blog. And it wasn't just Kate Rusby the far right seemed to latch on to. Spiers and Boden had a track on a giftshop album, the kind that might be sold as a souvenir at stately homes, entitled *A Place Called England* which featured Elgar and Vera Lynn, amongst others. The BNP took to selling it on their party website, the same website which used Show Of Hands' song 'Roots' as a soundtrack to some of their online publicity materials.

'It was such a shock, the whole BNP thing, as I don't think it had ever occurred to anyone that the folk scene was anything other than left wing. Because we all are!' Jon Boden shook his head.

In an interview with *The Guardian* in 2008, Eliza was keen to disassociate her passion for English culture and identity with any kind of far right sentiment, stating 'Jon Boden has had to stick a huge anti-BNP sticker on his fiddle, she says, 'so that every time anybody takes a photograph of him playing, there's this sticker telling the BNP to fuck off right next to his face.'[9]

A BBC News story claimed that Nick Griffin was hoping to start his own internet radio channel on which he would present a folk music programme. *Searchlight*, the anti-racism campaign group, stated that the BNP were looking for a 'political soundtrack', one which would differentiate the party from the old National Front's association with the steel toe capped boots of certain rock bands, such as Skrewdriver, back in the late 1970s and early 1980s: 'The modern BNP no longer has angry white teenagers in big boots. They have people between 35 and 55 years of age. So folk music with its ideas of land, tradition - the BNP are trying to get involved in that.'[10]

The folk scene needed a platform on which to publicly demonstrate that the far right was not welcome, that they had no right to appropriate the playing of English traditional music to support their extremist views.

In August 2009, two months after Nick Griffin and Andrew Brons were elected to the European Parliament as MEPs, Folk Against Fascism was launched at Sidmouth Folk Festival. A special concert took place, in which Eliza, John and Jon played alongside a whole host of other folk musicians, and the new alliance spelled out their message: 'that you can be proud of England's music, traditions and customs without being a bigot or a racist.'[11]

With only a small administrative team at the core, the campaign is largely grassroots activism: folk fans and musicians are encouraged to speak about the campaign when they can, wear branded t-shirts to gigs and hold FAF-themed events such as sessions and singarounds. Visitors to the website are encouraged to download their own stickers and posters, adding Twibbons to their Twitter profiles and banners to their homepages. The campaign also released its own double album with tracks contributed by some of the biggest players on the folk scene, including Eliza, Kate Rusby, Jon Boden and John McCusker.

Unfortunately, however, the media once again linked the British folk scene with the BNP a year later, forcing Eliza to speak out on the subject.

Guardian journalist Christian Koch sought to 'reveal which artists fill up the iPods and Spotify playlists of the world's most evil men.' Here, in an article the very epitome of no-news-January, Koch emphasized Nick Griffin's supposed love for traditional English music, stating 'In particular, Griffin (who penned lyrics for an album of "patriotic" songs entitled West Wind in 2007) is a fan of nu-folk poster girls Eliza Carthy and Kate Rusby.'[12]

Eliza was outraged: not only had her personal and professional reputation been insulted, but the field in which she worked, the very genre she had been instrumental in developing and furthering, had been illustrated to be old and stale, backward and, exclusive, in just two words: 'arthritically white'.

This was not the scene Eliza knew.

In a rebuttal published in *The Guardian* only ten days after Koch's initial piece, her anger at the original article was plain for all to read. Eliza explained how she feels that playing English traditional music is essentially a cultural invitation of 'you show me yours and I'll show you mine', as she plays across the world with musicians also showcasing their own traditional music.

But her sign-off truly illuminated how strongly she felt: 'Bollocks to Nick Griffin. And because talk is not cheap when it comes to this, bollocks to Christian Koch. It's just not funny.'[13]

The far right's apparent appreciation of the English folk scene, and the work that Eliza and her peers were doing, encouraged Jon Boden to think a little differently. 'It scared the shit out of me, really,' he shuddered. 'I've come to the conclusion that it's not a perfect situation that we're in, with people not understanding their music and that sort of stuff, but you have to be bloody careful not to play into the hands of the far right. It would be better if people used [English traditional music] more, because if you leave something lying around, you shouldn't be surprised that someone comes along and uses it for something you'd rather they didn't.'

As Eliza Carthy and the Ratcatchers, they released *Rough Music* on 18 April 2005 – exactly the same release date as Bellowhead's first output, *E.P. Onymous*.

Alongside their Ratcatcher commitments, John and Jon's Bellowhead was slowly beginning to emerge and garner the plaudits. The band first performed at the Oxford Folk Festival in 2004, a gig for which the new group had little time to prepare despite the prestigious Saturday night headline slot. A year later, prior to the release of their EP, they received the 'Best Live Act' award at the BBC Radio 2 Folk Awards, a ceremony they would go on to dominate over the next few years, winning Best Live Act in 2007, 2008, 2010 and 2011. The eleven-piece has also been the recipient of 'Best Group' twice, in 2007 and 2011. Further nominations followed in 2012.

Though the Ratcatchers were working on a follow-up to *Rough Music*, Jon Boden felt his workload was getting too large to manage, especially with the impending birth of his first child. He decided that he would need to leave the Ratcatchers to concentrate on Bellowhead and his solo material.

'For a while I was deliberating whether to leave Bellowhead and stay in the Ratcatchers because, in a way, it felt more significant. Bellowhead was throwing more genres into the mix and being more experimental, but what was great about the Ratcatchers was that we did the thing properly, with energy,' Jon explained. 'When we were on form, I thought we were a top band. In a musical sense, it felt like it was the most important thing I was doing. But in the end, having children and all that sort of stuff, I had to prioritize career over anything else and Bellowhead is the biggest thing, really.

'Being a performer, one's only security is that people recognize your name and come to your gigs, and that was never going to happen with Eliza's band: I was always only ever going to be in the backing band, which I had no problem with at all, I loved doing it, but from a purely long term career point of view, it was the most sensible thing to let go,' Jon expanded. 'It was really sad.'

Jon hoped the band would resume without him, and he suggested three potential replacements. At first, it seemed a possibility, as both Eliza and John Spiers were keen to continue. 'Creatively, I felt like we were just starting to hit our stride when it broke up,' she said. 'It took the wind out of my sails a little bit.'

The live bookings problem continued to dog the band, even though *Rough Music* was so well received. 'I remember bringing out *Rough Music* and reading in the Folk Awards blurb that it was the best thing I'd ever done, but I'd got all those awards for *Anglicana* and didn't get anything for *Rough Music*! We were putting aside a month for gigs and only coming back with twelve gigs. I just got more and more frustrated,' she remembered.

Some of this stemmed from the continued confusion of who Eliza's audience really was.

'[Nigel] kept trying to put me with what he knew, which was men of a certain age, so I was on the road with Billy Bragg, I was on the road with the Oysterband, he was trying to put me together with Joan Baez. It was an age and demographic that actually I wasn't interested in at all, and I love Billy Bragg so don't get me wrong, but it was an audience I wasn't interested in. They may or may not have had an interest in me. It completely alienated the audience that I had developed in 1998, an audience which was young and excited. For me, it just went down this whole AOR [album-orientated rock] path that I wasn't into, and things got harder and harder and harder.'

Even in 2012, Eliza still laments the what-could-have-been, stating on Twitter on 6 January, 'watching "my music", missing the Ratcatchers. If only anyone had ever been arsed to book us or come to see us. What a fucking good band.'

Gideon Juckes decided to move to Japan, not long after contributing to Bellowhead's first album, *Burlesque*, and Eliza and Ben Ivitsky broke up.

'The decision was made for us,' John concluded, sadly.

'I did want us to continue even after Ben and I split up, but I guess we weren't as big as we thought we were,' Eliza added.

SIX

What A Beau Your Granny Is

I'm a folk singer. I'm not trying to hide that,
but the folk scene is, in fact, very eclectic
Eliza interviewed by Stewart Lee, *Sunday Times*[1]

In the autumn of 2009, radio playlists were besieged by one particular song. It was almost guaranteed to appear within minutes of the radio being switched on, and seemed to be on hourly rotation. It had an energetic, incessant banjo *ostinato*, frenetic acoustic guitar and gravelly vocals rarely heard on commercial radio stations these days, where vocoders, autotune and X Factor warbling takes precedence. Zane Lowe deemed it his 'hottest record in the world' and the music press fell over themselves to claim Mumford And Sons, with their hit song 'Little Lion Man', as the new folk (or 'nu-folk', depending on the publication) generation.

Out came the folk clichés – finally, a band to save the genre from beards and sandals! journalists cried, as they nodded at the band's tasteful penchant for sporting waistcoats, ties, pointy boots – and as they delved deeper, they realized that Mumford And Sons were not alone: young music listeners also enjoyed their peers Noah And The Whale, Emmy The Great, Johnny Flynn, the US's Fleet Foxes, and the artist who has since become the darling of the scene, the 'folk princess', Laura Marling, who was later to walk away with Best Female Solo Artist at the 2011 Brit Awards.

Even better, the journalists collectively rubbed their inky hands together with glee, the bands seemed to know each other, tour with each other, work with each other. Was this a *scene*, a *real young folk scene*? Laura Marling had even been romantically linked with members of both Mumford And Sons and Noah And The Whale, the latter of which had written an album dedicated to the disintegration of their relationship.

And it was all too obvious why this quiet revolution had come about, they told us: the global downturn, the current economic climate of tightening purse strings had led to musicians reaching under beds to reclaim their dusty acoustic guitars and remember what music really is all about – a good voice, a poetic lyric; no need for expensive production, extensive lighting rigs and costumes. Instead, true musical prowess could simply be found in a troubadour clutching a notepad bursting with observations and a handy crowd ready to join in on the chorus, eyes closed and fists aloft.

Folk was back. But had it ever gone away?

To those frequenting the UK's longstanding festivals and clubs, or reading magazines like *fRoots* and *English Dance And Song*, this was perplexing. After all, they knew folk music was healthy – the live circuit boasts countless young acts, and folk-specific degree courses and summer schools are packed full of young performers, eager to reinterpret the songs and tunes that have enthralled them – but who were Mumford And Sons? Who was Laura Marling? And why did this not really sound like folk music as they knew it, more like 'Coldplay-with-a-banjo', as *The Independent*'s Nick Duerden so delicately put it.[2]

It wasn't long before Eliza, ever the 'presentable' side of folk and traditional music, was consulted on her view. 'Traditional music is passed through generations, so in that sense what they are doing is not folk,' she stated, 'but neither was Dylan.'[3]

Eliza used her own family's arrival to folk as an example. Her family had been prompted to find their own tradition by the skiffle craze and the increasing influence of American blues and folk. It was the very reactionary nature of pop music to want to change, subvert, the sounds that had come before it.

Though she is clear that, in her view, these musicians so quick to be heralded as the new folk generation aren't necessarily playing the music that she deems folk – the songs, tunes, techniques and styles passed down over time – she welcomes the contribution of new blood, and, of course, the five minutes of fame for the wider genre. 'There may well come a time, after the apocalypse, that one of Laura Marling's songs may very well end up being a traditional song. Give it a couple of hundred years. Folk has to take a long view.'

Of course, opening the debate which must rage in every musical niche, the time-consuming *what is folk?* debate, is unhelpful and, ultimately, pointless. We all know that categories and genre-monikers are unavoidable, for marketing, for sales, for casual reference, and there is a quiet joy to be taken in the journalistic coining of subgenres: a recent favourite is 'Witch House', and folk has had its fair share, too, with 'psych-folk', 'acid-folk', 'wyrd-folk' and 'folktronica'. (Should anyone be able to define the subtle differences, I would be an eager pupil.)

Eliza's open-mindedness towards Mumford And Sons, Laura Marling, *et al*, and their inclusivity in the folk scene, is perhaps not surprising given her back catalogue: her incorporation of different influences in her treatment of traditional music and her own brand of songwriting. It is for this reason, then, that Eliza has chosen to define herself as a 'modern English musician', rather than a 'folk musician'. This distance from the folk genre and folk scene prevents her from disappointing those that enjoy solely her trad. arr. material and approach. The label she has given herself insinuates that original songwriting is just as important and necessary to her and her career, and reinterpreting traditional music is not all she, as a musician, is concerned with. She has other strings to her bow.

It is only natural that 'modern' and 'English' appear in there, too; after all, she has spent her entire musical path making music which weaves in current influences and reflects her interests, heritage and culture. So often folk music is thought to be a preservation tool; a genre which looks back to keep tradition and voices alive. Eliza, though, is keen to prove that she is current, she is English.

Her own songs and tunes have peppered her back catalogue, right from her 1993 composition, 'The Wrong Favour', a self-proclaimed 'spleen-venting' song as she tells us in the liner notes. When her own compositions are side by side with traditional music, the listener 'rarely [sees] the join', as Stewart Lee commented, adding 'with her own material, you can see the elements of research and development that she's gained from years of traditional research.'

Her own songs that appear on the albums more heavily dominated by traditional material sound as though they could neatly slot in to the folk music canon: *Red Rice*'s 'Accordion Song' and *Rough Music*'s 'Mohair', for example, have the intricate melodies that arrangers bring to an old song, the kind of melodies that singer songwriters often sacrifice in favour of the plaintive pronunciation of words over choppy chords. It is often only the switch to a lyrical first person perspective that gives her own songs away.

But Eliza knows her listeners and the folk scene well, and has chosen – for the most part – to segregate her traditional material from her original songwriting, preferring to release and tour pure songwriting albums, before moving on to her traditional music collections. Jon Boden understands why she does this. 'You don't want to con people into seeing what they don't want to see,' he explained. 'Everyone knows that with her current band, they will hear her songwriting; the Ratcatchers, the name, especially, differentiated it, so you knew that'd be the traditional music. I did the same when I started the Remnant Kings, but I think there's a sense of wanting to do it for its own merit and not to have to apologize for your own material.'

Of course, her first songwriting album was *Angels And Cigarettes*, her only release on a major label to date and a poorly performing album. But following its release and the offer to record a second, Eliza and her band were already working on new material when she was dropped from Warners. They had fully formed demos ready to go, but with the implosion of the band and the desperate need for six months off to reassess and revaluate – and ultimately, to find a new way forward which resulted in *Anglicana* – these recordings were left untouched. After the success of *Anglicana* and *Rough Music*, and yet more personnel changes, Eliza was ready for something new

131

once again. Songwriting beckoned, but this time, it would be Topic continuing to take her forward.

'Tony had said that we could've done *Angels And Cigarettes* with Topic, but he wanted to see me do well and [Warners] seemed like a good thing for me to do,' Eliza remembered. 'He also couldn't have offered the budget that Warners had. But over the years, it became clear that a songwriting album was something that Topic would also consider. In the end, I told him that I had all this material left over [from the Warners period]. I asked him "how much can you give me to finish it?"'

And though Eliza and Ben were no longer a romantic partnership, Ben's heavy involvement in the writing and arranging of the demos and early recordings of the material following on from *Angels And Cigarettes* meant he was committed to the album that became *Dreams Of Breathing Underwater*; so much so, in fact, that he continued to work on it whilst Eliza was working away, gigging with her family in the United States in spring 2007 and subsequently throughout May, June and July of that year in the UK.

Though Eliza was of course grateful for his input, and for his efforts in moving the project on when she was caught up in touring, 'it was a source of tension in some ways, as I didn't think it should be worked on when I wasn't there.' But then, she reasoned, 'there were certain things I couldn't be there for, like I wasn't there when the strings were recording which was a shame as I wanted to be there for that.'

Nevertheless, the album was recorded and released, a launch party taking place at London's Madame JoJo's nightclub on 9 June 2008 with all audience members receiving a pre-release signed copy of the album. Reviewer David Kidman found the launch party rather unsettling at first: 'Several sex shops and a man handing out sticks of seaside rock in the centre of London's Soho – not the usual setting for a folk gig.'[4]

As with all her original writing, Eliza's collection of songs that became *Dreams Of Breathing Underwater* is reflective, contemplative, and, above all, personal. And it's clear that Eliza has a great deal to say, to work through, at this period in her life.

The album opens with 'Follow The Dollar', clearly a cathartic frustration at the disappointment felt towards Warners and the lack of artistic control she recognized under their stewardship, with lines such as 'we don't make our own decisions/but we follow the dollar all the day.' But it's not just artistic control Eliza rails against: it's the wanton consumerism encouraged by the mainstream music industry, the impulse to purchase and buy into brands rather than artists; artists which, actually, have become lazy in their controlled capacity and don't warrant the adulation they receive:

> *so you buy the rubbish like you just do*
> *put me in the limo like you must do*
> *in the VIP lounge, if you can get to me*
> *see me at the bar going far*

In fact, the title track, which didn't actually make it on to the final album, was even more explicit about her frustrations with the major label experience.

Eliza was, at this point in time, also experiencing difficulties with her manager, Nigel Morton. Morton had been Shane MacGowan's booking agent for a number of years, and had also worked with New Model Army and Oysterband. A Yorkshire native too, he had taken Eliza on once Kit Bailey had moved on to different things and Eliza had become unable to manage her bookings herself.

'Eliza had quite a busy schedule and a certain profile that it made sense to find someone who knew promoters and venues, and so on,' Sam Thomas remembered, 'and this guy had a track record so he came on board. But I always had a problem with him, he was classic manager material.'

In the sleeve notes to *Dreams Of Breathing Underwater*, it is Liz Lenten that receives a thank you. Having worked for many years with Shane MacGowan and the Popes, Liz had also spent time working alongside Nigel Morton. 'But I didn't know Eliza at all, I didn't follow folk, I didn't know anything about her family, but I did realize the respect with which Eliza is held. In fact, I still need a history lesson – it was only recently she mentioned her tour with Joan Baez, and I had no idea! She has done so much!'

It was during this time that Eliza and Nigel parted company, and Liz took on a new managerial role on Eliza's behalf. Alongside Liz's artistic management services, she also provides music education packages as well as being a vocalist and composer herself. 'We sat and sorted out this plan for us to work together. Step by step, blow by blow. She listens to my opinions but I work for her so she takes the final decisions. I'm very, very transparent, perhaps too much, but she's a dream to work with.'

It seemed that the feeling was very much mutual, with Eliza going on to thank Liz in the liner notes to later album, *Gift*, stating that without her representation, she would 'still be prey of the shark and the whale'.

It was only after the release of *Dreams Of Breathing Underwater*, in June 2008, that we really begin to catch a glimpse of the kind of professional and emotional turmoil Eliza has suffered courtesy of the Warners' legacy and the transitional period between *Anglicana* and *Rough Music*.

In *Time Out*'s 'Ten things you didn't know about Eliza Carthy' feature in late October 2008, she claims 'Things were much tougher three years ago – working really hard, not getting anywhere, big rotten divorce, big nasty splitting up with manager. The kind of stuff that makes you go: Fuck this I'm getting a job in Tesco kind of shite.'

Though Eliza and Ben Ivitsky weren't married (but they were engaged), this was the kind of relationship breakdown which felt like a divorce: there were their livelihoods to consider, hence the decision to continue working together on the album, and their home in the Scottish borders they had bought together, Eliza contributing the money gained from the Warners' pay out.

Eliza first met Ben through his brother, Conrad, the former bass player in Shooglenifty. 'I ended up going out with Conrad for about a year before I moved up to Edinburgh and started going out with his brother! And me and Ben were together for nine years. He was Willy, my [current] drummer's brother, too. There's seven of them all together, but I only managed to work my way through two!' she laughed her infectious dirty laugh.

But again, it's the inside of the CD that provides the clues to Eliza's real feelings: 'I'm not one of those people that can easily go back to talking about the weather.'

By the time *Dreams Of Breathing Underwater* came out, Eliza had found happiness with Aidan Curran and was looking forward to the birth of their first child six months later. Aidan, a singer and guitarist originally from Vancouver Island, had moved to the UK in order to study Folk and Traditional Music at the University of Newcastle in 2006. He met Eliza at a session at Sidmouth Folk Week and before long she was invited to contribute to *Sit On This*, the debut album of his band Park Bench Social Club.

As their romantic partnership blossomed, so did their musical output, with the pair playing a number of gigs together as a duo and Aidan's solo performance opening for her band shows. His guitar and mandolin work featured on *Gift*, and Aidan has since founded a new band, the No Good Sinners, to which Eliza also contributes.

Dreams Of Breathing Underwater also featured a jumble of different musicians each attributed to the different phases in Eliza's career to date. As mentioned previously, recordings made after the release of *Angels And Cigarettes* were kept in where appropriate, so Barnaby Stradling was surprised to hear his bass playing on the album, a number of years after he had finished working with Eliza. Similarly, Spiers and Boden, having decided to leave the band after the completion of *Rough Music,* played their part in the album on vocal and multi-instrumental duties.

But this was not a piecemeal collection from the past. Eliza had new songs ready to be showcased, a number of which she formulated during her stint as regular guest presenter on Mark Radcliffe's BBC Radio 2 show in 2005; a gig she was rumoured to have received thanks to an unlikely source – Noel Edmonds. 'I don't know if that's true or not,' she laughed, 'I'm not sure which album I was promoting, but I did an interview with Noel Edmonds on his show and we got on so well that apparently he recommended me!

'I really wanted to connect with songwriting again,' she continued, 'so I used to dare myself to write a new song to go on to the Mark Radcliffe show with. "Rosalie" was one of those and I played the whole thing on fiddle. I started off by seeing if I could write just to two chords, playing two chords and singing over the top. "Little Big Man" started like that. I finally realized that two chords weren't going to be enough and I needed to do other things. That's when I thought I needed a barbershop quartet, and I remember sitting around the table with Ben, Heather [Macleod] and Barney Strachan, the tape op for the album, and singing that bit for the first time, the vocal bit for "Little Big Man" and getting it all worked out and just being delighted. It was so much fun, working it out.'

Eliza's original songs are littered with references to the sea. Of course, it's a nod to her heritage; that she was born in Scarborough and grew up in Robin Hood's Bay, a village whose history has been dominated by its relationship with the sea. A wave breaking at the foot of her bed, like in 'Accordion Song', or the fish refrain in 'Little Big Man' is a subtle reference to the sea and a way of name-checking her friends, family and her own personal history when she is living away; in Sherwood Forest at the time of the release of *Dreams Of Breathing Underwater*, and previously in the Borders of Scotland, a location her dad had remarked was almost exactly the same as their home – remote, northerly, a folk festival down the road – but at least four hours north. Was it something he and Norma had said? he joked.

The sea is also a romantic setting for any song. The folk song canon is full of young sailors lost at sea, or sailors returning unrecognized after many years away. Women are left waiting at the shore, not certain as to the outcome of their betrothed's fate. There's the mystery of the sea, through the myth and legend of pirates, mermaids and enchantments. Its shore is also a debauched place, full of excessive drinking, promiscuity and an entire raft of unusual, eccentric characters perfect for carrying a plotline.

But for Eliza, there's also the glamour of the seaside. The *Dreams Of Breathing Underwater* inlay guides the reader through the attractions of the seaside town, from fairground rides and piers, to glimpses of snack bars, amusement arcades and the sea itself. At one stage, she even tells us 'Going to the Fair with my young man, or down the pub on the harbour anyway, for fish and chips and a snog. Whitby fish and chips is the cure for most things. Weston? What?'

Naturally, this British love affair with our seaside towns has changed in recent times, and as some seaside towns fall into disrepair, it is the ghostly echoes of the music hall entertainers, once found on the stage of every seaside pier playing to healthy crowds, that Eliza is taken with.

Eliza often soundchecks with 'Oh I do like to be beside the seaside', her big lungs powering every pregnant pause, her arms elevated as the music hall doyenne, and *Dreams Of Breathing Underwater* is paean to those entertainers who really could *sing*, backed by plenty of brass and gusto.

And though *Dreams Of Breathing Underwater* was deemed 'the soundtrack to her marriage break-up'[5] it is far from gloomy: instead, Eliza indulged her love of music hall and show tunes, milking her sultry vocals for plenty of glissando and brass oompah, particularly in songs like 'Oranges And Seasalt' and 'Little Big Man'.

Stewart Lee explained that 'she does those music hall swing songs like an entertainer would. We don't realize how lucky we are to have someone who can carry on that tradition, that doesn't have to court ephemeral fashions,' and he is right: Eliza doesn't aim to shoehorn her songs in to a particular genre. Martin Green illustrated further, claiming 'she's extremely open-minded musically; she doesn't see anything as "off limits". And with her own songs, if they suggest a certain flavour, then she's quite happy to explore that.'

As a result, Eliza found that after *Dreams Of Breathing Underwater* had been laid down and completed, she had almost a whole album's worth of excess material which dallied with swing. 'Yes,' she laughed, 'we could have released *Dreams Of Swinging Underwater*, too, plus loads of Irving Berlin and George Formby covers. I don't know what we're going to do with it all.'

Having worked within such a maligned, neglected genre for her entire life, Eliza has never seen any need to make music which is 'on trend', allowing her the freedom to write and arrange as she chooses, providing, of course, her own current experience is very much the nucleus. She knows that the pure quality of her and her band's musicianship and confidence on stage will win over audiences regardless of trends or fashions.

'I think after *Red Rice* there was all this pressure on her to become a marketable singer songwriter,' Stewart Lee added. 'Maybe if she'd become a pop star then, she would have peaked and now she'd not be out there anymore. The good thing about Eliza and her crew is that fashion is irrelevant. The trajectory for folk and jazz musicians is so much longer and with Eliza, you often feel like she's only just begun.'

In a 2008 interview with Carol McDaid for *The Scotsman*, Eliza made public the problems she was experiencing with her voice. Though she had been singing from such an early age, and thus knew her limitations and the ways in which she had to care for her voice, for the ten years leading up to the recording of *Dreams Of Breathing Underwater*, Eliza was experiencing the increasing regularity of hoarseness she had suffered as a result of 'overuse, damage from smoking and stress.'[5]

'The entire time with the Ratcatchers, I was finding it very difficult,' she explained to me. 'Like when we recorded *Rough Music*, I could sing the top B – or is it a top F#? – in "The Unfortunate Lass" in the studio, but I couldn't do it while we were touring; I think we did it live twice. We ended up having to take "Willow Tree" down; oh, and a lot of the songs on *Angels and Cigarettes* were also taken down. By the time we came to do *Dreams Of Breathing Underwater*, I couldn't sing "Hug You Like A Mountain" in the same key any more, either. Singing got more and more painful.'

As the instrumental parts of 'Hug You Like A Mountain' had already been laid down in the key Eliza once could sing, the entire arrangement had to be pitch-tuned to a lower key. 'There's some really funny low backing vocals in there; you're wondering "is that a man or a woman? Is that Anthony from Anthony and the Johnsons?" but no, it's just me being pitch-tuned down a whole octave!'

Though she feared that smoking was the biggest contributing factor, the specialists she consulted claimed that although her smoking was a problem, the steroids she took in order to control her asthma, as well as alcohol and the stress of touring, were all to blame.

She tried to change her lifestyle. Quitting the nicotine came first, and then she cast a critical eye over her pre- and post-gig routine, 'First of all, it was about doing warm-ups before gigs; then it became doing warm-ups before gigs and being silent after gigs. I had to give up drinking obviously, which I did to most success, although not after I met Aidan.

'But then I needed to be silent all day, then warm-up, then do a gig, then be silent afterwards and not to have a drink.'

As singing became more painful and hoarseness prevailed, her social life began to suffer, too. 'For a while, I could go to parties but I couldn't laugh out loud, so I developed this thing where I was shutting my mouth but wobbling my shoulders in laughter. Then, I could go to parties but not laugh out loud or speak to anybody, either! The Folk Awards was a nightmare if I had to sing; before and after, I could only nod and smile at people … and wobble my shoulders. People must have thought I was a nutter!

'And then when I did meet Aidan, we were big partiers to start with. I met a whole crowd of first years at university and trying not to drink around those people was just incredibly difficult. I had to let people know I couldn't smoke or drink, and they were all eighteen year olds, singing their heads off and having a good time. I couldn't do that, which was pretty hard for Aidan. I started to withdraw, really.'

I reviewed her performance at The Met in Bury for the *Manchester Evening News'* 'City Life' supplement in late September 2008 and feared the cancellation of the gig, such was the severity of her condition. With packets of Halls' Soothers at her feet, it seemed that, her voice rasping desperately to be heard, talking was actually more difficult than singing. And though she didn't reduce the amount of between-song banter, she was calmer, perhaps even more solemn, as the combined forces of pregnancy and illness forced her feet to remain firmly planted on the stage, her hips swaying gently to the music instead of her usual fit of flamboyant dance moves.

Her vocal problems had intensified when she became pregnant with Florence. The cyst which had developed over her left false fold grew more advanced due to water retention in pregnancy. And, of course, being pregnant meant that she couldn't take anti-inflammatories to keep it under control. Two months later, her voice had completely ground to a halt. The remainder of the tour was cancelled.

Eliza gave birth to Florence Daisy late on Christmas Eve 2008. She remained silent throughout the birth.

In March 2009, Eliza had the cyst lasered away at a hospital in Nottingham, her mum accompanying her during treatment. As she took in a breath after waking the next day, she felt the rush of air hit parts of her throat that she hadn't known in over ten years. Following treatment, Eliza realized that she needed to find a new way of singing, one that would better care for her vulnerable vocal cords. Already a low, earthy voice, Eliza found that after illness and treatment, her voice seemed lower still, retaining some of that rasping breathiness brought about by her condition.

'I remember her saying how much she had learnt from going into the studio day after day after day,' Kit Bailey said, 'learning a different technique of singing. It was an important learning development for her. And you can hear that in Eliza: her voice has got stronger, and rather than try and make an album that would be more accepted by the mainstream, she hasn't. She's just Liza and better. She's arguably a mainstream person now, without having to become a mainstream artist.'

'You know, people used to call me "sir" on the phone, as my speaking voice was so low and growly!' Eliza laughed, shaking her head in bemusement. 'But now I have the same, if not slightly bigger, range than I did when I was nineteen, though the tone is very, very different. It would've been different anyway, but this is really different as it has a real hoarse edge to it – though that's slowly subsiding as my teacher's teaching me to control it.

'I've got a lot of work to do, but it's great to have that range back. When I first got my falsetto back, I was completely blown away. I remember I was taking Aidan to work, he was doing some decorating just outside Sunderland, and I took him in the morning. I had this little red Golf that Ben's dad had sold me and it had a tape deck in it and after I moved away from Scotland, I'd found all these boxes of tapes. I'd dug out [George Michael's album] *Faith* and I was singing along to "One More Try", and it goes up this high note and I just shot up … it's not an octave leap, is it? It might even be a ninth, but it felt huge and all of a sudden I was singing this high, weedy falsetto note!'

Just a month after the operation, Eliza was centre stage at the St George's Day celebrations in Trafalgar Square, and her voice wasn't just back to normal: it was bigger, grander, simultaneously more honed and more controlled.

Her peers noticed the change, and welcomed it. Martin Green told me 'It's amazing how her voice sounds now, it's just incredible. It's not the same voice. As long as she makes use of that huge voice, I'm really happy whatever she chooses to do.'

Billy Bragg has found the difference between her earlier and more recent recordings markedly different, saying 'Now, listening to her records, the thing that strikes me most is her voice. I don't think that had quite come into its own in those days,' in reference to her support slot with him on tour in 1997. 'She was still a little bit exotic back then, you know.'

Eliza will never be completely recovered, though. Comparing herself to a runner who once sprained their ankle, her voice will always be susceptible, reminding her with regular tickles and coughs. 'If I get sick, my voice is the first thing to go. But I've been doing this a long time and I have to accept that there are some things I can do and some things I can't. Drinking lots and lots of red wine and expecting to be able to sing for two hours the following day is unrealistic,' she smiled, knowingly.

Unsurprisingly, once Eliza had recovered from the cyst in her throat, there was little respite before she embarked on her next project, despite having a very young child in tow. This time, however, she didn't have to stray from her parents' home for writing, arranging, rehearsals and recording.

Eliza and Norma decided to put together a collection of songs together that they had been singing for years, a true representation of the songs they had learned and arranged together. Though Norma, as a member of the Watersons and as a solo artist, has long been regarded as one of the finest purveyors of English traditional music, (she was awarded the MBE in 2003 for services to the genre), she finds herself regularly learning from her daughter.

'It has never been a one way system, it has always been two ways,' Norma explained. 'Eliza has taught me an awful lot about phrasing things. She has a great capacity for taking a song that you've heard millions of times before and phrasing it in a way that makes you go "why didn't I think of that?" She has a musicality which is really wonderful. Both Martin and I have learned things from her, and she has learned things from us. It has been definitely 50/50.'

But though the focus of the album was wholeheartedly mother and daughter, the extended family couldn't help but be involved. Eliza's cousin, Olly, was drafted in for recording and production duties, his studio a convenient distance for Norma to travel, whilst Marry, Oliver, Aidan and Martin contributed vocal and instrumental parts. Aidan also arranged the album opener, 'Poor Wayfaring Stranger', after 'Mam and Aidan sitting having a tune one night. Aidan led the arrangement, right down to trying to tell Danny Thompson what to play without being too scared,' explained Eliza.[7]

At first, Eliza was concerned about the progress of the album, telling *Bright Young Folk* 'The first week was a little slow. My mum's getting on a bit and I was worried it was turning into Liza's solo album, but it isn't, thankfully, and we've got some really nice songs.'[8]

The album was released in July 2010 and the artwork featured close portraits of both mother and daughter along with Florence. The front cover depicted their bejewelled wrists, their hands clasped together, whilst the back showed the pair through the window of the family kitchen. But this subsequent tour was also beset by poor health. This time, Eliza, expecting her and Aidan's second child, was well; it was her mother who suffered: really suffered.

Norma developed an infection in her knee partway through the tour in November 2010 and was taken to the nearest hospital in Warrington. Sadly, though, her condition quickly deteriorated. She contracted septicaemia and was referred to the Intensive Care Unit where she remained for almost three months, a tracheotomy in her throat and a dialysis machine and ventilator by her side.

A kindly promoter in Cheshire made a box room available to Martin, so that he could visit his wife at the hospital each day. Gigs, and therefore any form of real income, subsided.

By mid-November, *Gift* had been announced as one of *fRoots'* albums of the year in their Critics Poll. Keen to keep up morale whilst communicating Norma's condition to the wider public, Eliza turned to Twitter, stating, on 22 November, 'sleepy mam and me nominated for *fRoots* critics' poll album of the year 2010! she'll wake up for fabulous prizes … diva …'

When Eliza gave birth to Isabella Mary on 26 November, Norma was in too poor a condition to realize, still unconscious in the Intensive Care Unit in Warrington. Eliza and Aidan, with the new-born and Florence, were confined to their home just outside Edinburgh. Four days after the birth, Eliza tweeted 'two kids eh.two! mam awake today.i miss her a lot underneath the nappies and baby-love mist. howay the mammy.'

Thankfully, by 7 December, Norma awoke, with Eliza telling Twitter 'mam laughing yesterday. howay get out of my way the snow so i can drive to cheshire to see her … there's a baby needs a munch.'

But Norma remained incarcerated in hospital throughout the festive period and early 2011. Marry and Eliza kept fans updated: 'Aunt Norma speaking, no tracheo, drinking cups of tea and eating ice cream yippee, yippee!' [@marrywaterson 26 January 2011] and 'mother update: eating ice cream and mash (not together), learning how to swallow. good times'[@elizacarthy 2 February 2011]

Though the effect of critical illness on any family is enormous, for those who are self-employed, the financial burden of unplanned time out from work can also take its toll. For musicians, especially folk musicians who cannot rely on the level of royalties that come from the kind of radio play that rock and pop musicians receive, for example, not playing essentially means not receiving any money.

Despite Norma and Martin's combined stature as key players within the English folk revival, with large back catalogues and years of touring history, this is sadly no less the case. With Martin spending the majority of his time 150 miles away at Norma's bedside in Warrington, gigs were cancelled and income forfeited.

Rod and Danny Stradling, close friends of Norma and Martin, and Barnaby Stradling's parents, launched an initiative for folk music fans and fellow well-wishers to contribute to a series of benefit concerts, the proceeds from which would be given to Norma and Martin to help soften the impact of lost earnings over the period. The *fRoots* and *Mudcat* forums were used to advertise the plan, with links to the Stradlings' *Musical Traditions* website giving frequent updates of Norma's condition.

Folk clubs and communities across the country began to coordinative events, including an Imagined Village show at Cecil Sharp House, whilst those that couldn't attend a gig were encouraged to donate online. Eliza contributed to dedicated threads on message boards, thanking fans for their concern. It seemed that the folk music community was not just saddened to hear of the ill health of one of their finest singers; they were collectively shocked that such talented and prolific musicians could be left financially unstable after a period of illness. One *fRoots* forum member, Simon Hall, stated 'A welcome initiative, though I'm shocked, but not surprised, by reading between the lines that a family of such stature in our national music can be up against it financially after just a few months of cancelled gigs.'[9]

Norma was still in hospital by the time the BBC Radio 2 Folk Awards rolled around, on Monday 7 February. Following on from the *fRoots* Critics' Poll nod, *Gift* had fared very well in Folk Awards nominations, too, clocking up a nomination in the Best Album category. 'Poor Wayfaring Stranger' was also nominated for Best Traditional Song, whilst Eliza and Norma themselves had been selected for the Best Duo award.

The BBC Radio 2 Folk Awards has always held a rather difficult place for folk fans. On the one hand, there is the argument that it guarantees prime time radio (and sometimes even television) for a somewhat marginalized genre of music. It is a chance for folk artists to be heard on national radio outside of Mike Harding's show, and an opportunity to showcase the merits of the genre through celebrity endorsements and appearances from those not closely associated with the scene – comedians, actors, broadcasters – plus lively sets from nominated artists, a spangly backdrop and black tie dress code.

Then there are those who feel that the Awards fail to challenge the negative, outdated stereotypes of the genre by selecting 'safe' recipients of its awards: the same names cropping up year on year, or the attempt to inject more populist personalities – and thus more PR leverage – via tenuous connections to folk music.

During the BBC Radio 2 coverage of the buildup to the Awards ceremony, journalist Colin Irwin referenced this in conversation with Simon Mayo, stating that there were rumours, albeit tongue in cheek, of a stage invasion following the announcement of 1960s hippie Donovan's Lifetime Achievement Award that year. Of course, no Brit Awards-style posturing really took place at the Folk Awards, and when Nancy Kerr and James Fagan, previous collaborators of Eliza's, of course, beat her and her mother to the gong for Best Duo, it was likely that Eliza was genuinely pleased for them.

The 2011 Awards featured on Freeview's red button function and, on the announcement of the recipient of the Best Duo Award, the roving camera focused on Nancy at the table with James and their baby son, Hamish. Eliza was also sat nearby with baby Isabella. It seemed strange, somehow, that these two women started their career in a partnership together, before forging a more family-orientated musical career, resulting in, on this windy night in February, direct competition with each other. But Eliza wasn't empty-handed for long. As she went up to collect the Award for 'Poor Wayfaring Stranger' as Best Traditional Track, she tugged at Aidan's hand until he joined her at the lectern, Isabella notching up what must be her first television appearance. Eliza was understated, almost solemn, in her acceptance speech. She explained how ill her mother was, and thanked the audience for their support.

It was then the turn of one of the celebrity personalities to present the Album of the Year award. It materialized, as Joanna Trollope gave her tediously long introduction in a cut-glass accent, that some of the author's stories are set within the folk music community. As Eliza returned to the stage to collect the Award, it was only too obvious how she missed her mother, how she wished she was also on stage receiving her share of the whoops and cheers. 'When we were in the studio making *Gift*,' she began, 'sometimes she wasn't there. Sometimes she was making soup or looking over the baby and saying "you'll be alright". And she can't be here tonight. But she sends her love, as does my dad. This is smashing. Thanks.'

Norma's poor health prompted Eliza to decide to make the move back to Robin Hood's Bay. Eliza had lived away from her native Yorkshire for a number of years: over a decade in Scotland and a temporary move to Sherwood Forest, before moving back to Edinburgh.

And though her parents had a large extended family and circle of friends around them, Eliza felt she needed to settle her young family near to her parents so she could keep a watchful eye on them – and they on her. In spring 2011, Eliza packed up the house in Gorebridge, just outside Edinburgh, and returned to her parents' home.

Eventually, Norma was well enough to be transferred to hospitals closer to home; firstly to Middlesbrough hospital, then back to Whitby. This spelt relief for Norma: she knew Whitby hospital well from the many times Eliza had been admitted for her asthmatic attacks and was a convenient proximity to home, meaning that family members, neighbours and friends could drop in on a daily basis – and it also had a menu of some repute.

'It was lovely,' she told me, 'the food was fantastic. They've got a chef in Whitby hospital, because it's a small hospital, and they make everything homemade. So you get homemade soup every day; three, three-course meals every day, and it's done so it looks good as well as tastes good, so it encourages you to eat. When I arrived, the sister said to me "I don't want any of this no eating. On my wards, you eat." And I did!'

By May 2011, Norma was back at home. She received physiotherapy twice a week at the hospital, and she had to be put through a full routine of exercises at home every day. 'When I woke up, I had been unconscious for four months and I couldn't do anything,' she said, settled in a large armchair in the corner of the living room, baby Isabella asleep on her chest. 'I couldn't lift my head, I couldn't feed myself; I was like a weak kitten and Martin had to feed me.

'But gradually, with the help of the physiotherapists mainly, because they're brilliant, those girls, it's all coming back. The doctor examined me and he said the muscle tone is still there, that I just need to get it going again.' Her walking still troubled her, but she had been able to leave behind the zimmer frame, preferring to use a walking stick instead.

Also that month, Martin Carthy celebrated his seventieth birthday. A concert had been programmed to take place at the Queen Elizabeth Hall on London's South Bank, but following Norma's hospitalization, it was arranged to be a benefit concert, too, with all proceeds going directly to the couple.

And though Norma was still too weak to travel to London for the event, she was very much at the forefront of Martin's mind on this special occasion. In amongst sets provided by the guests, Dave Swarbrick, Tom Robinson and Eliza herself, he made sure he publicly praised the staff at the hospitals in which Norma had been so expertly cared for, expressing concern at the coalition government's threat of cuts to the NHS, and warmly thanking those who had held a benefit concert or donated to the fund.

Eliza, too, mentioned her mother when she was called to introduce the event. 'I've always had admiration for my dad as a musician,' she began, 'but now I have even more admiration for him, for taking such good care of my mum. And he takes good care of me.'

For many years, Eliza had mentioned in interviews that she was always surprised when people came up to her to tell her the profound effect her father's music had on their lives and their playing; that, as a child, she couldn't quite grasp what an impact he had made on not just folk music, but on rock and pop music, too. To her, he was her dad, and he happened to like playing the guitar and singing songs. But, here in the Queen Elizabeth Hall, in front of a sold-out crowd of fans, it seemed that she was now finally accustomed to her father's achievements and how well regarded he is by music lovers and guitar aficionados. Instead, she chose to say how she couldn't quite believe that her father – her own father – had turned seventy.

In the second half of the show, Martin welcomed Eliza on to the stage. Just before he passed the microphone baton, he talked to her quietly, out of earshot of the expectant audience. Once he left for the wings, Eliza revealed that she had asked him what she should play. He had replied 'Sing the one from Northumberland … or whatever you like.' The audience laughed at the vagueness of his suggestion and Eliza's apparent amusement. Suddenly, Martin shouted from the wing, '"The Snows They Melt The Soonest"'! He had remembered the title of the song he hoped she would play and the audience laughed again. Such is Eliza's confidence that she hadn't prepared a set, despite the grand setting, the capacity audience, the special occasion, and did as her father wished, playing her chilling interpretation of 'The Snows They Melt The Soonest' followed by her rendition of Billy Bragg's 'King James Version'.

Following Norma's gradual recuperation, she and Martin wanted to publicly thank their friends, family and fans for their support during a worrying, uncertain time. They turned to their friends,

Top left: Martin recording 'The Blowjob Song', which so impressed Van Dyke Parks.

Top right: Will I do? Eliza getting ready for her second Mercury nomination.

Above left: Norma and Eliza at the second Mercury Awards.

Left; Saul Rose and Eliza mid-gig at Vancouver Folk Festival Hangover Party, 1997.

Top: Lovely shot of Norma and Eliza clearly enjoying themselves at Vancouver Folk Festival Hangover Party 1997.
Bottom; Martin, Norma and the late Lal Waterson raising the rafters.

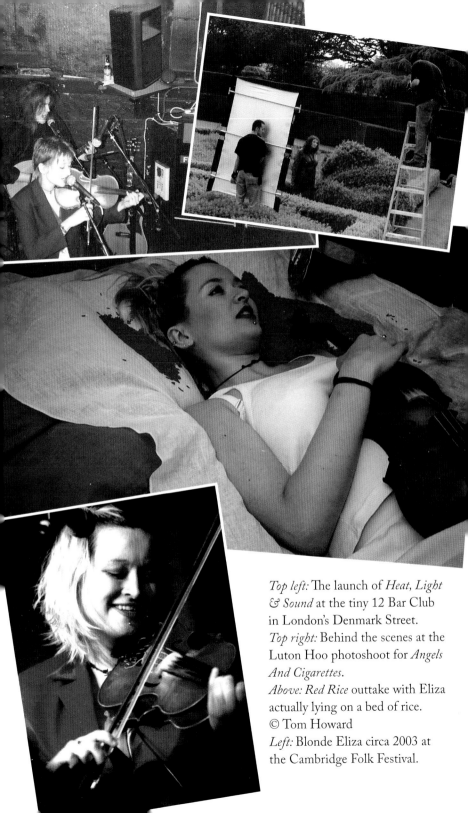

Top left: The launch of *Heat, Light & Sound* at the tiny 12 Bar Club in London's Denmark Street.
Top right: Behind the scenes at the Luton Hoo photoshoot for *Angels And Cigarettes*.
Above: Red Rice outtake with Eliza actually lying on a bed of rice.
© Tom Howard
Left: Blonde Eliza circa 2003 at the Cambridge Folk Festival.

Top left: The Ratcatchers at an airport somewhere in Europe. L-R Ben Ivitsky, Jon Boden, Eliza, John Spiers.

Top right: 'If I can make it there ...' Eliza, Martin and Saul Rose in New York. Snapped by Norma.

Centre: A summer camp teach-in Ashokan, NY, with Guy Broushard.

Right: McCabe's Guitar Shop, Santa Monica. Eliza's idea of hell!

Top left: Richard Thompson, pictured here in 1995 working on Norma's first solo album.

Top right: The Milkman Of Human Kindness himself calls on Norma. Billy Bragg, Glastonbury 1997.

Centre: Eliza looks surprised to be photographed with Joan Baez.

Left: Eliza, Bob Neuwirth and (the late) Kate and Anna McGarrigle rehearsing for a Hal Willner Southbank concert in 1999 … in a toilet!

Top left: Punk influenced bassist Barn Stradling cuddling flowers. Why? Because Elvis Costello gave them to Norma.

Top right: The drinking session that inspired 'Oranges And Seasalt'. Don't try this at home!

Below left: 'Mum, how do I get to the Albert Hall?' 'Practise, Florence.' Teenage Cancer Trust Benefit, 2009.

Below right: Saul Rose, whom Eliza describes as her musical soulmate, seen here in his Seven Champions dancing gear.

Top: This is the moment when the Imagined Village idea was touted. Simon Emmerson, with James and Francis from Afro Celt Sound System.
Above: Dhol maestro Johnny Kalsi and Martin having fun at the Big Chill in 2008. © Mark Bennett
Left: Eliza at the St George's Day celebrations at Trafalgar Square 2009. © Garry Knight

Right and below: Some things never change, like festival mud. Mud on her trousers and 'Mud On My Boots'.

Below: Eliza Carthy with The Imagined Village at WOMAD Charlton Park. Photographer: York Tillyer. © Real World Records Ltd

Rod and Danny Stradling, and asked them to publish a short announcement on the *Musical Traditions* site. It read:

Norma and Martin would like to thank everybody for their wonderful good wishes, cards and flowers; these certainly lit up Norma's continued stay in hospital, especially when she regained consciousness, and reminded Martin of how the folk community loves and values her.

Also thanks for the substantial financial contributions which you all made, making it possible for Martin to stay by Norma's bedside for almost the entire time she was there. This lengthy stay was, by the way, a stark reminder of the selfless dedication of ALL those nurses in all the hospitals, and especially those in the ICU in Warrington.

We would both like also to thank Rod and Danny who - entirely unbidden - took on the task of co-ordinating the fundraising for our benefit - No, don't delete this bit Rod (or Danny). You are true friends.[10]

SEVEN

In London So Fair

I keep getting asked to do things.
Eliza interviewed by Joe Lost, *fRoots*[1]

The sociable, participatory nature of folk music means that most new musical ventures are marked out around the table in the pub during a session or forged after the weekly singaround. Sessions at festivals might lead to an exchange of email addresses as a new project comes to life in the musician's mind. And as a folk musician's professional life is not swathed in riches, with a set of stadium gigs in the pipeline to keep up a bulging bank balance like their compatriots in the more populist genres, he or she must keep playing to earn their keep, tapping in to the UK's healthy network of folk clubs and festivals.

Many players on the current scene have a number of different bands, often used to develop or mine a particular field of traditional music and song. Some will perform their own solo work outside of their band commitments, to which members of other bands will provide backing. There are also numbers of one-off projects which tend to draw together a number of different musicians for a particular reason – to celebrate the work of Darwin, to explore the stories surrounding Hadrian's Wall or the life of Cecil Sharp for example – and record an album, perform a live tour and then lay it to rest. Many of these are commissioned by festivals or other music-oriented bodies, often with help from the Performing Rights Society (PRS) or Arts Council England.

Despite Eliza's prolific output of solo material, she has also found the time to contribute to a wealth of different projects, working to expand the reputation of both herself and the genre with which she is associated. One of her most unusual, and probably lesser known, collaborations has been accompanying crime writer Peter Robinson. Venture into any bookshop and Peter's prolific output will be apparent in the row of titles which often take up an entire shelf, a colourful demonstration of the fact that he has published at least one novel a year since his first, *Gallows View*, in 1987. He is best known for his *Inspector Banks* series which was televised in Britain in 2010, with Stephen Tompkinson in the lead role.

However, fans of his writing will know that he is also a folk music enthusiast, with references regularly creeping in to his work. Though now based in Canada, he was born and raised in Yorkshire and was a frequent visitor to The Grove folk club in Leeds, fostering a love for the Watersons and Martin Carthy from an early age.

Chris Wade, agent at Adastra and Artistic Director for the Beverley Folk Festival, was keen to commission a new partnership between a storyteller and folk musician, believing both art forms to complement each other and that their respective fans would appreciate the cross pollination. There was also the practical element too: a partnership of storyteller and folk musician could play at a range of different arts events, from folk festivals to the increasing number of literary festivals, from book shops to record stores. For those working in the arts and experiencing very uncertain times, this made perfect sense.

In 2006, Chris approached Peter and Eliza with the view to a performance at the Beverley Folk Festival that year and happily, storyteller and musician were keen to accept. 'I'm not really musical', Peter explained, 'I've not been in a band since my late teens and I'm used to working alone. She, on the other hand, is very mercurial; she'll go as the wind takes her with no great structure, which is so odd for me as I've got the words written out in front of me. That kept me on my toes!'

The partnership began with a short story of Peter's, 'The Two Ladies of Rose Cottage', a story which had previously won the Macavity Award. Eliza researched some songs and tunes that she felt suited the ambience of the story and when Peter paused in his reading, she played and sang. After a short interview at the end of the story, Eliza played an extended set. The Beverley performance was well received, a full tent being a testament to this, so they pressed on, booking at Yorkshire's Books And Boots festival, of which Peter is patron. Their confidence grew, despite the limited amount of time in which they had to rehearse.

'Later Eliza worked up themes for the some of the characters and certain situations, which worked very nicely. The fiddle would come and go, and then she'd come in at unexpected times and I'd pause at unexpected times; we'd be taunting and teasing each other,' Peter explained. The duo added another of Peter's stories to their repertoire, 'The Ferryman's Beautiful Daughter', no doubt a nod to the Incredible String Band, from his collection *The Price Of Love*, and returned to Beverley in 2009, to another full tent. 'She has a lot of fans,' Peter acknowledged, 'and there was a real mix of people who came to see us. I think they were just curious to see what we would be like together.'

It was no doubt Eliza's love of story, writing and literature that drew her to this partnership, and Peter's stories of criminal activity and brutality, not to mention his historical references and timespans, inevitably sparked obvious references to her knowledge of folk song.

This knowledge would also be put to the test in another literary collaboration, also in 2006, but this time involving some rather unexpected co-artists. Stewart Lee, '41st best stand-up of all time' according to Channel 4, which later gave him the name for his 2007 stand-up show, had discovered folk music in the early 1980s. 'I was in the Virgin Megastore in Birmingham in 1982 and someone was playing *Penguin Eggs* by Nic Jones and I asked what it was and bought it. Then I started borrowing all the old Topic Records from the local library,' he said.

He looked forward to Eliza's early material, having been a fan of her parents, and interviewed her for the *Sunday Times* ahead of the release of *Red Rice*, where he took great delight in learning of Eliza's love – and Norma's dislike – for the Orb, hoping for 'An Orb remix of the Watersons' *For Pence And Spicy Ale* album [which] would have been a record worth hearing.'[2] He became a fully-fledged fan, but it wasn't until an opportunity arose for his theatre work that he met Eliza: 'I was given a grant for a few days of research and development for a theatre piece. I'd been trying to write something about William Blake for years and in all the Blake biographies there's this common thread running through about him being mixed up with a couple of soldiers in the Napoleonic Wars, so I was really keen to do something on this but using folk music,' Stewart illustrated. His intention was to make a promenade piece, the kind of theatre where audience members are involved in the action, often having to physically follow the performers through the theatre space as the plot progresses.

'I asked Eliza to come in and help for three days. She came with this big old book of songs; it must have been the family book. She has such an encyclopedic knowledge of songs: I could ask her 'do you have a song about … er … doctors?' or something, and she'd know, she'd find one. It was unbelievable,' he marvelled. 'The thing is,' Stewart cleared his throat. 'You always feel a bit intimidated when you're with her … well, not intimidated, because she's not *like that*. But you always feel like you're wasting a genius' time!' But Eliza enjoyed getting involved in something different, telling me: 'I had a bit of a speaking part; I got to be a busty landlady character, a bandleader. And I got a dressing room and they had to sleep in the barn, I remember that,' she laughed, rather triumphantly.

Her father, an assistant stage manager before his music took him full time, must have been proud.

Comedian and actor, Johnny Vegas, was also involved. 'I had to teach Johnny Vegas how to sing a song, and it was very moving, actually,' she said. 'He made me cry, in a workshop space with bods from the National Theatre deciding whether or not we should go through with it. And Johnny Vegas, in an orange monkey suit, actually made me cry!'

'She got a great performance out of him; she always manages to get the best out of people,' Lee asserted.

153

As this tale demonstrates, Eliza does not solely work with musicians and artists performing within the genre with which she is closely associated. In fact, it could be said that she relishes the opportunity to work with artists from outside her sphere, in order to take her sound, her songs, her heritage to new audiences, furthering her own reputation whilst simultaneously flying the flag for the traditional songs and music she takes with her.

Singer songwriter and 6Music DJ, Cerys Matthews, grew up listening to folk music, collecting songs from the age of nine when she began to learn the guitar. After the demise of her rock band, Catatonia, she decided that it was time to focus her energies on the music she really loved, British and American folk music, blues, ragtime and old time. 'I wanted a clean break from having toured all my adult life in a rock band,' she told me. 'The folk roots are evident though even in my music with Catatonia, but I wanted to move on and go deeper into the music I'd loved for so long.'

In the year that Catatonia split, 2001, after their fourth album, *Paper Scissors Stone*, Cerys was invited to play at the Hay Festival for an elite audience which included former American President, Bill Clinton. 'I had been extremely happy to meet Norma and Martin, having read so much about them and their interest in folk music. So when I was invited to sing for Bill Clinton at Hay, it was an opportune moment to call the Carthy family.

'I thought a duet with Eliza would be perfect, since she had emerged from the bosom of folk tradition in England, and I from my own folk traditions of Wales and beyond. We would present a united front.

'And as her voice is very recognizable, I thought it would go well with mine. I chose the songs: "How Can I Keep From Singing", an American civil war song whose lyrics are so powerful, and "Ambell i Gân" from an amazing collection of songs by Peter Kennedy. I sang some verses in Welsh and played guitar, whilst Eliza sang some verses in English and played fiddle. My friend, Lisa Jen, now frontwoman for 9 Bach, completed our merry crew.'

Rehearsals took place in a pub in Hay, '[the performance coming] together very naturally and easily.' And the duo certainly made an impression, with founder of the festival, Peter Florence, declaring it in the *Western Mail* as one of his 'stand-out moments' in the history of the festival.

Just under a year later, Cerys and Eliza played publicly again, this time at the 2002 BBC Radio 2 Folk Awards, the year Martin Carthy won Folk Singer of the Year.

A few months later, Cerys moved to America, 'I ended up living in America for nearly six years. It was so refreshing, musically, going on endless road trips eating cat fish, hush puppies, ribs, and turnip greens, discovering more about blues and jazz and country right there where it began.'

Cerys also used her time in America to discover more about European folk music: 'I was also interested to see if I could follow songs from Europe that came to America with the people who emigrated there. There is a huge dollop of Scottish and Irish songs in Appalachian music. It was so interesting. Great songs outlive the people who sing them: they travel all around the world, they tell you so much.'

Now back in the UK, following her participation in 2007's *I'm A Celebrity ... Get Me Out Of Here!*, Cerys and Eliza see each other from time to time, usually at festivals. 'Last time we bumped into each other, it was our ten year anniversary of playing to Clinton at Hay [May 2011]. Nothing much had changed, bar the number of children we each had in tow. We both have a single-mindedness when it comes to music,' Cerys concluded. 'I don't think there's a choice but to do it.'

Billy Bragg popped up regularly in the young Eliza's life, having been a friend and admirer of her parents for many years. Like Stewart Lee, it was Topic records in the local library which led a teenage Bragg to the Watersons, and a realization 'that punk rock wasn't the only kind of political music out there.' Though punk had fuelled his early musical and political life, it was the frequent meetings with folk singers during the miners' strike, when Bragg spent time performing at gigs in the coalfields, that cemented his admiration for folk music.

'One of the first gigs I ever did, I went up there with my politics and my Clash head on, and there was this guy there, Jock Purdon. He was an old coalminer, singing these old political songs that really blew me away,' Billy remembered.

As his involvement and interest in folk music grew, around the time of his *Between The Wars* EP released in 1985, he found himself invited to play at folk festivals and it was then he met Martin and Norma. A subsequent request to put on a gig at the ICA saw Billy ask the Watersons to perform, and their friendship was bolstered. Billy remembers seeing Eliza perform at Cambridge Folk Festival in the early 1990s, when she and Nancy were just starting out. It was then he approached her parents with the idea of them performing together. 'I asked if their daughter would come out with me,' he laughs, adding hastily 'in the nicest possible way, of course. That sounds bad!'

Billy invited Eliza to perform with him at Glastonbury Festival's acoustic stage, an all-covers set performed by a ragged ensemble of different musicians with rehearsals taking place in his garage, before inviting her and her band to support him on his national tour. Though Billy's fans were accustomed to folk musicians accompanying him on tour – Kate Rusby had occupied a support slot, whilst Dick Gaughan had played some shows alongside him – Bragg felt that there was something definitely different about Eliza.

'What? A skinhead girl in Doctor Martens playing folk violin? [The audience wasn't] expecting it!

'It was a great tour, which culminated in general election night 1997. I can remember being in the dressing room with Norma, Eliza and my manager, and saying "What do we want from tonight?" We were saying "Wouldn't it be great not only if we won, but if Michael

Portillo lost his seat", and of course, at four in the morning, that's exactly what happened.'

Though Billy acknowledges that Eliza was already showing the signs of great musicianship, he remembers that she was definitely still in a learning capacity, still developing her own style and approach.

'She was feeling around the ropes,' he said. 'She was already an incredible fiddle player, but back then she was a little bit more traditional; she hadn't transcended that yet. She was still feeling her way round it. Was she writing her own songs back then? If she was, she wasn't playing many. It was only later she developed into a great songwriter.'

But despite the tour coming to an end, Billy was keen for Eliza to remain on board. When he was asked to contribute to a Pete Seeger tribute album, it was Eliza he drafted in for fiddle and vocal duties on 'If I Had A Hammer', and then came the Wilco and *Mermaid Avenue* project. Woody Guthrie's daughter, Nora, had unearthed a quantity of her father's lyrics that hadn't been recorded – in fact, the extended Guthrie family didn't know of their existence. As she searched through the files and boxes, she couldn't understand why her father hadn't worked with these lyrics, such were, to her mind, their power and poesy. She decided that she would approach a musician to bring them to life and, following a visit to one of his gigs, felt that Billy Bragg would be the best possible choice.

Nora was struck by Billy's political views and his straightforwardness, of course, but felt that his humour matched her father's. Though Billy respected and admired Woody Guthrie, Nora wanted someone who could approach his lyrics from their own standpoint – not an artist who would be compelled to replicate her father, but someone who could take his lyrics for what they were: Billy's understanding and interpretation of the words on the page.

Billy took up Nora's challenge, much to her delight, and he encouraged Wilco to participate, too, feeling that he needed to bring an American connection to the project. And it wasn't long before Eliza was also asked to join in.

'With the Pete Seeger [track], it was pretty straightforward, as we were working on a piece of music we were both familiar with, it was more like a meeting of minds.

'But with *Mermaid Avenue*, it was completely different because we were collaborating with Woody Guthrie: we had the lyrics, but no template to record the song. Really, it was a matter of trying what we thought fit, and I felt very strongly that Eliza could make an interesting contribution, and she did.

'She was the youngest person on the record; she came over to Dublin and hung out with me and Wilco, and whoever else was passing through, and came up with a few ideas. Her fiddle playing on the album is really brilliant, and there's some tracks that you won't have heard yet because they haven't been released. They will be coming out in 2012 for Woody's centenary.'

The album was released in June 1998 and received a Grammy nomination for Best Contemporary Folk Album the following year, eventually losing out to Lucinda Williams and her *Car Wheels On A Gravel Road*.

Though Eliza's contribution to the album is subtle, her wheeling fiddle solos, in 'Way Over Yonder in the Minor Key' and 'California Stars', for example, speak volumes: here is a twenty-three year old accompanying seasoned performers, yet her playing is confident and accomplished, knowing when to enhance and when to embellish. More importantly, though, is the happiness exuding from her violin: she is simply relishing reaching for those old-timey double stops and bends, soaring next to the lap steel.

Eliza has often been called upon to contribute a track or two to a particular project. There's no doubt that this is for artistic reasons: Eliza's vocals are immediately recognizable and her fiddle playing so versatile that the project curator will be assured that she will bring something honed yet distinctive to the table. But then there are the practical reasons, too: Eliza's wealth of knowledge of musical traditions, of songs and of players, not to mention how well networked she is and the fact that she can produce her own records and tracks herself, means she will need little preparation time ahead of the project in question – particularly valuable when there is little or no rehearsal time and next to no budget, which is quite often the case.

Richard Thompson had met Eliza on many occasions throughout her childhood, but it wasn't until his curating of the *Hard Cash* project came about in the early 1990s that he began to know her well. Originally conceived as a soundtrack to a television documentary programme of the same name, which told the stories of many workers throughout Britain and their experiences of exploitation at work, *Hard Cash* brought together a range of different folk musicians and singer songwriters together, including Martin Carthy and the Watersons. Though she didn't contribute herself, the teenaged Eliza would have undoubtedly enjoyed her time shadowing her parents' involvement in the project and getting to grips with how such collaborations evolve from seed right through to fruition, with all the challenges a menagerie of musicians brings with their varying influences, skills and, of course, egos.

So when Richard discovered Eliza was also on the bill for the Harry Smith Project, Hal Willner's plan to revisit the work of the great American musicologist and archivist, Thompson decided to get her in to contribute to his track, too.

'I was designated to sing "The Cuckoo" [or "The Coo Coo Bird" as it is also often known]. I knew Eliza and Garth Hudson were performing on the show, and I thought it would be fantastic to have them play on the song. I think we might have rehearsed for all of thirty seconds,' he smiled, wryly. 'But Eliza is a great musician, and I've never seen her need much in the way of direction. She tends to play the right thing – the right sensibility, the right number of notes, the right emotion.'

The Harry Smith Project made its live debut at the Meltdown Festival, at London's Royal Festival Hall on 2 July 1999, a performance set to include a range of different big name artists, the majority of which are not usually associated with folk and traditional music, including Nick Cave, Beth Orton and Bryan Ferry. As Eliza was only assigned one song on the bill, she decided to make herself available as a fiddle accompanist, should any of the others require it.

'I got this call to go upstairs, to the cafeteria on the top floor – there's been some good parties up there, that's a fun room – and I went up there and Van Dyke Parks was up there, with his wife Sally, along with Bryan Ferry and a couple of other people,' she said, her words tumbling out in excitement.

Bryan Ferry took her up on her offer:

I can't remember what song we had to do but it was just after Bryan Ferry had been ill, he was just recovered and he hadn't been singing. I think it was the first time he was due to be on the stage for ages and he had real stage nerves. We practised the song and I went back downstairs, back to the dressing room I was sharing with Jarvis Cocker and Beth Orton. Jarvis actually borrowed my eyeliner, it was brown and there was only a tiny bit left, but I kept the eyeliner for years afterwards! It was the eyeliner that Jarvis borrowed! Anyway, we were backstage and someone came in to the dressing room, an hour before the gig, and said that the running order had changed because Bryan Ferry was not doing his song. Maybe he'd had a bit of a freak out and so he wasn't going to do it. 'Fuck it', I thought, 'I'm going to write a note and put it under his dressing room door.' I asked Beth if she would help me and she said yes, so I wrote this thing, saying 'oh, I thought it was really good, you shouldn't be nervous, it sounded great' and we pushed it under his door and ran away, you know.

The gig went on, it dragged on and on. In the end, I thought it was about four and a half hours long. Beth was getting bored and I was *really* bored, so we started nipping out to the fire escape for a smoke. We came back in and someone came running out saying 'Where were you? Where were you?' I had no idea what they were talking about. They said 'Bryan Ferry was just on stage – where were you?' But nobody had told me he was doing it! Apparently he'd changed his mind – I like to think it was because of the note – but he went onstage to do his two songs and there was a fiddle solo in one of the songs and apparently he was singing away and then spun round to where I was supposed to be on stage and did this big air fiddle thing and I wasn't there! He stood there kind of going 'Oh'. I like to credit myself with Bryan Ferry's revival, of course, but I'm sorry I embarrassed him! I didn't even get to speak with him afterwards; that was it. I was just mortified.

Thankfully, it didn't seem to jeopardize Eliza's future involvement with the project or with Meltdown Festival itself. A Harry Smith Project album soon followed, featuring Richard and Eliza's interpretation of 'The Cuckoo', recorded live at UCLA's Royce Hall in Los Angeles on 25 April 2001, the US leg of the tour, and one of her recordings from the 1999 Meltdown, her interpretation of 'I Wish I Was A Mole In The Ground' with Bob Neuwirth.

She also returned to Meltdown in 2005, as part of Patti Smith's 'Songs of Innocence', an exploration of William Blake's *Songs Of Innocence And Experience*, and in 2010, when it was Richard Thompson's turn at the helm. He, too, invited Eliza to play, saying 'She's a great singer and instrumentalist. She can work in most situations, and doesn't step on other people's toes. Any project would be enhanced by her presence.'

In 2006, she was reunited with a number of the contributors to the Harry Smith Project for another Hal Willner production, this time *Rogue's Gallery: Pirate Ballads, Sea Songs and Chanteys*, a double album. But this time, things got a little more A-list: the project was initially conceived by every man, woman and child's favourite Hollywood hunk, Johnny Depp, and his *Pirates Of The Caribbean* director, Gore Verbinski, and featured Sting, Bono and Lou Reed, alongside the Thompson, Wainwright/McGarrigle and Carthy dynasties, amongst many others. Eliza's contribution, 'Rolling Sea', is an atmospheric aural experience, with the scene set from the very first seconds: creaking harmonics and subtle cymbal crashes bring to mind old, unaccompanied ships sighing in the harbour, waiting for their sailor inhabitants to bring them back to life, whilst fluttering bows on strings echoes sea wind playing upon sails. Her genial crew of shanty men, which included Ed Harcourt and the artist Ralph Steadman, join in at each chorus, grog leaping out of tankards – or, in this case, the Wild Turkey bourbon which Ed Harcourt had brought for the occasion. The band was led by Kate St John and included Bad Seed and Dirty Three's Warren Ellis on scratchy fiddle. But it is Eliza's assured vocals which make this a contribution to remember, with Thom Jurek pinpointing it as one to 'really shake up the decks'.[3] 'People are always asking me what Johnny Depp is like,' she smiled, 'but I never met him.' She did, however, meet Sharon Stone in the lift following the live performance. 'She told me I had a great voice. She is very tall,' Eliza mused.

It was the following year, 2007, when the fruits of the labour of one of her most revered lineups came into being. On the back of the eponymous Imagined Village album, the collective's first which was released on Peter Gabriel's Real World label, there is a bold statement: 'The Imagined Village is an ambitious reinvention of the English folk tradition, embracing modern-day culture in all its diversity.' It speaks of updating the tradition for a new generation. English folk tradition? Modern-day? Diversity? No wonder Eliza was scouted out as a likely candidate for participation.

The aural introduction to *The Imagined Village* is as curious as its written introduction. 'Ouses, 'Ouses, 'Ouses' features John Copper, a member of one of the most celebrated families in the English folk song tradition, fondly recounting his grandfather and great grandfather's memories of boyhood and working the land, recalling a landscape that has since changed dramatically, unrecognizably.

Fittingly, a tune entitled 'The Surburban Sprawl' soars and meanders underneath the spoken word, unsettling string drones indicating this isn't just an exercise in rose-tinted nostalgia. There's no 'ah, remember the good old days?' here. Alongside violin, guitar and Northumbrian pipes, the texture is augmented with bass guitar, programmed drums, samples and effects and keyboards. Sheila Chandra's vocals, drawing heavily on South Indian traditions, curl around the memories. The track draws to a close with a frank admission from John Copper:

> Old Bob would have been delighted that these young musicians have taken an interest in the material, he really would. He loved to share

the stuff with everyone. That's what they're for: to be enjoyed. Those chaps have carried on these songs through the thin years, when no one wanted to hear them. Old Jimmy Copper, and his father, and indeed my dad, Bob. They're the people that deserve the credit for these songs.

Long before the final participants were assembled, the Imagined Village was a concept, a seed, a conversation. It was around the year 2000, Simon Emmerson explained, that *fRoots* editor Ian Anderson made contact, hoping to get a project off the ground that was similar in taste and tone to Emmerson's Afro Celt Sound System, but which tackled the Copper Family Songbook: the collection of Copper family repertoire which was published in 1995. Anderson wanted to acknowledge the importance of these songs for the English folk tradition, and the family who helped keep them alive, by going a step further and reinterpreting them for a modern-day England: the stories and messages the songs dealt with, the sounds, the players and residents of England themselves.

In an email to Georgina Boyes, author of *The Imagined Village: Culture, Ideology and the English Folk Revival*, Ian Anderson spelt out the project: 'It's to make an album of English trad songs done by people whose music is certainly English, in that it uniquely evolved here, and who would approach the songs as songs without preconceived ideas of how they "ought" to be done. So they'd do them in their own way, which could be in be such uniquely English styles as drum and bass, bhangra or trip hop ...'

Georgina Boyes' academic assessment of the English folk revival of the late nineteenth and early twentieth century had certainly found an audience, one which was inspired by her findings.

In the BBC Radio 3 documentary, *A Place Called England*, which was first broadcast in March 2003, Simon Emmerson explained his fascination with her study and how it led to a project getting underway.

It was only once I read Georgina's book that I realized that these people who put these claims on authenticity are walking quite

163

reactionary footsteps. The idea that you can mix the ancient music of the British Isles with the modern folk tradition, and by that I'd include soundsystem culture bands like Massive Attack and Portishead and drum and bass, to try and find a meeting point, something that's exciting. And that's loosely what the project is.

Boyes' *The Imagined Village* states that the onset of industrialization, and the arrival of rural working classes to the ranks of city and town, set a trend for the English middle and upper classes to search for the pre-industrial 'innocent' culture, a harking back to the simple songs of the country 'folk'. The popularity of European, particularly German, music in the concert halls also drove individuals to seek out the 'real' English music which would ultimately unite the country's residents, summing up our collective character and spirit and with which we could fight against the 'vulgarity' brought on by industrialization. Eager collectors hopped on to bicycles and scoured the country for the old singers who could impart some of this ancient knowledge, notepads rapidly filling up with words and dots to be preserved as manuscript, rulebook, for industrial England.

Licentious, inappropriate lyrics were filtered out or tamed and diluted, much like a great many of the community folk traditions to mark the year – Whit and Mayday celebrations, for example – had before. More recent 'invented' traditions were excluded, under claims of inauthenticity, whilst the people from which the materials were sourced – the Folk themselves – were entirely forgotten; reinvented, reimagined in order to pursue a different agenda.

Without attempting to sum up Boyes' material, which is far too thorough and complex for a crude reinterpretation for our purposes here, it is an interesting starting point for a musical project. Boyes states that the turn of the twentieth century folk revival appropriated the songs sourced from the working classes and proceeded to set them in stone by noting them down, dictating, thenceforth, that this is how they ought to be done. And 'done' they were, but not by the Folk themselves: instead, these materials became something else entirely, such as parlour entertainment or genteel exercises in which to engage the middle classes.

The Imagined Village as Simon Emmerson's musical project then, was to take that material and hand it to those musicians and listeners who perhaps hadn't heard it before – or if they had, did not have a prescriptive approach to how the songs and tunes 'should' be performed. Emmerson's musicians would be English, yes, but their interpretation would be influenced by a whole manner of different things: culture, genre, age, just to get them started. In the same documentary, following Emmerson's introduction of the project, which had evidently only just begun in practical terms, Eliza was keen to reflect on her own music in reference to this theme.

'That's what *Red Rice* was about for me,' Eliza told Fiona Talkington. 'Everyone went on about that being an experimental album, but basically, as far as I was concerned, it was about getting a load of people who were from England who had never played English traditional music together before – people like Martin Green, who mainly played boogie woogie and Irish stuff and Eastern European stuff – get them to apply their techniques. Our bass player, Barnaby Stradling, grew up playing in fusion reggae bands with English traditional music as well but his main interests are in the punk and reggae areas.

'Get people from England who haven't come across it before and introduce it to them, saying here you are, that's yours, I know you're a good musician so just go ahead and do it.'

Simon Emmerson was taken with the Copper Family Songbook that Ian Anderson had handed him, and was keen to present an assembled band of English musicians with *a capella* versions of the songs so that they wouldn't have any preconceptions as to how they should be accompanied and arranged.

However, he felt that the Copper repertoire was light, generally quite uplifting. He asked Ian to show him some darker songs which could be added to the mix. Once the Watersons' repertoire was included, Emmerson was sold, and took it upon himself to assemble the lineup and produce the record, with Ian Anderson

165

and Martin Carthy as professional advisors and supporters. The project was underway. However, it didn't come to fruition until some time later.

'I remember being at the Afro Celt studio some time in around 2001, 2002, and Billy Bragg turning up,' Simon Emmerson said. 'Tim Whelan from Transglobal Underground had done a rhythm track to "Cold Haily Rainy Night", and not long after that, I went to Ian's [Anderson] house. He phoned Martin [Carthy] up who wanted Benjamin Zephaniah to do "Tam Lyn"; we wanted Martin to do "John Barleycorn". Martin came down to London and we had a meeting. I contacted Paul Weller, who said he'd love to be involved; Billy Bragg wanted to do "Hard Times Of Old England". The whole thing bubbled away for years.'

Some musicians who were approached during the developmental stages turned down the opportunity, fearing that the project would be viewed as simply a vehicle to engage pop singers with folk songs. They felt that the folk musicians might be misconstrued, as though appealing to mainstream pop artists to show them how to do it, to give the folk scene some unabashed kudos.

The inclusion of mainstream artists didn't worry Alan James, though, who wrote about the new project for *English Dance and Song* magazine: 'Passing on the baton, that essential and generous part of the traditional music scene, did not always confine itself to the folk world. British group Traffic heard the song "John Barleycorn" from Hull singer Mike Waterson. The song was carried out to a rock and pop audience on the band's classic *John Barleycorn Must Die* LP released in 1969, which is where Paul Weller picked up on it.'[4]

The material for the Imagined Village's first album came together as organically – as chaotically – as the project itself had been conceived. 'One of the conversations we had,' Ian Anderson recalled, 'was "how do you get a modern audience to listen to the story in a traditional ballad?" So we thought of someone like Linton Kwesi Johnson or Benjamin Zephaniah.'

'It took Benjamin Zephaniah a year from saying yes to actually doing it,' Emmerson smiled. Zephaniah took the tale of the young woman rescuing her true love from supernatural forces and chose to set it 'in the urban jungle of London club land where the timeless power of the yarn still resonates. The resulting musical style clash is English Dub Poetry meets English Roots Storytelling and in many ways encapsulates what the whole project is about.'[5]

Billy Bragg also revelled in his artistic license, coming up with new lyrics for his interpretation of 'Hard Times Of Old England', where the Countryside Alliance, the Post Office and Tony Blair were given a nod. And it wasn't just words which were given a reshuffle.

'The Tiger Moth track on the album started off as a Tiger Moth track from the late 1980s which Simon had been remixing for us,' Ian explained. 'He stripped it right back but got Rod Stradling in to re-record the melodeon. The recording of me and Ben Mandelson playing, though, was from the original track.'

The 'Worms Meet Moths (English Ceilidh Medley)' came about through a further recommendation of Ian's. 'I said that we should get Laurel Swift and her ceilidh band the Gloworms involved and the two bands ended up on the album, playing twenty years apart. Then we played together onstage at WOMAD.'

Of course, with all this reinvention and reinterpretation flying round, it wasn't long before Eliza's name came up. 'You've got to be really sure of who you are and how you fit in the lineup we use for the Imagined Village,' Billy Bragg explained. 'You need to be brave enough to go on stage with it, with people like Johnny Kalsi and Sheema [Mukherjee] who are coming from a completely different tradition. Eliza has a strong sense of Englishness and the ability to stand up and say that this is world music, too, which stood her in very good stead for the project.

'Simon Emmerson was pulling together the band at around the same time I was writing *The Progressive Patriot*, where I was talking about ideas of Englishness and how to articulate them, how to push the envelope, how to nudge the debate along a bit and challenge people's idea about what it means to be English. I was very pleased, I was very encouraged, that Eliza was getting involved.'

'I mentioned it to her and she was up for it immediately. She's been doing that stuff for ages, she's the real ground breaker. But she kept missing planes to come down to London and do some recording,' Simon laughs. 'On the third attempt she got down and played on "John Barleycorn".'

She knew a number of the other participants well, just through the music scene. Johnny Kalsi, for example, had first met her at Celtic Connections many years previously, then subsequently bumped into her pretty much every year at some festival or another.

Eliza did have some early reservations about the project, though. 'I thought [Simon Emmerson] was this big time producer. I thought he'd put synth washes over everything. And to be fair, he's put synth washes over quite a lot of stuff, and I never thought I'd be singing "Lark In The Morning" over a load of synth washes which is what we *did* do,' she said. 'And I think he thought I wouldn't be up for putting beats to the music.'

But even once the participants were signed up and the register was called, not all were present at each session.

'When I sang on "John Barleycorn",' Eliza illustrated, 'Paul Weller's parts weren't there. I see the Imagined Village as a train line that had a destination, but each of us were different stations along the way. We were all on the same track and Simon was the conductor, or possibly the engine driver. It's like I.V. the engine!'

'I ended up on a track,' Ian remembered, 'on which Eliza played the fiddle. But we weren't in the same room to record it!'

Though it was a collaborative project with a large number of musicians involved, Eliza was keen to make her mark.

'[The Imagined Village] is a very percussive line-up; Eliza could've simply been an ornament in that, rather than being an integral part in the centre of it,' Billy Bragg acknowledged. Johnny Kalsi agreed, telling me, 'It's not just her voice and her skills; it's her persona, her presence. She's an integral part of the band; there'd be a hole in the set if she wasn't there.'

As well as contributing fiddle and vocals to half the tracks on the album, in 'Acres Of Ground', she takes centre stage. Like something out of *Red Rice,* her interpretation of the 'Dilly Song' (often referred to as 'Green Grow The Rushes, O') is bedecked with bluesy guitar riffs, distorted vocal effects and bouncy tabla.

Of course, like all her live performances, her energy and enthusiasm triples, quadruples, and finally explodes when the Imagined Village take to the live arena. The ensemble performed 'Cold Haily Rainy Night' on *Later with Jools Holland,* broadcast on 15 February 2008. As Johnny Kalsi theatrically takes centre stage with his dhol, Eliza can be seen dancing from the very first beat, microphone in hand. As she takes the vocals, it is sensual: as she closes her eyes, lilts her body and raises her arms, she is more like a soul singer. When the breakdown ensues, Eliza is a match for Kalsi, kicking her legs and shaking her head.

Perhaps it was no surprise their rendition of 'Cold Haily Rainy Night' carried away the award for Best Traditional Track at the BBC Radio 2 Folk Awards in the same year.

After the success of the first album and tour, it was time to knuckle down and plan their next move.

Empire And Love was released in January 2010 on Emmerson's own label with business partner, Mark Constantine, the co-founder of Lush cosmetics. Sid Smith, writing for the BBC, saw this as 'de-cluttered of the likes of Paul Weller, Billy Bragg, the Copper Family, Benjamin Zephaniah and other musical worthies found on their 2007 debut album ... [the] basic plan remains in place: match-making folk tradition with the mores of modern life via a spot of pan-cultural genre-hopping'.[6]

Simon Emmerson, in fewer words, agreed: '*Empire And Love* came together as a band; we are writing as a band, now.'

And for many, critics and peers alike, the second album garnered better reviews for that very reason, with Andy Gill at *The Independent* awarding it five stars.

Opening with 'My Son John' and the inimitable lead vocals of Martin Carthy, it's clear that the Imagined Village is not just a trans-influence project – the mix of ages of the performers – from Martin Carthy's 70 years right down to the late twenties of recent recruit, Jackie Oates – goes some way to prove that folk music is not the domain of the grey beard as is constantly perpetuated.

'My Son John', the story of a young man who loses his legs during battle, also receives an update to its lyrics, referencing modern conflicts with Iraq and Afghanistan.

The album is actually brazen in its approach, choosing the songs that folk enthusiasts would naturally steer clear of, having heard them time and time again – 'Scarborough Fair', 'Lark In The Morning', 'Byker Hill' – in the hope that their collective reworking might make them listen again with a fresh outlook, taking them back to the very essence of why these songs have become so well known, whilst simultaneously attracting other music fans to whom the songs would present an easy opening through recognition of the tune.

But of course, it's not just about the fans: in tackling the very foundations of the English folk tradition – those songs that are in the collective consciousness – the Imagined Village is doing exactly what it set out to do: presenting a modern English music, in all its multicultural and inter-generational glory.

And this is Eliza's Anglicana in use, as the album repertoire not only covers English traditional music. Slade's 'Cum On Feel The Noize' is, in Martin Carthy's mouth, a mournful, morning-after-the-night-before contemplation, whilst Eliza pops it up on Ewan MacColl's 'Space Girl' complete with twinkly spaceship sounds.

In celebration of Eliza's performance, handmade cosmetics company Lush launched the 'Space Girl' bath bomb, describing it as 'Purple and sparkly [with] extra added Space Dust. Bathing in it is the closest to floating in space that most of us will ever get.'[7] Later, Jackie Oates was to receive her own Lush tribute, this time a foundation aimed at 'those with a typical English Rose complexion' which uses oatmilk in its base.

The Imagined Village's third album is well underway, with Eliza tweeting on 5 December 2011: 'Singing on new Imagined Village album doings today. Hoorah!' Jackie Oates, meanwhile, promptly uploaded a photograph to Facebook of an orange and yellow-striped tea cosy she had knitted during the course of her time recording with the Imagined Village.

Of course, for current pop and indie bands, real kudos comes with the writing of original material – covers, and the arrangement of songs already in the ether, are reserved for Glastonbury sets, Christmas gigs and encores. In the 1960s and 1970s, it was commonplace for bands to cover each other's work, no matter how recent the material, but today it is original music which builds bands up or knocks them down.

The Imagined Village is also writing original material together, with Eliza leading the charge. She has written two original songs for the pleasure of the Imagined Village, the recording taking place at her cousin's studio.

Though Paul Weller's involvement with the Imagined Village was constrained to the collective's first album, his interest in Eliza and her music continued. He had heard her version of his song, 'Wild Wood', on her *Angels And Cigarettes* album and was rumoured to have liked it, despite Eliza's embarrassment at getting the words wrong. 'I couldn't tell what he was saying!' she protested, smiling sheepishly. 'It was before the days of being able to look shit up online. Well, you could, I suppose, but I had a really awful internet connection, living on a hill in the Scottish countryside!'

They hadn't met during the recording of the Imagined Village album, with their contributions taken at different times, but Paul invited Eliza to contribute to his seventh album, *Studio 150*, which saw the singer tackle songs by a range of different artists including Gil Scott-Heron, Bob Dylan, Noel Gallagher and Neil Young. Eliza was tasked with adding fiddle and backing vocals to Gordon Lightfoot's 'Early Morning Rain' and the traditional song, 'Black Is The Colour'.

'I had a great time. He was a bit stiff to start with, but then he had a Stella and he chilled out after that. It was great being in the studio with him, and it was brilliant that he was there, him and his producer, talking me through it. I've never been a massive fan, but it was a real privilege to have his voice coming into my head; I really got to appreciate what an astonishing voice he has, a beautiful, beautiful voice,' Eliza said, before adding, 'He's quite foxy for his age, too,' a cheeky grin growing across her face.

Though she was given free rein within the studio to do as she pleased, the Dolly Parton-inspired backing vocal parts she assigned to 'Early Morning Rain' weren't met with great enthusiasm. 'His producer said "this isn't a duets album, actually, we just want you to do backing vocals and play the fiddle" and I was a bit gutted by that. But I was there to do a job, I did it and they liked it, and I enjoyed it,' she said, simply.

And though Eliza was forced to postpone accompanying Weller on *Later With Jools Holland*, he duly brought her in for fiddle duties when he was invited to perform for the BBC Four Sessions in November 2008. A satisfying collaboration indeed, then: accompanying the Modfather and impressing upon his fans.

As with her own music, Eliza seeks out collaborations that will take her – both her personal and professional reputation, and the music she has become known to represent – to different places, different audiences. She might be contributing a luscious fiddle solo to a top name from the rock and pop world under the dazzling lights of a prestigious venue or the glare of television cameras, or she may seek out a whole new project which will carry her name and her tradition to a new plane: sonically, socially, politically.

But at the crux of Eliza's work is the need for variety, for change, for constant challenge. She tires quickly, always keen to board the next ship. She wants to meet more people, try more new things. And, of course, this chapter only goes some way to uncover her plentiful collaborations over the course of her twenty-one years as a professional performer: there has been no mention of her work with Salsa Celtica, Patrick Wolf, her tributes to Peggy Seeger and Kirsty MacColl, for example, but, as she said to me in an interview for *FiddleOn*, 'I'm a pie eater[…] I always want more.'[8]

However, Eliza didn't have to look very far for one of her best-loved collaborations. It was with her parents that Eliza gained her first solid experience of touring and playing to large, expectant audiences aged sixteen and seventeen. In fact, it was these tours – including visits to Australia, New Zealand, the United States and Canada – that made up Eliza's mind: a professional musician's life was what she wanted. Sixth form, and the promise of 'A' Level certificates, fell by the wayside.

However, Martin, Norma and Eliza didn't set out to establish a family band; as with many of Eliza's collaborations, it was born out of a shared enthusiasm for music and spontaneous tune sessions around the house.

'We were invited to Elkins, West Virginia. It was a week-long thing and Norma was doing workshops on the music of the Watersons, trad stuff and the written stuff, and I was doing various things. I definitely did one on Scots singers, one on Irish and one on English singers. I think I did one on gypsy singers, too,' Martin recalled.

'Anyway, we knew that, at the end of the week, the lecturers would have to get up and give a concert for the students. We'd go to their concerts and criticize, and then by the end of the week, it was time to put your money where your mouth was. They could shout at us.

'A couple of weeks before we went, we worked out a little set … "Jacob's Well", "The Swallow", Liza sang something, Norma sang something else. I've still got the recording, it was absolutely fantastic.' Having enjoyed the performance, and following subsequent invitations to perform, the family band was formalized as Waterson:Carthy.

'It was Kit Bailey who actually called us that,' Norma remembered. 'She said that we were the only group with a colon.' 'A person needs a colon,' Martin mused, thoughtfully.

Their debut album, *Waterson:Carthy,* arrived in 1994, when Eliza was nineteen. Dedicated to Bampton Morris and the Goathland Plough Stots, it makes a feature of Eliza's frenetic fiddling accompanied by her father's steady guitar - something I like to think is reminiscent of the recordings she and Martin made only a few years previous for her music GCSE.

Though Eliza was, at that time, of course, much younger and inexperienced in comparison to her parents, she doesn't shrink from the limelight, actively taking lead vocals on both 'The Light Dragoon' and 'The Grey Cock', and taking centre stage in promotional images (a sultry stare into camera on the eponymous album; a pink and blue blur on 1996's *Common Tongue*).

It is these shots which emphasize Martin and Norma's evident pride for their daughter: presenting her as the 'next generation' as they, in the background, watch and endorse her ability and approach.

And Waterson:Carthy was a new chapter for Martin and Norma. Martin was almost 50 years old when he began to record with his wife and daughter and it presented a new flood of feelings and experiences. In the *Originals: Martin Carthy* documentary, he commented 'I'd had telepathic moments with Dave [Swarbrick]; with [Eliza and Norma] it goes far deeper. It's a mysterious business.'[9]

Even taking the stereotype of the teenager out of the equation, it is perhaps unusual for a young adult to want to spend considerable amounts of time with their parents, let alone form an artistic, professional bond. And, of course, musical collaborations with parents spell out more challenges: the frustrations of performing to a high standard when the parents have years of cumulated knowledge and experience, having performed on some of the biggest and best stages, with some of the biggest and best names; not to mention the living in close quarters and the post-gig socializing that touring commands.

But Eliza and her parents have always been very close. They speak to each other as they would friends and equals, often to the point of being painlessly frank. (Her parents' most poignant piece of advice for their aspiring musician daughter? 'Don't shag the band!'[10])

'They are all very close knit, they have great fun together,' Kit Bailey concurred. 'I have always really admired their relationship. Liza was working with her parents at a time when most older teenagers would do anything they could to get away, but Liza was never really like that. They seem like good friends.'

Being a family band though doesn't equate to a lack of ambition. The group, to date, has released six albums, and in the first year of the BBC Radio 2 Folk Awards, Waterson:Carthy won Best Group as well as Best Traditional Track for their interpretation of 'Raggle, Taggle Gipsies' which appeared on their 1999 album, *Broken Ground.*

Waterson:Carthy has also been bold in its live performances. Picking up where the Watersons left off with their *Frost And Fire* album, Waterson:Carthy took to organizing all-singing, all-dancing Christmas shows which incorporated mummers plays, brass interludes and the young vocal trio, the Devil's Interval. In 2006, Waterson:Carthy released *Holy Heathens And The Old Green Man*, a further exploration of Yuletide songs and music.

And, in 2007, to commemorate the fortieth anniversary of the appearance of the Watersons at the Royal Albert Hall, Waterson:Carthy, alongside other family members, performed at the legendary Kensington venue under the 'Mighty River Of Song' banner, a name also given to the 2004 release of a 4-CD and DVD Watersons box set.

Though first and foremost a family band, Waterson:Carthy has also welcomed the contributions of other musicians throughout their recording and performance history, many of which have happened to be Eliza's various musical collaborators over the years: Nancy Kerr and Jock Tyldesley play on the first album, whilst Barnaby Stradling, Maclaine Colston and Ben Ivitsky contribute to other records down the line. Saul Rose has also remained a regular fixture of the Waterson:Carthy lineup; an absence of leave plugged by Tim Van Eyken until he left to pursue other musical ventures.

'Waterson:Carthy is a fantastically important band,' Jon Boden enthused. 'I'm sure that their first album will be seen as one of the great folk albums of the whole revival, it's a fantastic album. I'm already amazed it's not seen on a par with *Penguin Eggs* or *Liege and Lief.* It's totally that important, as it's when the 1970s revival met the 1990s revival in a genuinely organic way. It's got all the earthiness and depth of the Waterson sound, the Martin Carthy sound, and even the Eliza sound.'

Though Norma's recent bout of poor health cast doubt on the likelihood of her returning to the stage and the studio, threatening the very existence of Waterson:Carthy, she has recovered significantly to begin booking live dates once again. And with her nephew's studio just across the road and a continually loyal fan base with a healthy appetite for future recordings, it would be no surprise if the family supergroup's discography continues to grow and grow.

EIGHT

Follow The Dollar

Now I take my baby. It used to be five dice and
a cocktail cabinet. Now it's cocktails of milk and water.
Eliza interviewed by Christopher Friedenthal
Bright Young Folk[1]

Though Eliza was no Rachida Dati, the French minister who returned to work just five days after giving birth in 2009, her maternity leave was remarkably short.

Unintentionally extended through the illness of her mother and the cancellation of the last dates of the *Gift* tour in November 2010, she started back at work shortly after the New Year, putting the finishing touches to her next album, her third songwriting album, which had a planned release date of May 2011.

Despite the arrival of the new baby *and* the care of her two-year-old, Florence, not to mention the added pressure of concern for her mother's health, Eliza made excellent progress, tweeting on 4 January, 'Two and a half songs completed today! Ahead of schedule and so far the baby is being a little star. Voice holding up too. Yay!' Nine days later, she added, 'Fourteen hour days in the studio with a nursing child? Ha! You don't scare me!'

Alongside the writing of the original material, which she had somehow found time to do in between the releases of *Dreams Of Breathing Underwater* and *Gift*, as well as their respective tours, this new songwriting album presented a new, more terrifying challenge: Eliza had decided to found her own label, HemHem, a nostalgic nod toward Heroes of Edible Music, the name she and Martin Green had given to the label on which they released *Dinner* a decade previous. Her new songwriting album would be the label's first product.

'Well, I want the money I earn to be my own, you know?' she replied honestly, in response to the question why. 'I've always been fortunate and had good deals, and I don't expect to be a millionaire off the back of this, but it's nice to be earning my own money, it makes such a difference.' And running the label means making all the decisions, a responsibility that has always appealed to Eliza. There's how the package looks and sounds, when and where it is to be put out, and how many to manufacture and issue. Of course, there's that initial financial burden to stump up, too, which becomes all the greater if sales are poor, but Eliza had calculated that if the forthcoming album sold as well as *Dreams Of Breathing Underwater*, she would break even.

'But, obviously, I'm hoping it'll do better than that because ... well, *Dreams* didn't seem to do anything else: it didn't take us to any new places, and I wanted it to do that. Not bigger places, necessarily,' she asserted, clearing her throat. 'Just different; it's a different kind of music. I don't want to be playing my own songs to people in folk clubs; I've always had a thing about that. I think that if you decide to be a singer songwriter, you should stay away from the folk clubs because they're for folk music.'

Eliza was keen, though, that while she would have a different vehicle for her new record, she would keep much of the same team behind her. In a don't-fix-what-isn't-broken fashion, she retained much of the traditional music-focused publicity, publishing and distribution specialists she had worked alongside previously, knowing full well that the vast majority of her fans would continue to access her material through these channels. Topic, for example, remained on board to own the publishing rights to her new material, whilst her regular distributor, folk and roots specialists Proper, invested money in her new project.

'What we've done is try to keep everyone involved. I don't want to slam my doors behind me and because I'm also keeping the traditional music going, I want to stay friends with everybody. And obviously if this does go very well, I'd like people not to think I'm leaving them behind,' she said. 'We put a new team together,' Liz, Eliza's manager, added, 'but our focus was that we didn't want to lose the old team, we wanted to keep the old team intact.'

The material showcased on the album, named *Neptune*, was also a mix of old, new, developed and adapted, too. 'Monkey' was another song, like a number on *Dreams Of Breathing Underwater*, which had been conceived during Eliza's songwriting challenge on Mark Radcliffe's show.

Eliza saw *Neptune* as an extension of *Dreams*, a building on the foundations that she had already laid.

'I realized I wasn't too good at chords. My dad had bought me a book for piano called *Songs Of The Forties* and I went through all the tablature and found all these pretty chords I liked and started putting them into songs. That's how "Romeo" came about; I loved the forties sound,' she explained.

Eliza has never taken to performing entirely solo, without a backing band, despite her previous manager's encouragement. 'Apart from anything else, I've got a giant in my dad who plays solo all the time, and I never felt like I could do that justice,' she said.

But, accustomed to singing songs that were so often delivered unaccompanied, songs with enormous, autonomous melodies still recognized hundreds of years after their conception, Eliza wanted her songs to stand up, too; for her original material to be melody driven so that her songs could withstand the test of time, regardless of passing phases in band arrangement and sound technologies.

And, years after the death of the writer, it would be an ear-catching melody, an eye-catching lyric that would help propel the song through time. 'I'd become aware of my previous material, like "Poor Little Me", which was completely reliant on the band. In traditional music, you're singing all these beautiful melodies all the time and you can do them without accompaniment, so I wanted my own songs to be able to do that.'

For the first time, Eliza felt like a musician, rather than a singer. 'I went in a room and just tried to come up with beautiful melodies, and I think this album really does have that. I did most of it on the piano and some of it on the tenor guitar. I was able to present the band with finished work, rather than going to someone, like Barnaby, with a song idea and for them to flesh it out.

'I'm beginning to feel like a musician now. I'm very slow. I still don't reckon I'm going to be any good for another ten years.'

And, as the album title insinuates, *Neptune* is an even heartier reference to the sea, the album packaging going to town on the theme. Promo shots for the album, including the album front cover, depict Eliza mermaid-like, a human piece of flotsam and jetsam. Her bare shoulders delicately sparkle with sequins and an enormous curly blonde-grey wig is the centrepiece, complete with entangled model ship and octopus. Eliza looks out from underneath its weight, gazing in to the distance. 'I had it made by this lovely woman whose 80-year-old mum helped. I've got photos of her mum wearing it!' Eliza told me, taking the wig down from the shelf and fingering the model ship. 'The ship's a replica of a famous one, though I must admit that I can't remember which.'

It was then Florence ran in from the living room to see what her mum was up to, and why she was *still* talking to the strange woman. 'That's mummy's hair!' she pointed up to the wig, proudly. She was right; it was. And though Eliza has long given up dyeing her hair, the almost-'fro suits Eliza well. The viewer doesn't turn a hair (excuse the pun) at the sight of the wig despite the fact we are now accustomed to Eliza's natural mid-brown, straight do.

The decision to sport such an unusual headpiece, though, came about via a little insecurity. 'Well, I was thinking about being post-pregnant. I'm the heaviest I've ever been and the thought of having my photo taken for the album sleeve wasn't appealing, so I wondered what I could do to distract people from that,' she said, smiling. 'Oh I know, I'll get a really, really big wig!'

Neptune's inlay is also an extension of *Dreams Of Breathing Underwater*'s homage to the sea through its glamorous, neon lit meander down the promenade. However, in *Neptune*, we're transported back through time. The inlay folds out and the reader-listener is entranced: we have our own antique map. Scrolls and flourishes on a tea-stained backdrop present song lyrics clustered in archipelagos across the page. Forget readability: Eliza has set us an aesthetically pleasing, authentic mission. Read the lyrics if you can, and you will find the hidden treasure – the window to her soul, Eliza's truth.

On the reverse, we are treated to a ye olde poster, advertising Eliza as the ghost entertainer of her lost seaside town. 'Neptune, in the stars', we are told, 'wants his bloody pound of fish'; Eliza and her 'fish-smelling friends' will tell us all.

Again, readability is thrown out in favour of Eliza's take on historic authenticity – tiny, elaborate typefaces are at work – but, of course, this is all pleasant folly: the contents of Eliza's album, the work that is advertised on the poster-inlay, is forward-thinking. It is her progressive original songwriting, with electric guitars and drum kits. Though there is that fleeting nod to the forties, and barbershop and show-tune, this is Eliza expanding and developing. This is Eliza now.

And, if you'd forgotten that, she will sing to you a wealth of different anecdotes, storytelling with truth, rather than fantasy, at the core.

Neptune opens with the tinkling ivories of 'Blood On My Boots', the tale of a rather undignified visit to the premiere of her friend Stewart Lee's infamous theatrical extravaganza, *Jerry Springer The Opera*. It is an account best elaborated on live, where the audience is set the scene: Eliza, feeling brave, decides to go to the London opening alone until temptation – in the form of breath-catchingly expensive glasses of champagne – takes hold and finally, there is a catastrophic downfall, summed up by the title. (And it's something that has played on Eliza's mind for a number of years, having retorted 'Really no thanks to whoever spiked my drink at Jerry Springer the Opera' in *Dreams Of Breathing Underwater*'s acknowledgements.)

Her subsequent broken nose and black eyes sadly prevented her from accompanying Paul Weller on *Later With Jools Holland* the following day. Thankfully, the host didn't seem to mind, promising that Eliza could return to his show for another performance, another time.

This episode, and its honest depiction, is another example of frank, overt storytelling: Eliza, we are told, is 'dressed to the nines', but, unaccompanied and a stranger to other audience members, is feeling rather uncomfortable in the setting of London (expensive, brash) and at a plush event (celebrities are in attendance) outside of her comfort zone (she is not accustomed to being in the audience; this is theatre and not music).

Though it is a rather exclusive situation – we might not all have experienced a London premiere – we can recognize and relate to her feelings of discomfort and awkwardness. As a result, Eliza becomes someone on our own level not the remote starlet. Of course, this is Eliza's training in folk music situations: much of the themes dealt with are concerning real people in real situations, but it is something that Eliza expands on throughout her original songwriting.

Eliza actively wants her listeners to join her in her world, and so initiates us through a series of in-jokes and scenarios that really did occur. Quite often, these situations are presented in the lyrics, backed up in the liner notes and explained during the live show, sometimes with red-faced band members denying their involvement.

In *Dreams Of Breathing Underwater*, it is 'Oranges And Seasalt' which is the most obvious example of this. The liner notes tell us that this song is the result of three separate drunken evenings, focusing on one in particular where oranges and coarse seasalt substituted the lack of lime to accompany tequila. As her poor cousin, Oliver Knight, discovered via heavy vomiting, 'oranges and seasalt don't go together'.

Sometimes, Eliza likes to include cryptic liner notes and acknowledgements which hint towards a hilarious happening, something which her contributing artists and bandmates will have also experienced. Akin to her references to the sea as a way of keeping her family and friends by her side, this bonds her and musician friends to the project by way of shared experience. It becomes not Eliza Carthy, but the Eliza Carthy Band: a group of musicians all investing in a piece of art, under Eliza's stewardship and guidance.

The album packaging for *Dreams Of Breathing Underwater* also harbours the secrets of some impenetrable scenarios and memories, such as 'the legendary Spit Roast Accident and the long-lost bathtub thieves gang', which only Eliza and her inner circle of friends and bandmates will be able to explain. Sometimes her bandmates also get in on the act: 'Ben would like it to be known that the majority of this track was recorded live in a ten-foot cube in Mortonhall.'

Heather Macleod, a regular member of the Eliza Carthy Band over the years, mentioned that hilarious situations and happenings were a common occurrence whilst the band was recording or on tour. 'The most memorable story of too many,' Heather began, already chuckling, 'was being escorted to the state line of Oregon by the police after being evicted from a hotel there by their fascist receptionist, Genevieve. The police had it sussed we were not an "out-of-control rock band" and, in fact, a "half-asleep folk pop band" and so paused for a photoshoot of Eliza on the bonnet of the police car, before escorting us off the state. Yes, memorable.'

This is immortalized in the acknowledgements of *Dreams*: 'Really no thanks to Genevieve at the Mark Spencer Hotel in Portland, Oregon, for calling the police at five in the morning and breaking Ben's fiddle.' The fact that both the hotel – a hotel which markets itself as 'Portland's Hotel to the Arts', no less – and its member of staff are named in rage, with no subtlety or discretion, indicates this is a story worth telling, something that neither Eliza nor her bandmates would forget in quite some time.

And, in fact, Eliza went on to write a song about their miserable situation in Portland, which was demoed ahead of the recording of *Dreams Of Breathing Underwater* but dropped. It purportedly had a breakdown which ran along the lines of 'Misery! Misery! Misery!' and was a favourite of drummer, Willy Molleson. 'But I won't be doing it any time soon,' Eliza smiled, cheekily.

What Eliza didn't mention in the liner notes of *Dreams*, but which occurred ahead of the Mark Spencer Hotel incident was another occurrence which actually frightened her. Perhaps her decision not to include a memory-jogger here goes some way to describing how laughs shared between friends – even in tense situations such as in the hotel in Portland – are the memories best kept: everything else is best forgotten.

Eliza had been in America on tour with her parents in 2001. The final gig was a hop across the border into Canada for a rousing finale at the Rogue Folk Club in Vancouver and then Eliza would be free for two weeks, before her Warners American tour began, with her own band.

In that luscious free fortnight, North America was Eliza's oyster. She planned on visiting family friend Roger Swallow, former drummer with the Albion Country Band, who had appeared on Norma's first solo album and lived in Topanga Canyon, LA, before Eliza's then boyfriend, Ben, would fly out and join her. The couple intended to see how they felt: maybe a trip down to Mexico? They would drive, explore, go with the flow and see where it took them.

Until Eliza tried to re-enter the US at the border. The border guard took an instant dislike to the lone musician, believing her intentions to be suspicious. 'He asked where I was going and I said "I'm on holiday, so I'm not sure. Maybe drive down to Mexico?" But everything I said, he got visibly darker and darker and darker,' she recalled.

Despite having two weeks left on her work visa, the border guard – named 'Randall, a thick-necked ex-Marine twat. Or maybe not quite tough enough to be in the Marines' – was certain Eliza wasn't telling the truth. Or even if she was, he liked teasing open the jobsworth-sized holes he tried to find in her story. 'He thought I'd disappear and go somewhere to get a job. I asked why on earth I'd do that when I'd just finished a month long tour and was about to start another one in two weeks' time. Why would I disappear and get a job as a waitress? I had work!'

Cheery Randall wanted the other part of her working visa, the part which would validate the new tour commencing in two weeks, but Eliza didn't have it. It was back in the UK, still being processed by her manager and, despite having supplied her schedule with the two weeks' holiday at the end of it to the embassy as part of her initial visa application, the border guard was not going to budge. Instead, he looked at her and said 'sk-edule', correcting her British-English pronunciation.

'I was all dolled up, I hadn't seen my boyfriend for a month, we were going to meet at LAX [Los Angeles International Airport], go on holiday and then start the tour. Instead, what happened was that I spent the night in Vancouver in the airport hotel, after being interrogated for about three hours, then flew back to London the following day, and then spent ten days in a shitty little hotel in London where we got taxis and had to hire a car and all this kind of stuff. I ended up spending every penny I'd earned on the Waterson:Carthy tour,' she remembers with a grimace.

As Eliza sat in the airport grill ordering a burger, Ben was in the air, en route to LA, and Eliza had no means of contacting him to tell him of her predicament and to warn him to turn back. 'California Stars' by Billy Bragg and Wilco, from *Mermaid Avenue*, came over the stereo; all too coincidental, given both Eliza and Ben had contributed to it. Eliza had no alternative but to ask her father to call a friend who lived near to LAX Airport and beg her to meet the hopeful Ben, who would be eagerly awaiting his girlfriend and his American adventure.

'Dad told her: "At 3.30p.m., a Scottish man is going to walk off this flight, looking for Eliza. We can't send you a photograph of him, all we can do is describe to you what he looks like, but he'll be wandering around looking for Eliza. You've got to find him". She went to arrivals, met the plane and guessed who he was. Luckily, she found him, took him home and gave him breakfast, then put him on a flight back to the UK the next day.

'It was heartbreaking, absolutely heartbreaking. Thankfully, it didn't go down in my passport as refused entry as that would have been devastating for my work,' Eliza said.

Though this memory – recalled furiously even now, a decade on – is vivid, it seems that Eliza's cataloguing of memories through her album notes is a way to document her time, like a kind of public diary, because years of touring and travelling to different places have taken its toll on her memory. 'You know when you're a kid and in the back of your mum and dad's car, and they're driving, and the scenery goes whizzing by? That's what I feel like when I think back to past tours,' she admitted to me, with an almost melancholy air.

Neptune, of all her songwriting albums, has fared best in the eyes of the critics. It seemed her development work had paid off, with *The Guardian*'s Robin Denselow deeming it 'Her bravest, most original work to date.'[2] In fact, a whole range of different reviewers raced to claim *Neptune* as the culmination of years of hard work, realizing that her songwriting apprenticeship is now firmly completed with best practice and masterful composition shining through. The BBC's Rob Hughes comments that Eliza as 'Folk scion finally finds her sea legs'.[3] Fan and music writer, Adrian Denning, goes further, wondering if 'Eliza could wind up "the greatest" of all the family.'

However, I was disappointed to discover that the gig I went to as part of the *Neptune* tour, at Bolton Albert Halls, was poorly attended. Perhaps the policy of segregating her original and trad. arr. material had finally filtered through with the larger proportion of her fans casting themselves as folk music enthusiasts, thinking that her new album – and hence her latest tour – would hold little for them.

In contrast, one audience member felt that the gig hadn't been well publicized. 'I work in Bolton town centre,' she said, 'and I purposefully had a wander round today to see if there were any posters or flyers about, and I couldn't see a single one.'

Whatever the reason, Eliza acknowledged the turnout as she closed the evening, making light of the situation by commenting 'Thank you so much for having us; you've been a great audience. Come and see us again – but next time, bring your friends!'

Eliza can always count on the loyalty of her fanbase, however small the occasion. As I observed the trestle table in the grand corridor of the venue, laden with copies of every single album from her back catalogue, it was Eliza herself that audience members hoped to encounter, rather than her recorded work which they probably owned already.

Fans bustled about the table waiting for a suitable break in the conversation to launch their own agenda. The questions came thick and fast. How is her mother? How is Florence doing? She is fine, Eliza told them, at home with her dad, though she misses her dearly despite it only being a week. She has another three weeks to go. The questioner sympathizes; she, too, has a granddaughter the same age and hates it when she doesn't get to see her for a week. 'And what is the name of the new one?' the woman asks. 'Izzy,' the woman's own daughter tells her, before Eliza has even had chance to reply, instead nodding in surprise. She tells the pair that Izzy is back at the hotel, not quite settled into the touring lifestyle.

A teenage girl bounds over to Eliza. 'I'm Becky from Twitter!' she exclaims expectantly, and Eliza gives her a hug.

'And you're learning the fiddle, aren't you? How's it going?' she asks.

'I'm just about to do my grade seven, actually,' Becky replies.

'Seven? That's great!' Eliza says, genuinely. 'I think I made it to grade two!'

Another woman comes up, clutching something rather nervously in her hands. 'I've brought you along a present,' she tells Eliza, 'it's a bit silly really, but I've made you a bag.' She holds it up to Eliza who is obviously delighted at this stranger's gesture. Eliza thanks her profusely and the pair pose with the bag in front of a friend's camera. The woman apologizes for her present; it's apparent she's now inwardly cursing her motive to bring along a gift for this musician whose music she adores. She's probably secretly chiding herself for this Beatlemanic moment. But Eliza bats away the fan's awkwardness: 'It's absolutely lovely, I love getting presents from fans. When Florence was born, I had all these people coming up to me and giving me *Magic Roundabout* toys for her. It was lovely.'

The woman is pacified and smiles back at the photograph displayed on the digital camera screen.

'Are you coming to sing for us at Whitby [folk festival] again this year?'

'What's your partner's name?'

Eliza takes each question in her stride, speaking to each fan as if she's known them for years. In some cases, of course, there are some regular faces that she has grown to know and they greet each other like old friends. She is comfortable here, giving updates on her and her family's lives, plans for the next tour, what festivals she's taking in this season. Some musicians would be mortified at this prospect: many wouldn't dream of encouraging this interaction by manning their own merch stall in the venue, let alone enjoying it. But for Eliza it works, and the sales sheet is full of tallies and the money tin is light with notes.

In the toilets, some women are discussing the gig. 'I could hear you cheering!' one says to the other, teasing her gently.

'I know, I know, but I felt like I had to do more this time, as it was a bit quiet,' she defends herself.

'It's such a shame. She's so lovely.'

I realize that the woman teased for cheering is the same woman who brought Eliza the bag. The feeling of having to 'do more' is the kind of loyalty that Eliza can inspire in her fans.

Seven months after the gig, however, and the disappointing attendance is all too apparent. Though Eliza is stoic, held aloft by the excellent critical reception *Neptune* received, the six-month review of her new company – comprising of label, parent label, manager – proved an anti-climax.

'We're about 50% down on where we'd expect to be, which I wasn't quite prepared for so I was quite shocked,' Eliza shrugs, obviously dissatisfied.

But Liz sees it differently. 'We [manager, label and parent label] realize that in the current climate, the album actually did incredibly well for sales, especially without much airplay support. It has definitely helped to develop a new audience for Eliza as a singer songwriter, and has changed the public perception of her as "just" – ridiculous word! – a folk singer.'

Nevertheless, *Neptune* has provoked Eliza into thinking about the future a little differently.

'The tour we just did – and we've got a new agent, a new business and all that kind of stuff – and the new agent and the new promoters at the new venues we were going to were all very happy, but this year [2011] I'm celebrating my twentieth year as a professional and I don't know if I want to be playing to 150 people at the Anvil in Basingstoke which is a 700-seat venue. I don't know if I can do that and leave the children at home, I don't know if it's worth it. I actually don't know if it's worth it. I thought it would go differently to this.'

Perhaps unsurprisingly, *Neptune*'s lyrics hint at her newfound responsibility as mother, and the impact her travelling lifestyle has on her children. During the BBC Radio 2 show, *The Verb*, presenter Ian McMillan caught wind of this, and drew attention to the lines 'oh the baby she distrusts my suitcase / so I put it away in a safe place / so she wouldn't see it and think I was fleeing' found in 'Thursday'. McMillan particularly liked the use of the word suitcase, something he felt wasn't commonly found in songwriting, to which Eliza replied, 'maybe it's because it doesn't rhyme with much … fruitcase?' she offers, to the laughter of the studio audience.

McMillan felt that 'Thursday' seemed like an unusual song to be written from a female viewpoint, given that so many love songs which yearn for their love over distance – impending journeys, leaving lovers behind – are from a male standpoint. Was this Eliza's chance, given the lullaby feel of the song and the child subject, to redress this, bringing the travelling woman in to view?

Eliza wasn't sure it was intentional; it is just something she has come to experience since becoming a mother. 'When I was thirteen,' she told the presenter, 'I pictured myself [travelling to gigs] with my baby slung on my back, but it's not always that practical; sometimes you do have to leave them.'

Sadly, *Neptune* also received little airplay, something Eliza puts down to mainstream shows filing the album away, believing it to be folk, something Mike Harding would cover, whilst the folk-orientated shows probably found it wasn't quite to their tastes, with no real trad. references to draw them in.

It's the kind of disappointment that leads you to look beyond your immediate horizons.

'I've been thinking that I'm a couple of years away from retiring; well, retiring from touring, with Florence starting school. So I was really hoping to spend the next two years having some really fulfilling work but actually, things have been really difficult. Live, it's been really difficult,' Eliza exclaimed, her forehead wrinkled in frustration. 'Honestly, without being too miserablist about it, I've been quite discouraged by it, the last few months. I was all about new beginnings, but actually …' She let out a big raspberry sigh, 'the world's not having it. I'm trying not to be too down about it.'

And, surprisingly, Eliza wasn't too down about it. In fact, she was decidedly pragmatic, stating her need to diversify, to change her approach, to try new things, at a time when her fellow artists were probably thinking along the same lines. As her peers offer singing weekends tutoring eager adults in their skills and repertoire; head to the theatre with touring shows and musical accompaniment; compose for radio documentaries and set down tune books, Eliza knows that her future can't quite mimic her past.

'I just don't know if there's a market for me anymore. The new business is set up really well and our new colleagues are fabulous, they're really supportive, but I'm not sure I can fight it anymore with having the children. If things had gone differently … I've still got eighteen months or so, to … I don't know if turn things around is the right phrase …' she tailed off with another timely shrug.

As *Gift* marked the tenth anniversary of her aunt Lal's passing, so, too, did *Neptune* come to carry a landmark moment. The novelty, fun-filled album inlay bears a sombre message: 'This album is dedicated to my glorious, genius uncle, Mike Waterson, playing on the laces of his shoes.' Sadly, Mike Waterson, still resident in the home he had helped to build at St Ives, the family farm just outside Robin Hood's Bay, died on 22 June 2011 aged 70, having suffered from pancreatic cancer.

NINE

Stumbling On

[Her fans] would be happy if she released another Anglicana,
*her acclaimed 2002 album, every couple of years or so.
But that's not what Eliza Carthy does. What she does
is constantly push forward, challenge and change.*
Jeremy Searle, *Americana UK* [1]

Of the 'big name' artists associated with the mid-twentieth century folk revival, still celebrated for the part they played in developing and progressing traditional music, a great number were women. They led bands, recorded seminal albums, collaborated with global superstars and wrote songs which are continually referenced and reinterpreted today. Their focus was song, their musical careers defined by song in fine voice – the voices which have gone on to characterize the sound of a genre. Though many of the women accompanied themselves and others with guitar, piano, banjo, perhaps a strum of an autoharp, it was for their singing, songs and songwriting they became known.

Now, however, the British folk scene boasts a great many female musicians playing a whole host of different instruments. There are a number of all-female, multi-instrumental bands making albums and gigging the length and breadth of the country, and an unquantifiable amount of women influential in folk music tuition across the UK, from beginners workshops right through to degree level and beyond. Of course, much of this is largely thanks to grassroots initiatives on the ground across Britain: schemes and bodies like Folkworks and Wren; the profile of competitions like the BBC Radio 2 Young Folk Award; the ease of accessibility to tunes and tuition thanks to advances in technology, not to mention the wealth of instrumentalists visiting schools, running festival workshops and teaching young people.

And though Eliza initially sang traditional music before she played it, she has become known as one of the finest purveyors of the English fiddle tradition. She and her immediate peers, though few in number at the beginning of their careers – Nancy Kerr and Kathryn Tickell, for example – are fine instrumentalists as well as singers, where tune sets dominate airtime as much as songs.

But young people undoubtedly need role models: techniques to aspire to, styles to emulate, and it is inevitable that many regard Eliza Carthy as a fiddle hero. In fact, even one of her peers – and former bandmate – admits that it was Eliza who became his fiddle idol as he was learning repertoire and honing his technique. 'She was a massive influence on me as a fiddle player,' Jon Boden told me. 'It was stylistically that sort of ballsiness, that gravitas.'

The notion of 'having balls' – determination, nerve – often rears its head when in conversation about Eliza: it's the very reason former bandmate, Barnaby Stradling, admires her, claiming 'She's got big balls. There's a danger of twee-ness in the folk scene, but Liza is a very good example of what I like about folk music. I like women with balls, those who don't make things beautiful and pretty.'

Eliza saws at her violin, notes clashing and blending, the bow hairs eating away at her strings. When she wants lush and smooth, she can achieve it, but her playing is always full-bodied and soaring; it is rarely sweet and never apologetic. Tunes, though, are when she comes into her own: she likes them fast and furious, rhythm and punctuation as important as – if not more than – melody.

Though Eliza began her career as a singer, she is now beginning to feel like a musician, as her playing, arrangement and songwriting takes centre stage. In fact, on 7 January 2012, she stated on Twitter 'I think I may be developing into a violinist.' This illustrates a newfound confidence in her largely self-taught ability: that she is now not an accompanist, or simply a purveyor of tunes, but capable of far more, of holding her own in a band, as a soloist. She is now making more of the possibilities of the violin and reaching far beyond the genre to which she is famously associated.

And it's not just the sounds her fiddle makes: there's her stance and body language. She feels the sentiment and the pace through her entire body, dancing and swaying whilst utilizing each joint, each muscle. Don't expect girl-group steps from side to side; Eliza plays the fiddle with her body. Perhaps the 'folk babe' tag was coined immediately after a journalist had witnessed one of her pelvic rolls, feet apart and fiddle wielded like an electric guitar.

To state that a woman has 'balls' is, of course, asserting she possesses male characteristics; that for her to play as she does, she is expressing masculine traits. Once Eliza's vocals are taken into consideration, it is understandable why this description comes up time and time again: she has a low – lower, following the treatment for the cyst in her throat – voice, earthy and bold. Her vocal vibrato is much like her fiddle vibrato, with plenty of depth, whilst her emphasis is power and truth, rather than sweet affectation. It's all rounded off with a good dose of her Yorkshire accent; she sings much as she speaks.

'There is a tendency,' Billy Bragg explains, 'for women on the folk scene to be fragrant and sweet. But not Eliza. I'll never forget when she was playing with me at Glastonbury and it was a particularly muddy year. She was wearing white and right before we went onstage, she went out the back and put mud in her hair and all over her clothes! I thought it was great. Go, sister!'

Then, of course, there is the material she tackles, too: a repertoire 'which has balls (or its excellently named female counterpart "clitzpah")' as her father, Martin, comments in the liner notes for Waterson:Carthy's *Common Tongue*. To sing from a male viewpoint – the soldier, the sailor, the tradesman – is commonplace, and the fact that Eliza, as singer, is female never comes into the equation: instead, the listener is taken with her emotive delivery; she is the subject of the song regardless of gender.

Eliza had told me that a boyfriend had joked that 'Sometimes I think I *am* a bloke; I'd make a great man, I'm a rubbish girl', and though in jest, the statement indicates Eliza's predicament: after all, the music industry – even the microcosm of the industry that is the folk world – is still male-dominated with predominantly male fellow musicians, sound engineers, promoters, agents and managers, label owners, distributors, pluggers, journalists, broadcasters … even fiddle makers! Eliza, in order to succeed and drive forward her musical mission, has had to make herself heard – both verbally and musically – and understood whilst inexplicably being 'the other': a young woman.

But, of course, for Eliza, who began her musical career at a tender age, and spent her formative years on the road and in the recording studio, having 'balls' – courage, mettle, pluck – is part and parcel of the job, whether the artist in question is male or female. To survive and thrive as a professional musician requires a steely determination, not to mention a unique selling point amidst the masses, which, in Eliza's case, is a potent blend of talent and attention-grabbing progressiveness. And with her signature red lipstick, skirts, boots, throaty laugh, it is clear that 'having balls' is just shorthand for a decisive, ambitious musician, keen to challenge herself and take risks to further her own and her music's reputation and understanding. She explains:

> I don't know if I wish there had been more girls around when I started working, I put together my first band out of people I really admired, and they were all blokes slightly older than me. They didn't take me seriously to begin with … But you have to man up – girl up – and be the boss. There was one incident, when Nancy and I were playing a rural gig. Nancy was wearing fishnets and I had on one of those all-in-one 'bodies'; they're back in now. It was red satin and I had some loose tights on, so I ended up putting the body over them. Then, at the end, this old farmer bloke came up to us and said 'heh-heh I was calling you two red knickers and fishnets!' and it was just horrible. I thought to myself, 'I'm seventeen and that's really inappropriate'. But it was before I learned about people's sightlines! Then there was a particular promoter in Scotland who really didn't like young

women and made it very, very clear. I wrote to him to apologize for something and his reply really opened my eyes, and I didn't like that at all. I was about eighteen or nineteen. We were working with Kit Bailey at the time who was a young woman starting her own agency, and yes, I felt we were being looked down on and expected to behave in a certain way. It's obviously a man's world, but less so these days. I really like having a woman as a manager, because I'm able to talk to her about things that I couldn't with others. Things get done in a different way.

Eliza's opinions – outspokenness, when the subject in question is something she cherishes, as we saw at WOMEX – are always proffered; she rarely suffers in silence. It is this forthrightness which has undoubtedly seen her through:

I've always been opinionated and when I've had my ideas; they've always been very strong and I've tried to communicate them as clearly and as strongly as I can. If I don't like something, I have to say 'no, please don't do that' and that's got me in to trouble a few times. Like the time I spent many hours trying to get Tim Van Eyken to play a rusty old organ for the beginning of 'Just As The Tide Was Flowing' [on *Anglicana*]. I told him I wanted him to sound like a wheezy old organ but he had spent two and a half grand on a handmade accordion. He got very angry with me about that. He said, 'what did you get me in for then? Why didn't you get someone who plays a wheezy old organ instead of this beautiful three grand handmade accordion, an Italian work of art!'

Folk musicians and singer songwriters, outside of the scene at least, tend to be conveyed as sensitive souls, a collection of timid emotion-barers wearing their hearts on their sleeves, cuffs drenched in tears for a misty-eyed yearning for the past. Eliza couldn't be further from this caricature. Though her soul is frequently laid bare, through lyrical frank observations, worrisome reflections and honest anecdotes, it is in her pursuit of truth, of the every-day.

Pretension holds nothing for her. It is for this reason that she takes such issue with the musicians – and fans – who look to perpetuate this stereotype through smock- and beard-wearing nostalgia trips.

Though she might be singing songs that are centuries old, she delivers them with a very current sentiment and experience. She has never been a gallant hussar or a bold privateer, a plough or fisher boy, a sailor or miller, but she tells their stories with conviction and empathy, and certainly with no nostalgia for times gone by, stating, to Alex Petridis in *The Guardian:* 'What bit of the past was good? Slave-based capitalism? Syphilis?'[2]

So Eliza's legacy, then, is to prove that traditional songs and tunes have as much relevance to current audiences, as they did to past. Though the literal characters and scenarios of which she sings may be playing out in an unrecognizable landscape, the sentiment – the emotional exchange – is understood by the song's subject, the singer and the listener.

Eliza makes sure that the aural landscape in which she presents her song is also relevant to the audience, encompassing instrumentation, arrangement and influence very much of the now. She adheres wholeheartedly to Ian Anderson's summing up of the timeless process, 'musicians always took what they liked and rejected what they didn't. Whatever was fun and worked, was adopted.'[3] Above all, how she appears on stage – her courageous playing, the inescapability of her gutsy voice, her love for a story – is very much how she appears off-stage, too. Whether that is sharing a joke or speaking about her family with fans, telling-it-like-it-is to the music press or campaigning for traditional music to be heard, she is determined, opinionated and passionate. So many of her interviewers over the years have commented on her rousing, hearty laugh, her tendency for swearing and her love for a good, dirty joke. They have commented on her smoking, been impressed with her apparent grasp of popular culture (South Park finds its way into one interview, much to the amusement of the interviewer) and have retold her drinking stories. This proves that Eliza not only bends the stereotype of the 'folky', she subverts it, balls and all.

The culmination of this challenge to the typecast female folk musician, however, is ultimately embodied in Eliza's appearance. Reviewers, commentators and interviewers alike have swooned over her dyed hair (from red, to green, to blue, to platinum blonde), her piercings (multiple ear, nose, labret) and her dress (bold colours, chunky footwear, baggy jeans). Her dress has never been a costume, a device to enforce a stage persona – she was just a young person in the 1990s, and hair dye, piercings and Doc Martens were everyday garb for everyday people, much as they remain today.

Though her hair dye has since been washed away, her hair instead curled into a nod to the 1940s, and her clothing now veers towards the chic and vintage-inspired, again this just reiterates how Eliza as musician does not seek to perpetuate a persona: she is who she is, on- and off-stage, as is her music. 'I guess I dress more conservatively,' she told one interviewer, 'I mean I'm 35 and I've had two kids. There's only a certain amount you can get away with at my age.'[4]

This reinforces the fact that although she makes music regarded as outside of the mainstream, Eliza isn't an oddity. Conventional media began to trust her: here was actually quite an interesting modern young woman, who could play well, with some stimulating things to say. Maybe she was worth a listen? In fact, maybe she was worth a watch, they thought, tempting her to broadcast on the television as well as radio.

It was almost as though they were counting her achievements on their fingers: two Mercury nominations, collaborations with a host of household names ... before wondering aloud 'Maybe this folk stuff isn't so bad after all?' holding out their Dictaphones to capture ... 'hang on, was that a *swear word?*'

'She didn't have to go and discover this stuff and make herself,' Martin Green asserted. 'She just appeared like that. The people who haven't grown up in folk music will understand many of the non-musical things about Liza, even if they don't understand the musical. That manifests itself in how she dresses and how she speaks. She speaks very well, she's a very eloquent woman, and that helps.'

All of this adds up to paint the picture of a rather inimitable persona: unique vocals, an extremely energetic live performance, a willingness to speak her mind, to wear and play and sing what she pleases.

'It's a great surprise that Eliza hasn't influenced more people in a direct way, in the way Kate [Rusby] has,' Jon Boden wonders in amazement. 'Not just singers, but the tune arrangements, too. It's strange that Eliza is so widely admired, looked up to and seen as a great authority, and yet there aren't any musicians who you can look at and say "yes, they're copying Eliza here". It's not a voice you can emulate, really [...] I can't think of anyone else modelling themselves on Eliza and I think it's a great shame.'

Nevertheless, there are younger musicians who claim Eliza as an influence on their own performance and material. Lucy Ward is a folk singer and singer songwriter in her early twenties who has recently released her debut album on Navigator Records. She was awarded the Horizon Award for the best breakthrough act at the 2012 BBC Radio 2 Folk Awards. Regularly sporting hairstyles of all different shapes and hues, I thought she seemed an obvious candidate to be have influenced by the Eliza Carthy legacy and it turned out that my hunch had been correct.

'I remember being ten years old and looking around the record shop. I'd seen all this red hair on an album cover and nagged my dad into buying it; I was so taken with this red-headed, pierced woman. It was only later I began to realize who she was,' Lucy laughs into the telephone. 'She's a bold woman, and I loved her lip piercing and scaffold. I realized that I didn't have to "look like a folky". I'd seen the natural hair, the promo shots in a wood and I thought "Eliza Carthy doesn't do that, so why should I?"'

Accordion player Hannah James was of a similar age when she witnessed Eliza for the first time, too. 'I was ten or eleven when I saw Waterson:Carthy at a festival. I had just started playing and I bought their album. I couldn't get over Eliza and Norma's singing, and I learnt the whole album. They never do a duff version of anything, really.'

For Hannah, who started her musical career with the band Kerfuffle aged thirteen, Eliza's image was also appealing. 'I had fifteen piercings and red and black hair when I was a teenager,' Hannah smiles, 'so I thought she was very cool.'

And though neither Lucy nor Hannah play the fiddle, it's clear to see from their stagecraft that Eliza's influence is more than outwardly appearance; it is musical approach and self-presentation, too. For Lucy, that means the way in which she blasts out her words in bold, unflinching tones which emphasize her Derby accent, softening the edges with a sophisticated vibrato, and the material she chooses to reference: at 2011's Shrewsbury Folk Festival, she sang Pulp's indie disco hit, 'Common People', complete with deliberate enunciation for extra comedic effect.

And for Hannah, it's 'her interesting arrangements and the fact that she's such a gutsy performer, really different. I think she's more rock 'n' roll than girly, and I really like that.'

Hannah has recently formed an all-female trio with instrumentalists and singers Hazel Askew and Rowan Rheingans. Though their initial intention was politically driven, to form a young, all-female singing group which would be a vehicle to showcase younger female talent and prioritize female-orientated material, the trio wanted a feminine name which would be instantly recognizable from the ballads 'but not too girly'. Lady Maisery was duly chosen, and Hannah's ear for unusual arrangement, as she praises Eliza's 'interesting arrangements', is all too apparent: Lady Maisery collectively pride themselves on the unexpected, with vocal twists and turns and a penchant for 'diddling', the singing of instrumental tunes.

Hannah is also an outstanding clog dancer, clogging for the Demon Barber Roadshow and their recent touring show, Time Gentlemen Please!, which combines English folk dance with street and hip hop dance, as well as leading workshops in clog tuition.

Though Eliza's own dancing has been limited to a few appearances, primarily with Nancy Kerr, the Goathland Plough Stots and support for Bampton's Whitsun celebrations, it has helped to highlight the importance of the English folk dance scene – for the development of the musician, as well as the profile of the dances (clog, longsword, Morris) and dancers themselves.

'[Eliza's] been an outstanding asset to the British folk scene,' Bevvy Sister and a regular member of Eliza's band, Heather Macleod ascertains. 'For many young people, she made traditional music a viable music and cool to play. However, it is, after all, traditional, so anyone breaking boundaries has the capacity to "annoy" the fundamentalists. Good on her, I say, noise it up!'

And it is undoubtedly the legitimization, the reinvigoration, the reworking, the progression, of the performance of English traditional music for which Eliza is best known – and her legacy in this area will only become more celebrated as time goes on.

Of course, to deem this a single-handed feat would be insulting and incorrigibly incorrect – she was influenced by her family and the source singers they introduced her to, not to mention the repertoire learnt from an early age; she and Nancy Kerr, in the early days of their careers, drew material and inspiration from Chris Wood and Andy Cutting, amongst other performers, and she and her immediate peers – Spiers and Boden, Bellowhead, to name but two – have all collectively worked together to ensure that English traditional music can enjoy the kind of popularity that Irish and Scottish music continues to have, inspiring the next generation to embrace the English traditional music canon and run with it.

But it is the forward-thinkingness of Eliza's take on English music which makes her contribution to the genre so great – her ambition to drive it forward and take it to avenues it hadn't yet visited: unusual instrumentation, arrangements and textures; her readiness to incorporate diverse stylistic influences, some of which appear, on paper at least, too contrary for subtle, functional integration; the assimilation of English-influenced songwriting. For Eliza, there is no prescribed way to do it.

In summer 2011, *The Guardian* ran a feature which documented fifty landmarks from the history of world and folk music. From the moment when Cecil Sharp met the Headington Quarry Morris

Men, one snowy Boxing Day, to the time that Topic Records issued its first release, the fifty events were accompanied by a downloadable playlist including some of the songs brought to life by the key events mentioned.

And at number 48 was September 1998: 'The Eliza Carthy Crusade.' It told us that she:

'... persuaded a new generation to take folk songs seriously and reinvigorated the whole genre.'[5]

Of course, such features are meant to give an overview of a genre: cherry picking a wide range of key happenings from a diverse array of sources whilst appealing to as large a readership as possible. But her inclusion here is significant: it demonstrates how Eliza, above her peers, and even above her esteemed family, has become a figurehead for the resurgence of interest in English traditional music. No other musicians concerned with the genre are featured in the landmark events documented throughout the 1990s and early twenty-first century.

But Billy Bragg is not surprised. 'The Watersons were central to my sense of what English music was about,' he said, 'and to have someone [in Eliza] who is from that place but is going to more interesting places, she's taken heritage and she's going forward with it, she's running with it. She could've just stayed within the family and carried on doing what they do, because what they do is incredible and like a mighty oak in the centre of our tradition, but she's going forward with that and I have such respect for her.'

The coining of the word 'Anglicana' has given to England, English music and English identity what American music, in Americana, has enjoyed for years: a home for musicians who interpret roots music through reworking, experimentation and original songwriting.

You don't have to be American to play and enjoy Americana: indeed, there is even *Americana UK*, a magazine comprising a full countrywide gig guide, album reviews, artist interviews and news for Americana artists, regardless from where in the world they are derived and making their music. It is simply that the musicians make music which is American-influenced.

Similarly, with Anglicana, Eliza is hoping to recognize those artists who don't simply play the English tunes as written on the manuscript in front of them, or regurgitate English songs in the manner they think they ought to be delivered, but weave in contemporary sounds and styles, and present their own songwriting which is influenced by the English tradition. To Colin Irwin, she explained herself more explicitly: 'People don't realize that when I talk about Englishness, I'm also talking about Ray Davies and Ian Dury and Kate Bush.'[6]

Whilst introducing the concept in the four-part series she presented on the topic for BBC Radio 2, back in 2004, she said, 'It can mean the music of singer songwriters, or rock music or folk music, or it can mean them all.'[7] The last installment of the documentary homed in on the modern folk scene, and Eliza's signposting of the musician Jim Moray, 'whose sound relies a great deal on computer technology and rock guitars but is rooted firmly within the tradition [...] making music which is as referential to Radiohead as much as the Voices of the People series'.[8] It is this kind of musician that is from the Eliza Carthy school – and one, with rapper Bubbz guesting on his version of 'Lucy Wan', she would firmly place within the Anglicana genre.

Similarly, Eliza has long been a champion of Brighton-based singer and songwriter, Mary Hampton. Mary reinterprets traditional song alongside her own weird and wonderful compositions, each understated and sinisterly creaky, like serendipitous records found in an attic.

Describing her material on her MySpace page as 'Experimental / Folk / Melodramatic Popular Song', her peculiar vocals give voice to her bizarre observations, accompanied by unexpected instruments (hand claps and stomps; a chamber ensemble of string and brass players entitled the Cotillion) and it is this kind of artist which Eliza knows will go on to appeal to wider audiences. Mary performed a live session and interview on Marc Riley's evening 6Music show in autumn 2011 and has released records on Rough Trade, for example – introducing 'cold' listeners to English traditional music.

Eliza is always looking for new audiences, inhabiting unfamiliar territories, to air her own music, introducing them to Anglicana through her arresting performance. She hopes, that through the utilization of her Anglicana concept, other performers will do the same.

As someone who has always liked to direct her own career, taking full responsibility for her writing and recording, often right through to production, as well as managing her band, the decision to found her own label was not unexpected. Part of this choice was to enable Eliza to better manage her back catalogue. Though she already has a 'Best Of' CD, aimed at giving the inquisitive listener a taste of her music, Eliza feels it misses the mark.

'*The Definitive Collection* is a toe-in-the-water kind of record,' she says. 'There's some good stuff on it, I suppose, and it's been constructed to be a low price record – you're not supposed to pay more than £4.99 – but there really does need to be a thorough 'Best Of' and a good live DVD and live album. That's the kind of thing you need for people that aren't hardcore fans, for people who are just a little bit interested, and those people have been held back in my life. There's not one thing with all my excellent shit on it, because I've got some excellent shit that I'm really proud of.'

As we near the end of the interviews for this book, Eliza had a great idea: how about she releases a 'Best Of' to coincide with this very biography, neatly celebrating twenty-one years as a professional musician? 'Sometimes people think Best Ofs and live albums are a bit throwaway, and I suppose they can be,' Eliza reasoned, 'but I need a good gateway album, for people to listen to something that is representative of me and representative of, for want of a better phrase, my vision.'

Although getting a book and an album out at the same time is feasible, there are distribution, copyright and marketing issues to overcome and the book and CD missed each other, but only by a couple or three months.

And though Eliza has made clear her 'vision' – as a modern, English musician – from the very beginning of her musical career, she wants to make sure that her listeners don't just see her as a singer, writing catchy original hooks or arranging age-old ballads, but as an innovator and a campaigner on behalf of English music, creating music with a point and a purpose. That said, it's difficult to predict exactly where she will turn next.

She has grown up immersed in traditional music, fighting long and hard for it to be heard, and it will remain something to which she is forever attached: learning new repertoire, finding new vehicles for it to be delivered and interpreted, returning to the research and development that she treasures. It's something we cannot imagine her without; similarly, we can't imagine the folk scene without her cropping up from time to time.

'But folk,' Martin Green acknowledges, 'pure traditional music, has never been fashionable so it's never really unfashionable. It's just there for you to play around with. I think Liza has wandered away and wandered back so many times that she can carry on doing that for as long as she likes. What keeps her interested is floating between these things. She'll keep floating.'

'She'll never leave [traditional music] behind, it's such a big part of who she is,' agrees Kit Bailey. 'It's running through her veins; it's not like folk music is something she came to because it was popular. With traditional music, it sometimes seems like she's written those songs, too, as they are so much a part of her, her own tunes, her own stories.

'But I hope she does more songwriting. She's an arresting performer in front of a band, she's one of the few people who can stand up in front of what is essentially a rock and roll band and lead it. She doesn't follow the band, the band follow her. It's because of her strong personality, and she's an amazing fiddle player. She still seems like she's not really lived a huge amount of her life yet, but she's done so much!'

Three albums in to her songwriting challenge, which is almost how she sees it – daring herself to start at two chords then progress, giving herself deadlines to cultivate new original songs, and so on – and she is enjoying critical success and her confidence is growing, beginning to view herself as a musician as well as singer.

Then there are her collaborations: we have seen how in demand a musician Eliza is, and how open she is to new projects and experiments. Her networks expand far outside the folk world and she may well be summoned by any number of musicians working within all kinds of different genres to contribute her distinctive voice and dervish playing, not to mention her encyclopaedic knowledge of traditional music, to all manner of diverse ventures. She has already mentioned a new endeavour on the horizon, a new ensemble comprising of herself, Kate Young and Lucy Farrell, recent graduates from the University of Newcastle's Folk and Traditional Music degree, and Peak District singer Bella Hardy, all of whom who are singers as well as fiddle players. What her new ensemble-mates don't match in Eliza's years of professional experience, they make up for in a similar approach to music.

'We were asked to play together at The King's Place and then The Sage in Gateshead as part of a Folkworks fiddle singers collaboration,' Eliza explained. 'So we got together for a few days and did a thing for them, and it went so well and we all got on so well ...

'I love Bella to bits, she's a really funny woman. And though I don't know Lucy Farrell's music that well, she's been getting some excellent praise for her songwriting. It strikes me that every member of this line-up has a peculiar approach to the material, number one, and to the fiddle, number two. I'm exactly the same. Bella doesn't think of herself as a fiddle player, and neither did I for a very long time.'

Following the concerts, Eliza and her new, all-female lineup were keen to take the ensemble forward. 'It's going to be a lot more than "hey everybody, let's play 'The Irish Washerwoman' at the end" kind of fiddle band; it's not going to be that. It's already not that; we're not doing so many tunes, it's mainly songs, though we will do some tunes for the album which we're going to be recording. We're going to work on it slowly, working on it all year. We all want the time to play together, to investigate more.'

Another songwriting album is also in the offing and she is also planning to make a record of traditional music with her dad: more than just the songs and tunes that they might jam in the kitchen once Florence and Izzy are asleep. 'Me and Dad are really going to blitz some traditional stuff. We've got nine tracks that we know that we want to do already; we just need to play together [to work out the arrangements]. We've got some ideas for accompaniment, some big ideas, conceptual ideas that I'm really looking forward to exploring. Concept albums seem to be doing really well at the moment, people like something they can get a handle on, a story to talk about, so we've got some great ideas about rhythm accompaniment that we're going to explore. There is the whole "why don't you sit and play fiddle and guitar" kind of thing, which we're definitely going to do, too, though, of course.'

But for Eliza, it's not just about what she can achieve: she wants to see others involved in the scene, taking things forward, her peers actively participating. She knows that she is not the youngest musician on the circuit any more, and will become accustomed, no doubt, to being labelled a 'folk veteran' or, worse yet, a 'national treasure'.

She will continue to admire and encourage emerging artists who develop and reinterpret the music she loves and respects, helping them in any way she can: from a timely piece of advice backstage at a festival, to a tune shared at a session, or even via a release on her own HemHem label.

'I'm kind of church mouse poor at the moment so I can't really think about that now,' she smiles, 'but when I'm rich and famous … I'm always saying that. I recently read an interview I did around *Red Rice* and it was one of those question and answer sessions and it asked me where I saw myself in ten years' time. I replied "on a beach, somewhere hot, eating pineapple."

'I'm still not there! That was more than ten years ago and I'm still not fucking there!' she laughed her throaty laugh, but there was definitely a hint of genuine yearning. 'I can't remember the last time I was on a beach, I can't remember the last time I was somewhere hot. I'm so bloody white, I'm minus-white now. It's living in Scotland for too long.'

Now that Eliza is a mother to two small children and essentially her own boss, she is hoping to develop a strategy which will see her use her time more wisely – if she doesn't decide to retire from the touring life completely, that is, like her own mother did when Eliza was small.

'Motherhood has definitely changed her; she's got more sense of responsibility, especially towards her own mum, funnily enough,' her manager, Liz, illustrates. 'I think when you have kids of your own, you really realize how much your own mum did for you.

'But she's a touring musician, at the end of the day. Even her recording tends to need some kind of touring to get it moving. So when the kids start school, she will know exactly where she's going to be and when from very early on. That's the plan, anyway!'

'Now that she has babies,' her mother, Norma, concurs, 'it's different. She worships her babies; she's a really good mother. I don't know [what Eliza will go on to do next], I've no idea. She has said to me at certain times, "oh, I might retire" or "I might go back to school". I would like it if she went back to school. She was offered a couple of things in Ireland and she just never had time to do them, it would've been good if she had.'

Despite not taking her 'A' Levels, Eliza has been offered a teaching position within the Arts, Humanities and Social Sciences school at the University of Limerick. Its Irish World Academy offers thriving courses in Community Music, alongside Irish Traditional Music Performance, Ethnomusicology and Ritual Chant and Song, and the more conventional music courses such as music and education and music therapy. 'When they offered it to me, I said "what about the fact that I didn't get any 'A' Levels?" but I was told I could actually study while I was working there. It's a year's post, a Masters

In Residence thing, and I was asked almost ten years ago. Though I couldn't take it at the time, it's in the back of my mind; it's something I would like to do,' she ascertained.

The decisions that Eliza made as a teenager, as a young woman, are still resonant for her today. Though she feels pride in the fact that she chose an unusual path – to become a musician working within or on the periphery of a marginalized genre – she has come to acknowledge that the decisions she made then haven't always made for an easy adult life.

'When I was seventeen, I actively chose the path less travelled, I actively did that, but because I was seventeen, I didn't know what that meant; I didn't know that choosing the difficult path would be incredibly hard. Because it is incredibly hard,' she said, leaning forward onto her knees. 'Unless you do the Michael-Barrymore-everyone-sing-along kind of thing, of course. And if you're in three or four different lineups, like I am, then people are always going to go to see the one with the most immediate reward for them, the easiest reward, something like the Imagined Village or Waterson:Carthy; that's always going to be a choice for people. There's nothing I can do about that, and I'll try and not be too upset about it. I'm not upset, angry or bitter.'

And, true to her word, she certainly doesn't show any outward signs of these negative emotions. Instead, she gets her head down – preferably with the purpose of working on another new project. 'These ceilidhs that she does are brilliant,' Norma smiled in wonderment. 'She gets together as many musicians as she can, and they all get dressed up and they all do it in proper ceilidh time so the dancers can still dance but it's all pop music. The Abba one was fantastic! They were all dressed up in those silly costumes.'

Eliza's ceilidhs began as part of her activities as patron of Whitby Folk Festival. She decided to tailor the annual patron's ceilidh to pop music, beginning with Abba, which later travelled to London's Southbank Centre. Though she had the idea, she felt her knowledge of ceilidh etiquette and set writing was limited, so called in frequent collaborator and former brother-in-law Saul Rose and the

Glorystrokes' Tom Wright, who had both cut their teeth in ceilidh bands, continuing to play ceilidhs throughout their respective careers. One of the most revered callers on the ceilidh scene, Martyn Harvey – who has his own Facebook fan club, entitled 'Martyn Harvey is the coolest caller ever!' – was also ensnared to play his part.

The ensemble built their ideal ceilidh set list of dances – 'now we do a Strip The Willow, now we do a Dashing White Sergeant, and so on' – and then assigned the Abba songs they felt would fit best.

Following on from the success – and intrigue – of the Abba ceilidh, the ensemble grew and performed ceilidhs around the songs of Queen and the Beatles before hitting on a real crowd-pleaser: Motown. 'I have to admit that playing "Smooth Criminal" as a jig is one of my favourite things in the entire world. And who'd have thought "Master Blaster" or the Jackson Five would make such great ceilidh tunes? Some things, like "I Want You Back", work absolutely brilliant by themselves, you don't have to touch them; you just play them as is. We did "My Girl" as a waltz which was just lovely. And Dogan Mehmet's impression of Stevie Wonder is quite wonderful, for a young Turkish lad!'

And for the curious, yes, there are a couple of videos languishing on the internet, showing Eliza's band in full swing as the energetic crowd whirl and jive before them.

Though Eliza's diary is looking extremely full with new recording and touring projects, she is also not sure what the future will bring. She hasn't a plan, a vision or manifesto for the next few years. She realizes there may be major changes ahead – the need to take on new, perhaps non-performance-based skills in order to make a living as the music industry continues to suffer; the change to established routine as her children start school – but she is taking each year as it comes. And who knows what idea, what project, will reach out to her in the interim, intent on taking her, her outlook and her music down an altogether different route?

More importantly, as the very first paragraph of this book illustrates, she is taking the time to take stock of her career to date

– all twenty-one years of it. 'It's just I've always taken it all very seriously. I feel the defeats, though there haven't been many. I have done very well,' she says, inspecting her nails. 'But it has been very hard work, though I did it to myself; I've done it on purpose. When I was seventeen and said that I don't want the easy life, I had no idea what that meant. Look what I did to myself!'

You can almost see her processing each chronological occurrence, both the obstacles to be challenged and the achievements: the endless touring with different groups of friends as an emerging artist, the break-ups and, sometimes, the subsequent lack of make-ups; the process of signing to a major label and feeling the impact of its ultimate unlucky failure; the managers, agents, promoters and collaborators who have come and gone, some leaving more of a legacy than others; the problems with her voice that she eventually overcame; the critical acclaim, the critical silence.

'In some ways, I really feel like I've been thrashing around in shallow waters with my work for ten years. I've had a lot of critical success but the on-the-ground work, the live work, the administration work, has been very difficult and very inconsistent. I thought I sounded profound saying that I was making all the hard choices. I had no idea what that was going to do to me, nearly twenty years later; that it was going to knacker me out and make me feel really pissed off. I am very proud of the fact that I haven't made easy choices, though I think it might be time for me to start making easy choices now.'

For the Eliza Carthy fan – or even the general music fan, who knows something of Eliza's music, her Mercury nominations, her Folk Awards, her family, her reputation – it's a difficult thing to imagine: that this row of CDs taking up an entire shelf in the alphabetized CD rack has been the very source of blood, sweat and tears over twenty-one years.

But, as Eliza herself has said, she does take her work incredibly seriously. She cannot help but dwell on the difficulties she has encountered since embarking on the road aged sixteen, often to the point that the interviewer forgets that Eliza has ever had any success at all. Until, of course, you lean back and remind yourself why you're here, and why you have had such a long list of personalities so keen to share their thoughts and memories about working with Eliza, about her legacy and influence.

And as she contemplates the past, she inevitably looks to the future. Though she may not know exactly what music she might be creating, where or with whom, or even whether she will be creating music at all, she knows that her future will be rather different to what she has become accustomed in her career to date. Her immediate physical landscape might now be homely and familiar, but her musical landscape is forever shifting, its vistas expanding as she continues to take in different sounds and styles, influences and impacts. And as the labyrinthine music industry continues to beckon, its walkways increasingly knotted and overgrown, she will no doubt find her own route through it, regardless of who is watching or waiting at the end of it.

Eliza sums it all up rather neatly:

> My mum always said that after you turn thirty and have babies, things start to get really interesting. I was always a very uncomfortable young person; I didn't always enjoy my teens and my twenties, so I've been really hoping for that. I enjoyed the things that happened, lots of fabulous things have happened to me in my life, in fabulous places, but I've always been looking for something. It's that cliché of me moving back to this place, to Robin Hood's Bay, the place you call home. I think I'm really going to be able to relax, and I think I need to. I've got a lot to give, but I came very close to giving up, very close to giving up. I'm glad I didn't.

Afterword From The Fans

I discovered Eliza quite serendipitously, drawn in by some curious album artwork. Before I knew it, I had discovered a whole new genre about which I previously knew nothing.

I wondered if there were others who had trodden the same path: was Eliza a route in to folk music for them? For some, is her musical output the sole representation of a folk influence in an otherwise largely non-folk collection? Are her fans lifelong Watersons or Martin Carthy followers, learning to love Eliza along the way?

And what was it that attracted them? And kept them coming back? What albums caught their eyes and ears?

In a very unscientific – and wholeheartedly nosy – fashion, I asked some friends, acquaintances and loiterers on Eliza's Facebook fan page whether they would be kind enough to answer a few burning questions about their experience of Eliza Carthy and her music.

Their comments are pretty much unabridged, barring a few stylistic tweaks here and there.

Matthew Gannicliffe is a songwriter from Stockport and member of Manchester's Single Cell Collective.

Would you describe yourself as a folk music fan, Eliza Carthy aside?
Everything is pop music to me. I didn't grow up in a close community where the old songs were handed down; I grew up on a new estate with John Peel and *Top Of The Pops*. At twelve I learnt Lancashire songs from a guitar teacher called Jean Applegate who ran a folk group. But if you're a child of mass media you can't go off and pick a tradition to belong to; well, obviously you can, but that's pop culture. 'Folk music fan' has a whiff of snobbiness; there can be this pride

213

that it's more authentic than something like techno, which it isn't. Hip hop fans are Keeping It Real but some folk fans really believe they are keeping it real!

When a historian like Ronald Hutton picks apart the evidence for traditions like witchcraft you find that it's actually a very modern idea, re-imagined and invented for the needs of our time. Folk music seems similar to me. It's authentic because it expresses something we feel now, not because it has the historical coherence we seek in it.

How did you discover Eliza and her music? When you learned of Eliza, did you know about her parents and their music? Were you a fan of their music?

My elder brother played me the Watersons but I was too young. It had this fierce austerity, like Joy Division or Leonard Cohen, artists he also liked, but felt forbidding to me at that age. Years later he returned from a Waterson:Carthy gig talking about their punky daughter. I was entranced by the two songs she sang on that album. 'The Old Grey Cock' and 'The Slaves Lament'. They still floor me. I've listened to them hundreds of times. Still get the shivers. So I followed her career after that.

Have you ever seen Eliza live? Do you enjoy her live performances? How do you think she compares to other folk performers?

She can be hilarious, or grumpy, or hilariously grumpy – or anything in-between; you can never guess. She appears to let the audience in on her world: current obsessions, in-jokes or arguments, and that sense of intimate spontaneity is hugely endearing. People really love her.

There are flipsides to this; I've seen her seem openly resentful of being there, which is sad if you've spent all your money on the ticket. Other times she tells the same anecdotes the next year and I realize she's not actually my mate, she's at work and it's routine. So what do I want from a performer? The truth about how they're feeling, or a show that best satisfies my feelings about them? I dunno.

In seated venues, it's tricky sitting still. At The Met in Bury, it's hilariously sub-dom; a super-polite audience being mocked and cajoled by this huge personality who then flails her fiddle with utter abandon as we sit there very nicely.

*Have you bought any of Eliza's albums? In your opinion, how do her self-penned albums (*Angels And Cigarettes, Dreams Of Breathing...*) compare to the albums where she plays mainly traditional (trad. arr.) music?*

I love all the albums. The exception is *Angels And Cigarettes* where for me the programmed electronic elements let the songs down. Beat-making is like learning the violin – it genuinely is that skilled and people who are great at it have invested a similar amount of time.

Critics pointed out the similarity to Madonna's zillion-selling *Ray Of Light* album, which came out a few years earlier, but the difference is Madonna had William Orbit programming.

Dreams ... is a wonderful record. AC/DC dream of writing album intros as electrifying as 'Follow the Dollar'! It makes me punch the air and do a horrible Liam Gallagher face. Come on! It reminds me of what Johnny Marr said about the Smiths' 'Bigmouth Strikes Again' being their 'Jumpin' Jack Flash'; one big rush that says We're Back. It's Eliza's 'Jumpin' Jack Flash'.

In your opinion, what kind of an impact or influence has Eliza had on the folk scene and the wider British music scene?

She's the antidote to cutesy hipster folk, the whimsical waifs getting all pastoral and spooked about vague ex-partners. Nothing wrong with that. Loads of it is great. But there's so much of it, it can feel contrived and fey. Like reading a shop-full of Hallmark greeting cards. Then I hear Eliza again and it's like finding a card with sharp edges that cut your fingers and a Ted Hughes poem inside covered in soil.

Have you ever listened to any of her collaborative work, such as the albums made with Nancy Kerr or the Imagined Village? Do you enjoy these as much as her solo work? (Or maybe more so?)

They're fine records but you know if you're really craving olives, or cheese, you just go and eat them; you don't make pizza with them. It's like a choir with Kate Bush in it; you wouldn't be immersed in her sound-world. When you want to hear Jacko you don't reach for 'We Are The World'.

The ideas behind the Imagined Village feel like the heart of that project, they're so important. I've spent more time thinking and reading on the website than listening to the records. What struck me at an Imagined Village gig was the power of lone song versus the almost proggy (dif)fusion of the collective. Chris Wood just demolished the Bridgewater Hall. I'll never forget that line about death in 'Come Down Jehovah' where he pauses and everybody in that concert hall was thinking about the most intimate and solitary thing, the moment of their passing, but also united in sharing that experience with everyone else. Incredible. He transformed the venue into an atheist cathedral. Then a whole bunch of my heroes come on stage and the power is gone. But that's not the point. Good on them.

How do you think - broadly - that Eliza's musical career will continue? What kind of projects can you see her tackling next?
I just hope she's able to release her music as she chooses without anyone telling her what to do. That said, playing Fantasy Folk Manager and paying for studio time, I'd wave my cigar around and demand that she takes 'Follow The Dollar' as the starting point for an album that would re-invent folk-rock. Not folk-rock in the rolling Fairport-ian style. Like the Pixies! She's got loads in common with the Pixies. The dynamics, those sections of sparse beauty that weave into complex mayhem then cut away. There's a classic album for you. Buy her a Telecaster.

The downside to those roots in the folk scene is getting fenced in there. I'd love more mainstream recognition of her as one of our great unique musicians. It might horrify her, but at some point they'll whack a blue plaque on her saying National Treasure. It's happened to Elbow in recent years and now their work has the wider audience they deserve.

In the immediate future, she's going to sing all the songs on my album because you're going to make her, Sophie, in return for answering these questions!

Eleri Evans is an aforementioned Facebook fan and recent convert.

Would you describe yourself as a folk music fan, Eliza Carthy aside?
Eliza captured me for every mood. She hugs me when I'm sad and then kicks me and makes me dance. It's a best friend in a CD.

How did you discover Eliza and her music?
My local record shop was playing her CD in the background and I found myself dancing involuntarily, I couldn't keep still!

When you learned of Eliza, did you know about her parents and their music? Were you a fan of their music?
Since being gloriously infected by her music, I have Googled her family. What an amazing bunch they are!

Have you ever seen Eliza live?
I WISH! I can only imagine that she is brilliant!

Have you bought any of Eliza's albums? Which?
I only have *Neptune*. I am an Eliza virgin, but I am also now an Eliza addict. I never thought that folk music could be so funky and sensual and exciting!

In your opinion, what kind of an impact/influence has Eliza had on the folk scene and the wider British music scene?
Massive. She has taken away the Morris dancing, odd-ball idea and made it her own. It's so unique; she has the soulful voice which, combined with folk and amazing foot-tapping music, she has made it addictive.

You are talking to a girl who only loved Michael Jackson and hip-hop. Eliza has opened up a whole new world! She sings about what we know in such a funky way (like 'Blood On My Boots') so I'm spreading the word!

Have you ever listened to any of her collaborative work, such as the albums made with Nancy Kerr or the Imagined Village?
No, but you have just given me a great idea …

How do you think - broadly - that Eliza's musical career will continue? What kind of projects can you see her tackling next?
Please don't let her be too commercial, she's too good.

Jen Blacker is a melodeon-playing, clog and rapper-dancing firefighter. She also co-runs The Village Folk Club.

Would you describe yourself as a folk music fan, Eliza Carthy aside? If yes, is it English folk music you are particularly interested in?
I'm a fan of all types of folk music, from traditional English/Scottish, etc, to singer songwriter, bluegrass, Americana and contemporary. I feel strongly about English traditional music though, as I'm afraid it will die out. Like when you say to people 'I like folk music' and they say "Oh, you mean *Irish* music" … I want to scream! "NO - folk music is not all from bloody Ireland!!!"" Ha ha.

How did you discover Eliza Carthy and her music?
I was listening to Andy Kershaw back in 1996. I discovered Eliza and Kate Rusby at the same time and I was hooked.

When you learned of Eliza, did you know about her parents and their music? Were you a fan of their music?
I knew nothing of her parents or of folk music before hearing her.

I became a fan of Norma and Martin and the Watersons later. If it wasn't for Eliza, I might never have become so involved in folk music or discovered her family and their music.

Have you ever seen Eliza live? Do you enjoy her live performances? How do you think she compares to other folk performers?
I first saw Eliza in 1996/7; I can't remember exactly. I've seen her countless times since. I've always enjoyed her performances and she's improved her fiddle playing greatly since I first saw her. She always puts on a good show – and she's funny, too, though not as funny as Kate Rusby!

*Have you bought any of Eliza's albums? In your opinion, how do her self-penned focused albums (*Angels And Cigarettes, Dreams Of Breathing...*) compare to the albums where she plays mainly traditional (trad. arr.) music?*
I've got pretty much all of her albums. My favourites are all the traditional ones – this is where her strength lies. Though there are some good tunes on her 'pop' albums, I'd still much rather listen to *Heat Light And Sound* and the other trad. albums.

In your opinion, what kind of an impact/influence has Eliza had on the folk scene and the wider British music scene?
I think she has been important in bringing folk music to a wider audience, just by being part of that generation of younger folk musicians. Also by not being afraid to add contemporary stylings to her music – bringing folk into the 21st century.

Have you ever listened to any of her collaborative work, such as the albums made with Nancy Kerr or the Imagined Village? Do you enjoy these as much as her solo work?
I have her early work with Nancy Kerr and absolutely love it. I'm not familiar with the Imagined Village, though – I saw one performance on the TV a while ago and it didn't inspire me to get the CD. I also have most of the Waterson:Carthy discs and I

219

really love them too. *Gift* is excellent and my favourite disc of hers for ages.

How do you think - broadly - that Eliza's musical career will continue? What kind of projects can you see her tackling next?
I imagine her career will continue strongly, with much collaboration in many different avenues of music. I don't know how motherhood will affect the immediate future of her music or projects, but with Liza anything is possible!

Becky Travers was born in 1995, two decades after Eliza, and a decade after myself. Becky is currently a student and an aspiring musician.

Would you describe yourself as a folk music fan, Eliza Carthy aside?
I wasn't actually a big folk fan before I was introduced to Eliza's music. I liked the occasional song; however, after listening to Eliza's music, I am now much more of a folk fan. Her music has influenced me a lot. I didn't know about her parent's musical ability until after I had discovered Eliza Carthy. But after talking to relatives they assured me how much of a talented musical family they were.

How did you discover Eliza Carthy and her music?
Well, I discovered Eliza through my family, around six months ago. My relatives have been to see Eliza a few times in the past and have purchased several of her albums. I had borrowed a couple of albums off my relatives to listen to and loved them! So when it was announced that Eliza was coming to perform in Bolton, I was very pleased to say I was attending. Her live performances are brill! It's not just the music, but also the way she has a little bit of a dance around the stage and a laugh. She's a real audience pleaser!

What was it that attracted you to her music?

I was attracted to Eliza's music by her use of instruments and her amazing voice! She is a very talented lady, able to play the accordion, guitar and violin, as well as sing. She uses a variety of instruments from song to song – sometimes playing two or more instruments in one song! This made me want to pay more attention to Eliza's music.

Was Friday 20 May 2011 at Bolton Albert Halls the first time you've seen her live, or have you seen her elsewhere?

That was the first time I have seen Eliza live, but I am more than prepared to go again on her next tour!

*Have you bought any of Eliza's albums? In your opinion, how do her self-penned focused albums (*Angels And Cigarettes, Dreams Of Breathing...*) compare to the albums where she plays mainly traditional (trad. arr.) music?*

I personally don't own any of Eliza's albums. However, I've borrowed *Heat Light And Sound*, *Red* and *Neptune*. My favourites are Eliza's older tracks. This is merely because I enjoy listening to the fiddle as I play the violin myself.

I do enjoy her own material as well as her traditional music. I enjoy rock music as well as folk music, and so listening to her own original material is great because of her voice, the drums and the acoustic guitar.

I also thoroughly enjoy watching Eliza play the violin, mainly so I can steal a few sneaky techniques of hers – and so her traditional music is best for this.

You've been playing the violin for a long time yourself. Is Eliza an influence on the way you play and the material you play?

Yes, I have been playing the violin for six years now (obviously nothing compared to Eliza!) At the moment, I am studying for my grade seven and so I am fairly limited as to what I am playing. However, as soon as I have completed my grades, I will be playing along with a few of Eliza's tracks at home!

She is definitely an influence on how I play. At the gig, I thoroughly enjoyed watching the way in which she expressed the music through the movement of her body on stage. I really liked the way in which she plays the technical bits, such as double stops, and this will help me in my exam to come. Her confidence really inspires me.

What do you think makes Eliza different from other musicians?
She displays a variety of different musical tastes and abilities, whereas most other musicians stick to their one type of music. This demonstrates how Eliza isn't afraid to come out of her comfort zone.

Michael Doward is a sought-after double bassist, playing with Samson and Delilah, Last Harbour and the Woodbine and Ivy Band. By day, he sells all manner of different instruments. He also performs his own material under the moniker Crazy Man Michael.

Would you describe yourself as a folk music fan, Eliza Carthy aside? If yes, is it English folk music you are particularly interested in?
I am a folk music fan, most certainly; my mum used to listen to bits of folk and folk rock when I was little (including a memorable trip to see Steeleye Span when I was twelve) and I completely rejected that as I got into music and when I went to university.

But, slowly, I began to get into folk music after university. The way in was mainly through the English tradition and the folk rock of Fairport and the Albion band particularly; since then my tastes have broadened and I'm into folk from a lot of different cultures.

How did you discover Eliza and her music? Did you know about her parents and their music?
My mum was a big fan of the Carthys and their music, and memorably I saw Eliza Carthy perform with Martin a few days before her seventeenth birthday. She played 'Seventeen Come

Sunday'. When *Red Rice* came out, my mum got it and I think it was one of the first folk records where I thought, 'Oh yeah, this is pretty good'. I became aware of Norma when her first solo album came out. I can't say I was a fan of Norma and Martin's music when I discovered Eliza's but I've certainly become so since.

Have you ever seen Eliza play live? How do you think she compares to other folk performers?
I've seen Eliza play on quite a few occasions. First time was Band On The Wall in probably 1997 or 1998. It was supposed to be a Waterson:Carthy gig but Norma was poorly so Martin and Eliza played. My girlfriend at the time ended up chatting to Eliza about hair dye. I saw them again at Glastonbury one of those two years and have seen her, both solo and with Waterson:Carthy, now and again since – most recently at the Priddy Folk Festival last July [2011].

*Have you bought any of Eliza's albums? In your opinion, how do her self-penned albums (*Angels And Cigarettes, Dreams Of Breathing...*) compare to the albums where she plays mainly traditional (trad. arr.) music?*
Ha ha, how embarrassing. I don't currently have any of her albums – because my mum's a fan and has most of them, I tend to listen to them when I'm at my parents. I have purchased most of her albums, but as gifts for my mum!

I think she excels at both ends of that spectrum. Her original material is inventive and challenging and isn't frightened of stepping outside the folk genre – *Neptune* being the most extreme example to date. In turn, I think her musical inventiveness comes across in her interpretation of traditional music and makes those some of the most exciting interpretations in contemporary folk music.

In your opinion, what kind of an impact has Eliza had on the folk scene and the wider British music scene?
I think she's been incredibly important in making folk music acceptable and palatable to a younger generation of nascent folk

fans. She provides them with a way in to more traditional folk because she incorporates contemporary styles of music into traditional arrangements – and conversely uses folk stylings in her original music.

On the downside, I think it means she hasn't been as successful as she should have been because a lot of traditional folkies are turned off by that use of contemporary influences and a lot of younger listeners will still see her as 'folk' and therefore 'uncool'. A case in point of the former was Priddy last July at which she played an incredible set. I think a lot of the older audience members were turned off by the almost 'show tune' feel of a lot of the songs and didn't get it or felt it wasn't folky enough.

How do you think – broadly —that Eliza's musical career will continue? What kind of projects can you see her tackling next?
I very much hope she continues to be creatively diverse and experimental. I hope she'll go on following her muse and whatever direction she feels she wants to take her music or her music takes her. I hope she will, much like Martin, receive proper recognition and acclaim for doing what she does and being a vital, eclectic and iconoclastic part of the folk music scene.

Chris Long is a proud beard owner and Yorkshireman, who is also a journalist and producer on the wrong side of the Pennines.

Would you describe yourself as a folk music fan, Eliza Carthy aside?
Well, I am a latecomer to folk in general and it was through an ex of mine, as it tends to be, you find music through other people. Her father's actually a folk singer from a family of folk singers. And, being with her, I got used to being around folk music and suddenly, you discover this family that exists, this other world and all these amazing experiences. It's very friendly.

And of course, there's always two names that come up: Waterson and Carthy. So you go down that road of excavating, as you do with any music; one musician leads to another. But what you find with those two names is that they are at the centre of one world.

How did you discover Eliza and her music?
So I remember that Waterson:Carthy played a gig at the Lowry, perhaps six or seven years ago, maybe longer, and I thought that as I was doing music reviews at the time, why not? I'd go along to whoever, Coldplay, Kings of Leon, whoever, and [W:C] were essentially at the same level, but in folk. So why not? They're your stadium rockers of folk.

I was aware that it was the family band, Norma, Martin, Liza, Tim Van Eyken, and I sat down and they came out. Your eyes are drawn instantly to Liza. Norma comes out, a beautiful, handsome lady; Martin comes shambling out with his guitar. But Liza, I think at the time had blue hair and massive boots on and I thought 'wow, that's not what I expected from folk.'

You hope that you don't think in clichés, but the reality is ... I grew up as a rock and indie music fan, into Nirvana and people like that, that's the world I inhabited as a teenager. To that world, folkies were bearded, jumper wearing ... and as much as you think that's not gone in, it's there at the back of your head.

So the first time you see Eliza, you think 'wow, I don't know where I'm going with this, my head's going to explode!' and it was just mesmerizing, the whole gig. The whole of the family are mesmerizing, but particularly Eliza: she is exactly as she should be, a combination of Martin and Norma. She's got the voice, the playing, the humour – everything comes together with her. And from that moment, I thought that I've got to know more: back catalogue and following her from that point onwards. I just think that she's such a fantastic musician, a stunning musician.

225

Have you ever seen Eliza, aside from your first experience of Waterson:Carthy? Do you enjoy her live performances? How do you think she compares to other folk performers?

Yes, I've seen her live by herself and it is a different experience. She's a very individual performer. You only see Eliza Carthy; you're not thinking 'who does she sound like?' or 'where has she got that from?'

Blue hair, or pink hair, or sometimes it's just the normal coloured hair and that really weirds you out, but she is who she is. You get that a lot more when it's just her because when she's on stage with her mum and dad, there's a certain 'you saw me in my nappies' type thing. She cuts loose a lot more when she plays solo, and without wanting to sound belittling to her, she's a lot more adult when she plays her own gigs for obvious reasons. When she's in charge, it's a different experience.

She's a brilliant fiddle player, but she's not the best you'll ever see. She's a brilliant singer, but she's not the best you'll ever hear. What brings it all together is her personality, her emotion, everything that she puts together in her songs. And I just think it's the complete package, from the massive boots to the fiddle playing. It's the honesty, I suppose.

She knows she's not the best singer: for one reason, she's Norma's daughter, so she's not even the best singer in her family, so it's that knowledge and self awareness that makes her a special performer.

*Have you bought any of Eliza's albums? In your opinion, how do her self-penned albums (*Angels And Cigarettes, Dreams Of Breathing...*) compare to the albums where she plays mainly traditional (trad. arr.) music?*

The *Dreams* album is phenomenal; it's so varied. It's not just about being an interesting musician at the forefront. One of the best things about that album is 'Mr Magnifico' which is actually very little about Liza – she's actually just orchestrating it. That's very interesting as it shows someone who is happy to stand back from their star. And I suppose that does come from being in folk: you're never going to be a superstar in folk music because at the end of the day, someone will say 'come on, let's go to a singaround' and then you'll be a nobody. They'll sing like the rest of us, and then there'll be some guy who can't sing at all and he'll get as big a round of applause as what you'll get.

The thing that I like about Eliza is that she hasn't been just influenced by the folk world – in the same way that Norma hasn't and Martin hasn't – they don't just live in a bubble. I would compare Liza to someone like Bjork. When you look back at their whole body of work, yeah, there are some bits that have dated badly, there are some that have dated but still sound great. That's the point of being a classical musical adventurer. If she hears something interesting, she wants to get involved with that.

The status she has within the scene means she can record it and sell it, but even if she didn't have the status, she still would have made *Red Rice*; it just probably wouldn't have been heard.

Does she stand by it now? I don't know. She probably thinks exactly the same as we do: that it sounds of its time, there's nothing wrong with that. There are plenty of songs that have a timeless quality to it, and no artist can live outside the time when they are creating music if they are prepared to be involved with the music around them. Just because she's investigating something from 150 years ago, doesn't mean that she shouldn't investigate drum and bass when that was happening. And to get a bit Radio 4 about it, that was the folk music of the day. So why wouldn't she be involved in it?

In your opinion, what kind of an impact has Eliza had on the folk scene and the wider British music scene?

She never disguises herself in someone else's songwriting, even if they may be 100 years old, or 150 years old. She'll have investigated them, she knows the history of them but the nice thing about her is the same thing about her wider family: they don't treat the songs with reverence, and that's important.

227

There's no getting away from the fact that if you're singing about a handweaver's daughter, you're not likely to be a handweaver's daughter and you haven't a clue how to use a hand loom, you've no idea at all. So if you treat that with too much reverence, it doesn't feel realistic.

If you get stuck in like the Waterson Carthy family does, getting right into the bones of the song, you feel more attached to it. And that's what Eliza does, she gets right into it. It's ridiculous that she's singing about a guy going away to war to fight Napoleon, she doesn't know anyone who has done that. But she looks inside it to find the real emotion of the song and it's that she pulls out. So essentially the words might be about a guy who's going away to fight Napoleon, but she's bringing in her own experience: leaving someone on a platform, or whatever.

Have you ever listened to any of her collaborative work, such as the albums made with Nancy Kerr or the Imagined Village?
You're never surprised at any of the Watersons and Carthys turning up in things; they're musical adventurers all over. Always open to a new idea, and if someone presents an idea to Eliza, she probably thinks, yes, why not? Why wouldn't I want to be involved? You're always going to, especially if you come from that tradition of everyone comes with an idea, everyone comes with a song. I sing mine, you sing yours, and eventually we come together and out of that ramshackle night, we either get hangovers or an album.

Inevitably, an album like the Imagined Village's is going to be a glorious failure. It can't encapsulate England today, it can't represent everyone, but there's nothing wrong with trying that. As long as you've all had a crack, you've all had fun, and there's something you can be proud of there, as long as you put your heart and soul in it, I don't see a problem.

There are elements of it that just don't work at all; there are elements that work nicely. But as you look back on it, you might think that's 'an' England, not *the* England of the day, but 'an' England of the day.

How do you think - broadly - that Eliza's musical career will continue? What kind of projects can you see her tackling next?

I think the beauty of Liza is that it is impossible to tell. With Kate Rusby, you can look at her and think yeah, I pretty much know where you're going next. I'll enjoy it, it'll be great and you're a great live singer, but you know where she'll go.

And I genuinely don't with Liza.

She's had a baby, so maybe she'll write a song about motherhood, or maybe she won't at all, maybe she'll ignore the fact that she's had a baby completely. That's the beauty of it. I never saw *Gift* coming, or *Dreams*. From a journalistic point of view, when an Eliza album lands on my desk, I wonder what it's going to be. That's the luxury she's found herself in, she's found it through talent and hard work.

She's a very giving musician, she is happy to work with other people. She's true to that tradition of 'bring along your violin and we'll see where it goes'. The reality is that with record deals, however open and folky they might be, they are still record deals and there is only so much you can do it that way these days.

Tim Powell-Jones is a disciple of His Bobness and dances an idiosyncratic dance to the tune of his own bass. He also likes a good dose of the Welsh language.

Would you describe yourself as a folk music fan, Eliza Carthy aside? If yes, is it English folk music you are particularly interested in?

Yes, but mostly weird folk music as opposed to serious young men with beards and acoustic guitars (i.e. preferably wouldn't sound out of place on *The Wicker Man* soundtrack). And yes, particularly English folk music, as it's more relevant to me than someone singing about highways and chain gangs.

229

How did you discover Eliza Carthy and her music?
Through you, Sophie!

When you learned of Eliza, did you know about her parents and their music? Were you a fan of their music?
I was aware of them and had heard them on folk compilations, and possibly BBC Four, though that could have been later. Liked it and do like it now, but heard Eliza first.

Have you ever seen Eliza live? Do you enjoy her live performances? How do you think she compares to other folk performers?
Yes, Manchester Academy 3. It was amazing, and completely converted [my girlfriend] Mel to thinking she's great too, despite initial scepticism about being taken to a folk gig.

Have you bought any of Eliza's albums? In your opinion, how do her self-penned albums (Angels And Cigarettes, Dreams Of Breathing...) compare to the albums where she plays mainly traditional (trad. arr.) music?
I am bad and don't really buy albums, but I think I prefer the more trad. arr. stuff ... but if you ONLY play trad. arr. stuff then it's hard to see how it can ever develop beyond Ewan MacColl with his finger in his ear.

In your opinion, what kind of an impact/influence has Eliza had on the folk scene and the wider British music scene?
She's one of the people that helped remind people what was good about folk music in the first place, and that it's not just for old folks.

How do you think - broadly - that Eliza's musical career will continue? What kind of projects can you see her tackling next?
I'd imagine as you get older you drift further and further back to your roots (like Bob Dylan has been doing) ...

Claire Godden is a nomadic fiddle player and is licensed to operate chainsaws.

Would you describe yourself as a folk music fan, Eliza Carthy aside? If yes, is it English folk music you are particularly interested in?
Before I discovered Eliza Carthy I was a fan of 'folky' sounding music such as Nick Drake, Joni Mitchell and Bob Dylan. As a child I enjoyed listening to a tape of traditional Irish dance tunes that my Irish neighbour gave me and my favorite tape was by Tim Laycock, a traditional English folk singer that'd visited my school. But until I discovered Eliza Carthy, I didn't really know that English folk music existed in any kind of scene. In the days before the internet, lack of exposure meant that I simply didn't know what existed or what was out there.

I have since become interested in English folk music and have started learning traditional English tunes on the violin. I thought English tunes would be a good place to start, as they are slower than the Irish tunes, therefore a bit easier to learn. Also, as I am English, I thought I should start with my own tradition.

Now I am particularly interested in English folk music, in a large part thanks to Eliza Carthy. Eliza Carthy is like a gateway drug, making English traditional music accessible, current and addictive. Listening to her music has led me on a trail of discovery of all sorts of traditional English music.

I now enjoy all kinds of folk music. I have recently been learning some traditional Breton tunes and Klezma and enjoy listening to Scottish songs and tunes.

How did you discover Eliza Carthy and her music?
I discovered her through a friend who'd borrowed her CDs from Manchester Central Library.

When you learned of Eliza Carthy, did you know about her parents and their music? Were you a fan of their music?
I'd never heard of her parents or their music before I discovered Eliza Carthy. I have discovered her parents through her.

Have you ever seen Eliza live? Where? Do you enjoy her live performances? How do you think she compares to other folk performers?
I first saw her live at the Bury Met with the Ratcatchers. I saw her there again doing her own penned songs and songs from *Dreams Of Breathing Underwater*. I've also seen her live at Band On The Wall with the same band doing a similar set of mostly self-penned songs. I've also seen her doing a solo performance at Festinho festival. And I've seen her at the Bridgewater Hall with the Imagined Village.

Her solo performance at Festinho festival was very moving. Stripped to bare bones of voice and fiddle, her talent is allowed to speak for itself. Her playing style, where the fiddle becomes an extension of her voice, and her instinctive arrangements of songs make her a powerful live performer. Her performance with the Ratcatchers wove crunchy arrangements with infectious musicianship, razzmatazz and showbiz. Moving ballads worked side by side with hearty stomp. Her small band managed to sound like a whole folk-plunk orchestra.

I've been disappointed by some of her recent gigs where she's performed some songs from *Dreams Of Breathing Underwater*. I absolutely love listening to the album, but her live sets have felt like a hotchpotch of songs that don't flow together into a coherent show. In moments, they have flown into a magical spin, but not consistently. She has complained about being on tour, and even opened her set at Band On The Wall with a song about the trials of live performance. When you've paid £15 to see a show, you want to be tricked into believing that the performer believes enough in what they're doing to want to share their material with you. These gigs have lacked direction but I'm sure Eliza will return to form when she finds a new project that inspires her.

*Have you bought any of Eliza's albums? Which? In your opinion, how do her self-penned albums (*Angels And Cigarettes, Dreams Of Breathing...*) compare to the albums where she plays mainly traditional (trad. arr.) music?*
My favourite albums are *Rough Music* and *Dreams Of Breathing*

Underwater. I can see why she keeps the two different strands separate, as they encompass very different styles. I think she is top of her game when playing the traditional arrangements. Eliza has a knack of choosing fantastic traditional songs. I find some traditional songs rather annoying. She manages to stay clear of these, or maybe they are no longer annoying when shaped by her. I'd like to hear her 'pop' songs produced by some top pop producers.

In your opinion, what kind of an impact has Eliza had on the folk scene and the wider British music scene?
Eliza's music is free from whimsy and she's carved a musical space that is honest and bold in contrast to the saccharine sickly girly sweet singers that are the norm and the stereotype of female folk singers. Most women folk singers are expected to sound like good-as-gold-butter-wouldn't-melt angels, but Eliza's voice is devilishly free, blokily-deep and true to herself. In her refusal to be constrained by conservative expectations, she has helped create a platform for other original, innovative and unshackled musicians. I suspect she has encouraged great bands such as Lau and Bellowhead to make the sort of albums that they really want to make, anarchically free from constraint. She has helped to create a fine tradition of expressive innovation.

Have you ever listened to any of her collaborative work, such as the albums made with Nancy Kerr or the Imagined Village? Do you enjoy these as much as her solo work?
I enjoy listening to Eliza's solo work more than her collaborations with the Imagined Village and Nancy Kerr, but I don't think she'd have made such varied solo records without having had the experience of collaborating with other musicians. Her work has matured since her early albums with Nancy Kerr, she has grown in confidence and her delivery is now more professional, subtle and stronger.

The Imagined Village was successful in inspiring my imagination of a real or fictitious England, picturing its evolving traditions and interwoven influences. I found the concept hugely inspiring, setting my brain into a whirr and encouraging me to follow thought-threads set in motion by the project and the collaborators. However, for me, the music wasn't as inspirational as the idea itself. Maybe the concept was just too huge to tie down into an album or two of music. I think they set themselves an impossible task; how do you fuse together a whole generation of music without muddying the styles? I'm glad they've set the ball in motion and hopefully they will have inspired others to take on similarly inspiring challenges.

How do you think - broadly - that Eliza's musical career will continue? What kind of projects can you see her tackling next?

I'm excited to see what tack she will take next. One of the refreshing things about her music is that she takes it in surprising and unpredictable directions. I do think she needs something new to get her teeth into; the last few times I've seen her live she's seemed to lack a coherent direction (or maybe just enthusiasm for gigging.) I'm sure that something new is brewing, and I look forward to seeing what it is.

I'd also like her to collaborate with Janelle Monáe, please … Oh, and I'd like her to make an album of songs and rounds for campfires and sing-songs … Or she could collaborate with top European folk singers … She could do a concept album about Robin Hood … She could write a musical about pirates … She could do a collaborative live show with Kate Bush, Bjork, and Joni Mitchell.

Shelley Rainey is a singing teaching assistant, one-third of the Bailey Sisters, Social Editor at *Bright Young Folk* and a Bellowhead fanatic.

Would you describe yourself as a folk music fan, Eliza Carthy aside? If yes, is it English folk music you are particularly interested in?

Very much a folk music fan, my first 'discovery' being Steeleye Span, in the 1970s. I remember seeing them on *Top Of The Pops* and thinking [of Maddy Prior] 'I want to sing like her!' I suppose I am primarily interested in English folk music, (Bellowhead have become a bit of an obsession), but I like some of the crossovers that have emerged in recent years, and like to hear traditional music from other countries, too. I particularly love the music of the Québecois trio, Genticorum.

How did you discover Eliza and her music?
According to Cropredy t-shirts I own, I saw Eliza Carthy and the Kings Of Calicutt in 1997, and the Eliza Carthy Band in 2001, but somehow they didn't register. I can't think why (although having three young children with me may have been a factor)! I first consciously saw her live with her dad and Saul Rose at Saddleworth Folk Festival a few years ago (Norma should have been there too, but was ill. I didn't see Norma live until Sidmouth last year, as a member of Blue Murder), I loved Eliza's playing and the way she stomped around the stage. She has a fantastic stage presence.

When you learned of Eliza, did you know about her parents and their music? Were you a fan of their music?
I was aware of her parents' music, (and her dad's involvement with Steeleye Span, of course) but I hadn't really heard any. I'm filling in gaps in my knowledge now.

Have you ever seen Eliza live? Where? Do you enjoy her live performances? How do you think she compares to other folk performers?
As I've said above, Eliza has a fantastic stage presence. She tells some great stories, too! I've seen her as part of Waterson:Carthy, with the Imagined Village and also with her own band (at least three times). She is one of several artists on the folk scene at the moment I would happily go and see again and again.

*Have you bought any of Eliza's albums? In your opinion, how do her self-penned albums (**Angels And Cigarettes, Dreams Of Breathing...**)*

235

compare to the albums where she plays mainly traditional (trad. arr.) music?

I'm buying her albums backwards, I think! *Dreams Of Breathing Underwater* was the first one I owned. I heard her interviewed about it on Radio 4(!) and was intrigued. I bought the album when it came out and loved it. I'm now working through her back catalogue in a rather haphazard manner. (*Anglicana, Kings Of Calicutt ...*) I know some of my friends have been disappointed with her self-penned material, but that hasn't happened to me because I heard that first! She is a talented arranger of traditional songs and tunes though, and has worked with some great musicians.

In your opinion, what kind of an impact has Eliza had on the folk scene and the wider British music scene?

I would hope that people who would not usually listen to folk would hear her original material and want to find out more, and would then discover the wonderful world of folk music.

Have you ever listened to any of her collaborative work, such as the albums made with Nancy Kerr or the Imagined Village? Do you enjoy these as much as her solo work?

The Imagined Village is such an exciting project, bringing together so many different musical styles and traditions. Exciting enough to listen to on CD, but live – wow!

How do you think – broadly – that Eliza's musical career will continue? What kind of projects can you see her tackling next?

I expect she will continue to develop her own songwriting (I believe *Neptune* is all original material – don't have a copy yet) and the Imagined Village. I believe projects like these bring folk to a wider audience as people will want to know more about the musical backgrounds of the people involved.

Matt 'Wayland' Copley tells stories across Britain and Europe and seems to be rather fond of our Eliza!

Would you describe yourself as a folk music fan, Eliza Carthy aside? If yes, is it English folk music you are particularly interested in?
Yes, I love traditional music in general, not just Eliza. I love folklore, you see, and feel we are very lucky to live in a country with such a rich and intriguing folk tradition. For me, Eliza and her ilk are as much a part of that tradition as fairies, the devil and Dick Turpin! You see, I'm a storyteller, and see myself as part of the same tradition that Eliza belongs to. Make no mistake though – she is far more proficient than I!

So I guess I like songs best that remind me of folklore. Songs about the Battle of Waterloo, about hares, about ghosts, about troubled lovers (those sad songs!), songs about pirates! Eliza does an awesome song about Captain Kydd. 'My parents taught me well/ to shun the gates of 'ell!' You see, there's history and there's folklore and they go side by side. One is what happened, while the other is what didn't happen. Folk tradition is the stories we, as a nation, tell ourselves about our shared past.

I like quite a few modern acts like Eliza and the Unthanks, and the generation before them like Maddy Prior and the Watersons, but the songs are the things, and some of them are hundreds of years old. I enjoy Irish and Scottish Traditional music, too.

I think that Eliza is a great ambassador for England and Englishness. I know that she despises the racism of the BNP and was extremely cross when Nick Griffin said he was a fan of hers a few years back. Eliza is very well rooted in the traditions of this country, but at the same time she is a modern person, and not nostalgic about some Arcadian age in British history. She understands that we are a multicultural nation and always have been. So Eliza takes a very strident stance against racists who want to legitimize who is British and who isn›t. She is anti-anti-immigration, and shows there›s a way you can be English and not indulge in petty prejudices.

How did you discover Eliza Carthy and her music?
Well, I discovered Eliza's fellow Yorkshire lassie Kate Rusby first, and loved her, then I saw an Eliza collection in HMV. This is a few years ago, and I think I had heard the name, but didn't know any of her stuff. I got it, and did quite like it, but I've got to admit it took me a while to get into it. I think it's because Kate's music and playing are much more straightforward, whereas Eliza's voice and her fiddle do unexpected things and come in from unexpected directions. I still really like Kate, but bless her, she does wilt a bit next to Eliza, because Eliza is a better musician, a better singer and about 50 times as charismatic!

When you learned of Eliza, did you know about her parents and their music? Were you a fan of their music?
It was the other way around. For me Eliza came first, then I discovered her parents. I was given *Frost And Fire* for Christmas and fell in love with it. That family really is hogging all the talent! Leave some for the rest of us, you lot!

As much as I adore Eliza, Norma is actually my favourite of the family. That voice is one of the greatest ever English voices, but it's more than that. I love Norma's wisdom, her benevolence and her lovely kind face! There is something almost elemental about singers like them, almost like their voices come from the land itself. In one of Norma's songs, she sings about being, 'up where the eagles fly', which sums her up perfectly for me. She is like the wind singing! Eliza's voice is like that too, but hers is more earthy.

Have you ever seen Eliza live? Do you enjoy her live performances? How do you think she compares to other folk performers?
I saw Eliza and her mother in Bath in November 2010 when they were doing the rounds promoting *Gift*.

Eliza compares very well to other folk performers, because she is talented and wonderfully witty so puts on a real show. It's also that great presence she has onstage. She's just so damn sexy as well! (Easy tiger! – Sophie)

I always liken her to a rock star. She looks like a rock star, has rock star charisma, and has that rebellious streak to her nature. What is appealing, though, is that she is not like a rock star, because she is still just a normal person, like you and me. When I saw her and Norma, I enjoyed the bits in-between the songs just as much, if not more than the songs themselves. They are both wonderful storytellers. I guess what really makes her special is that onstage she is so obviously having such a GREAT time! So, I have seen the Unthanks and Kate Rusby, but found these two to be better.

I have never met her, but I have met her dad a few times. I could have gone and had a chat to her in Bath, but was too nervous!

Have you bought any of Eliza's albums? In your opinion, how do her self-penned albums (Angels And Cigarettes, Dreams Of Breathing...) *compare to the albums where she plays mainly traditional (trad. arr.) music?*

I have a few of Eliza's albums, but mainly the traditional ones. They are the ones I'm most interested in.

I really respect her for diversifying so much and constantly proving that she is definitely not a one-trick pony! I do think 'Britain Is A Car Park' is a great tune, though. I think I will buy *Neptune*, because I almost feel a bit churlish not buying it! "Oh, I love you sooooo much ... but I only have a couple of albums!"

I've got *Anglicana*, *Red Rice* and *Gift*.

In your opinion, what kind of an impact has Eliza had on the folk scene and the wider British music scene?

Well, this one's a bit of a tricky one to answer, because I'm not really an expert on music as a whole, but I think there was an idea for years that folk music was for middle-aged, middle-class people, that it was neither youthful nor cool. I can remember being mocked at school for liking the Dubliners, when other kids would dance an 'Irish' jig for me! Eliza has certainly helped that image. She is young and she is cool. So Eliza, like her good friends Mr Spiers and Mr Boden, has been a great ambassador for folk. I guess she also shows other traditional musicians what the possibilities are; that you can stretch the art and do different things with it.

Have you ever listened to any of her collaborative work, such as the albums made with Nancy Kerr or the Imagined Village? Do you enjoy these as much as her solo work?
As to her collaborations, I've only really listened to her stuff with her family. I have watched an Imagined Village video on YouTube, 'Cold, Rainy, Haily Night', and love it. *Gift* is a truly wonderful record, and what's special is that it's the mother and the daughter together, sharing and doing what they do best. If Norma never does record or perform again, there could be no better way for her to retire. So, yes, I think Eliza's best work is when she's with Mom and Pop in Waterson:Carthy.

How do you think - broadly - that Eliza's musical career will continue? What kind of projects can you see her tackling next?
I imagine Eliza will continue to do what she's been doing, a combination of traditional and her own material. I heard her joking to Mike Harding on Radio 2, 'When I do my own stuff, I really miss the traditional stuff, and when I'm doing traditional I really miss doing my own!' As an artist Eliza does what she feels like. I can't imagine her doing a jazz album or something like that, though!

Finally though, the real reason I love Eliza is a rather simpler: she's gorgeous! EVERYTHING I like about women, she's got 'em covered!

Do you have any titles for the book in mind? *The Fearless, Full-figured, Fiddle Player* perhaps?

Endnotes, Sources & Further Reading

Chapter 1

1 *Originals: Martin Carthy* documentary, BBC Four, first broadcast Saturday 29 July, 2006.
2 Cummings, Tim. 'Stand and deliver!' *The Guardian* Tuesday 26 April 2005.
3 Anderson, Ian. 'Doing The English.' *fRoots 155* May 1996.
4 http://www.hunmanby.com/ceshall.html
5 Parkes, Sophie. 'Authenticity Doesn't Exist.' *FiddleOn*, Issue 17 2005.
6 *Ibid.*
7 *Ibid.*
8 Crossley, Neil 'Keeping It Reel' *Musician*, Summer 2005.
9 'Ten things you didn't know about Eliza Carthy' *Time Out London*, 30 October 2008

Chapter 2

1 Anderson, Ian. 'Doing the English' *fRoots* 155 May 1996.
2 Irwin, Colin. 'Young Arise.' *fRoots* 130, April 1994.
3 *Ibid.*
4 *Musicians' Stories*, Radio 3 Broadcast January 29, 2002.
5 Knowles, J. *A Northern Lass: Traditional Dance Music of Northwest England* . (Out of print).

Chapter 3

1 Irwin, Colin. 'The Village People.' *fRoots* 290/1 August/September 2007.
2 Petridis, Alex. 'Topic Records – 70 years of giving a voice to the people.' *The Guardian*, Sunday 23 August 2009.
3 Nickson, Chris. AllMusic.com
4 Anderson, Ian. 'Doing The English.' *fRoots* 155, May 1996.
5 'The Way I See It' *New Statesman*, 26 June 2008.
6 Crossley, Neil. 'Keeping It Reel' *Musician,* Summer 2005.

Chapter 4

1 Lost, Joe. 'The Anglican.' *fRoots* 233, November 2002.

2 *Originals: Martin Carthy* documentary, BBC Four, first broadcast Saturday 29 July, 2006.

3 *My Music,* Channel 5 documentary, May 2008.

4 http://www.folkmusic.net/htmfiles/webrevs/tscd2001.htm

5 Lee, Stewart 'Eliza Carthy.' *Sunday Times,* 7 June 1998.

6 Denselow, Robin. *Once In A Blue Moon.* BBC Radio 4, 9 November 2010.

7 McDaid, Carol. 'True Eliza.' *The Observer,* 10 September 2000.

8 *Ibid.*

9 Lost, Joe. 'The Anglican.' *fRoots* 233, November 2002.

10 McDaid, *The Observer. Op. Cit.*

Chapter 5

1 Anderson, Ian. *fRoots* 155. May 1996.

2 Cummings, Tim. 'Eliza Carthy: A New England' *The Independent,* 1 November 2002.

3 Avison, Ben. 'Eliza Carthy.' *The Living Tradition,* Issue 55 March/April 2004.

4 *My Music,* Channel 5 documentary, May 2008.

5 Sweeting, Adam. *Anglicana* Review *The Guardian,* Friday 1 November 2002.

6 Irwin, Colin. *Anglicana* Review *fRoots* issue number 233.

7 Petridis, Alex. *The Guardian,* Thursday 8 July 2010.

8 'Boyd, Joe. 'Gold badge: Eliza Carthy.' *English Dance And Song,* summer 2007, volume 69, number 2.

9 Petridis, Alex. 'Sod 'em!', *The Guardian* Friday 27 June 2008.

10 BBC News, Saturday 8 August 2009 http://news.bbc.co.uk/1/hi/8191094.stm

11 http://www.folkagainstfascism.com/about.html

12 Koch, Christian. 'Osama Van Halen and the 50 Cent dictator.' *The Guardian,* Saturday 16 January 2010.

13 Carthy, Eliza. 'Traditional English song has no links to the far right or Nick Griffin.' *The Guardian,* Tuesday 26 January 2010.

Chapter 6

1 Lee, Stewart 'Eliza Carthy.' *Sunday Times,* 7 June 1998.

2 http://www.independent.co.uk/arts-entertainment/music/features/sound-of-summer-meet-the-new-faces-of-nu-folk-2021011.html

3 http://www.telegraph.co.uk/culture/music/worldfolkandjazz/ 8421564/ Folk-music-A-quiet-revolution.html

4 http://www.folkandroots.co.uk/reviews5.html

5 McDaid, Carol. 'Coming up for air.' *The Scotsman* 22 June 2008.

6 *Ibid.*

7 *Gift* liner notes

8 http://www.brightyoungfolk.com/gigs/video/eliza-carthy-norma -waterson-new-cd-interview.aspx 13 July 2009.

9 http://froots.net/phpBB2/viewtopic.php?t=5812&highlight= norma

10 http://www.mustrad.org.uk/editor.htm

Chapter 7

1 Lost, Joe. 'The Anglican.' *fRoots* 233, November 2002.

2 Lee, Stewart. 'Eliza Carthy.' *Sunday Times,* 7 June 1998.

3 Jurek, Thom. 'Rogue's Gallery.' http://www.allmusic.com/album/rogues-gallery-pirate-ballads-sea-songs-chanteys-r847368/review

4 James, Alan. 'The Imagined Village' *English Dance and Song* Autumn 2007, volume 69, number 3.

5 *Ibid.*

6 http://www.bbc.co.uk/music/reviews/6f9p

7 http://properblog.wordpress.com/2010/01/15/imagined-village-giveaway

8 Parkes, Sophie. 'Authenticity Doesn't Exist.' *FiddleOn,* Issue 17. 2005.

9 *Originals: Martin Carthy* documentary, BBC4, first broadcast Saturday 29 July, 2006.

10 Parkes. *FiddleOn. Op. Cit.*

Chapter 8

1 Friedenthal, Christopher 'Eliza Carthy on recording a new CD with her mother.' 13 July 2009. http://www.brightyoungfolk.com/gigs/video/eliza-carthy-norma-waterson-new-cd-interview.aspx

2 http://www.guardian.co.uk/music/2011/may/05/eliza-carthy-neptune-review

3 http://www.bbc.co.uk/music/reviews/6cpn

Chapter 9

1 http://www.americana-uk.com/reviews-cd-live/latest-cd-reviews /item/ eliza-carthy-neptune]

2 Petridis, Alex. 'Sod 'em!', *The Guardian* Friday 27 June 2008.

3 Talkington, Fiona. 'A Place Called England', Fiona Talkington, BBC Radio 3, Monty Funk Productions, 19 March 2003.

4 http://www.morethanthemusic.co.uk/interviews/interviews-eliza -carthy/

5 Irwin, Colin. 'The Eliza Carthy Crusade.' *The Guardian* 16 June 2011.

6 Irwin, Colin. 'The Village People' *fRoots 290/1* August/September 2007.

7 'Eliza Carthy's Anglicana: the rise of British folk music from 1960s to present day' BBC Radio 2, first broadcast Summer 2004.

8 *Ibid.*

Bibliography

There are some big, overarching themes which Eliza's music and approach aims to interrogate. I have only scratched the tiniest of surfaces within this biography, and I feel I have so much more to learn. Many of the sources I list below explore these ideas in far greater detail and with more rigorous authority than I can ever hope to do, and I am grateful for the wisdom and information that these minds have shared. Please note that all interviews were conducted by the writer unless otherwise stated.

For an exquisitely comprehensive discography of Eliza's musical career to date (and a whole host of other musicians besides), song by song and tune by tune, please visit http://www.informatik.uni-hamburg.de/~zierke/ eliza.carthy/index.html

Articles

Anderson, Ian. 'Doing The English.' *fRoots, 155* May 1996.

Avison, Ben. 'Eliza Carthy.' *The Living Tradition*, Issue 55 March/April 2004.

Boyd, Joe. 'Gold badge: Eliza Carthy.' *English Dance And Song*, summer 2007, volume 69, number 2.

Bray, Elisa. 'Eliza Carthy - A second coming for the saviour of British folk.' *The Independent*, Friday, 6 May 2011.

Carthy, Eliza. 'Traditional English song has no links to the far right or Nick Griffin.' *The Guardian*, Tuesday 26 January 2010.

Crossley, Neil. 'Keeping It Reel.', *Musician* Summer 2005.

Cumming, Tim. 'Eliza Carthy: A New England.', *The Independent* 1 November 2002.

Cumming, Tim. 'Stand and deliver!' *The Guardian* Tuesday 26 April 2005.

Denselow, Robin. 'Neptune.' *The Guardian* Thursday 5 May 2011.

Duerden, Nick. 'Sound of summer: Meet the new faces of nu folk.' *The Independent* Sunday 11 July 2010.

Florence, Peter. 'Hay founder Peter Florence on the festival's stand-out moments' *Western Mail* May 21 2011.

Gill, Andy. *Empire And Love* review, *The Independent*, Friday 8 January 2010.

Hodgkinson, Will. 'Rhythm In Her Roots.', *The Guardian* Friday 13 February 2004.

Irwin, Colin. '*Anglicana*.' review, *fRoots 233* winter 2002.

Irwin, Colin. 'The Eliza Carthy Crusade.' *The Guardian* 16 June 2011.

Irwin, Colin. 'In-Depth: Legend of The Watersons.' *Properganda* 2011.

Irwin, Colin. 'The Village People.' *fRoots 290/1* August/September 2007.

Irwin, Colin. 'Young Arise.' *fRoots 130,* April 1994.

James, Alan. 'The Imagined Village.' *English Dance and Song* Autumn 2007, volume 69, number 3.

Koch, Christian. 'Osama Van Halen and the 50 Cent dictator.' *The Guardian*, Saturday 16 January 2010.

Lee, Stewart 'Eliza Carthy.' *Sunday Times,* 7 June 1998.

Lost, Joe .'The Anglican.' *fRoots 233,* November 2002.

McCormick, Neil. 'Eliza Carthy: How folk knocked rock off its perch.' *Daily Telegraph* 3 June 2011.

McCormick, Neil. 'Folk music: a quiet revolution.' *Daily Telegraph,* 1 April 2011.

McDaid, Carol. 'True Eliza.' *The Observer,* 10 September 2000.

May, Julian. 'Fiddler on the hoof.' *The Independent,* Friday, 9 February 1996.

O'Brien. Lucy. 'Sandals are out, piercing is in.' *The Guardian,* Thursday 24 August 2000.

Parkes, Sophie. 'Authenticity Doesn't Exist.' *FiddleOn* Issue 17.

Petridis, Alex. 'Sod 'em!.' *The Guardian,* Friday 27 June 2008.

Petridis, Alex. 'Topic records – 70 years of giving a voice to the people.' *The Guardian* Sunday 23 August 2009.

Rogers, Jude. 'Norma Waterson and Eliza Carthy: "Everything's in a cycle, isn't it?"', *The Guardian*, Thursday 8 July 2010.

Schofield, Derek. 'Eliza Carthy: The singer, song and source' *English Dance And Song* Winter 2005, volume 67.

Smith, Sid. 'Empire And Love review.' *BBC* 6 January 2006.

Sweeting, Adam. '*Anglicana* review.' *The Guardian*, Friday 1 November 2002.

'Ten things you didn't know about Eliza Carthy.' *Time Out London*, 30 October 2008.

Books

Boyes, Georgina. *The Imagined Village: Culture, Ideology and the English Folk Revival*. No Masters, 2010 (reprinted version).

Bragg, Billy. *The Progressive Patriot*. Bantam Press, 2006.

Irwin, Colin. *In Search of Albion: From Cornwall to Cumbria: A Ride Through England's Hidden Soul*. Andre Deutsch, 2005.

Reynolds, Simon. *Retromania: Pop culture's addiction to its own past*. Faber and Faber, 2011.

Sweers, Britta. *Electric Folk: The changing face of English traditional music*. OUP, 2005.

Online resources

www.adriandenning.co.uk

www.afolksongaday.com

www.americana-uk.com particularly Jeremy Searle's review of *Neptune* from 6 June 2011: http://www.americana-uk.com/reviews-cd-live/latest-cd-reviews/item/eliza-carthy-neptune

www.bamptonmorris.co.uk

www.brightyoungfolk.com particularly Christopher Friedenthal's interview with Eliza at The Big Session in 2009, posted on the site on 13 July 2009: www.brightyoungfolk.com/gigs/video/eliza-carthy-norma-waterson-new-cd-interview.aspx

Cox, Jo 'Interview with Eliza Carthy' *More Than Music* www.morethanthemusic.co.uk/interviews/interviews-eliza-carthy/

www.dvdtalk.com/noraguthrieinterview.html

www.efdss.org

www.eliza-carthy.com

www.elizanet.org.uk

www.frootsmag.com and the lively discussion in the *fRoots* forum

www.goathlandploughstots.co.uk

Hendry, Tony '*Red Rice* review' www.folkmusic.net/htmfiles/webrevs/tscd2001.htm

Hughes, Rob '*Neptune*' www.bbc.co.uk/music/reviews/6cpn

www.hunmanby.com/ceshall.html

http://www.informatik.uni-hamburg.de/~zierke/eliza.carthy/index.html

Jurek, Thom 'Rogue's Gallery' http://www.allmusic.com/album/rogues-gallery-pirate-ballads-sea-songs-chanteys-r847368/review

Kidman, David 'Eliza Carthy, Live at Madame Jojo's' www.folkandroots.co.uk/reviews5.html

www.mudcat.org

www.mustrad.org.uk

Nickson, Chris *'Heat Light And Sound'* www.allmusic.com/album/heat-light-sound-r260503

properblog.wordpress.com particularly the article about Lush: properblog.wordpress.com/2010/01/15/imagined-village-giveaway

Turner, James www.zyworld.com/albionmagazineonline/music1.htm

www.watersoncarthy.com particularly useful for the comprehensive gigography

Wood, Chris 'Not icons but jewels: music and loss in England' www.englishacousticcollective.org.uk/JMI/index.html

Radio

Carthy, Eliza. 'Eliza Carthy's Anglicana: the rise of British folk music from 1960s to present day', Smooth Operations, BBC Radio 2, first broadcast summer 2004.

Denselow, Robin. *'Once in a blue moon'*, BBC Radio 4, November 2010.

McMillan, Ian. *'The Verb'*, BBC Radio 3, Friday 13 January 2012.

Reinhardt, Max. *'Musicians' stories'*, BBC Radio 3, 29 January 2002.

Talkington, Fiona. *'A Place Called England'*, BBC Radio 3, Monty Funk Productions, 19 March 2003.

Television

BBC Radio 2 Folk Awards 2011 coverage.

Eliza Carthy: My Music, Channel 5 2008.

Originals: Martin Carthy documentary, BBC4, first broadcast on Saturday 29 July 2006.

Some of the other artists mentioned throughout the course of this book

http://www.bellowhead.co.uk/

http://www.myspace.com/thebevvysisters

http://www.thedemonbarbers.co.uk/

http://www.hannahjamesmusic.co.uk/
http://www.jimmoray.co.uk/
http://www.johnmccusker.co.uk/
http://www.katerusby.com/
http://www.kathryntickell.com/
http://www.kerrfagan.com/
http://www.ladymaisery.com/
http://www.lau-music.co.uk/
http://www.lucywardsings.com/
http://www.myspace.com/maryhampton
http://www.myspace.com/mysteryjuice
http://www.shoogle.com/
http://www.spiersandboden.com/
http://www.watersonknight.com/

Author Biography

Sophie Parkes lives in Manchester and has been a fan of Eliza Carthy since her teens. She contributes to a number of different folk-orientated publications and websites, including *FiddleOn, fRoots, English Dance and Song (EDS)* and Spiral Earth. She also plays violin in a band called Air Cav.

This is her first book.

She blogs at http://www.forfolkssake.org.uk/

Visit http://www.eliza-carthy.com/ for news, tour dates and online shop. Eliza tweets @elizacarthy